Oxford studies in education

Assessing Language Development

Andrew Wilkinson, Gillian Barnsley,
Peter Hanna, Margaret Swan

Oxford University Press 1980

Oxford University Press, Walton Street, Oxford OX2 6DP

Oxford London Glasgow New York Toronto
Melbourne Wellington Kuala Lumpur Singapore
Jakarta Hong Kong Tokyo Dehi Bombay Madras
Karachi Nairobi Dar es Salaam

Andrew Wilkinson is Professor of Education, University of Exeter
Gillian Barnsley is Lecturer in the Department of Curriculum and
Teaching, Rusden State College of Victoria, Australia
Peter Hanna is Principal Lecturer, Roehampton Institute of Higher
Education, London
Margaret Swan is Associate Professor and Deputy Principal, Nova
Scotia Teachers' College, Truro, Nova Scotia, Canada

Printed in Great Britain
by Biddles, Guildford

Contents

Acknowledgement

This book is based on co-operation between teachers in schools and staff of a university. The writers would particularly like to express their gratitude to the pupils in Devon, particularly from Hayward Primary School and Queen Elizabeth Lower School, Crediton, whose writing formed the material of the research. The project has been strongly supported by the Devon L.E.A., and by its English advisers, Rodney Lyons and John Gulliver, by the heads, John Brown and Geoff Woodford, and staffs of the schools concerned. For cordial co-operation and advice we are indebted to teachers in these schools, Derek Rackett, Vicky Rollason, Pat Sneddon, Keith Taylor and Dick Thomas; and to John Morgan formerly of Uffculme Comprehensive. Help during the writing of the book is gratefully acknowledged from Mary Croxen, Anne-Marie and Dick Glasheen, and Margaret and Robert Protherough.

We should also like to express our appreciation of the support given by our publishers and W.H. Mittins who assessed the book in typescript. Not least we wish to give our sincere thanks to Sally Williams who typed with great patience and accuracy a difficult manuscript.

AMW
GB
PH
MS

April 1980

Introduction

1 How to read this book

This book is intended for a variety of readers: those with more knowledge, those with less; those with more time, those with less; those with more patience, those with less.

The second part of this introduction, entitled 'What this book is about', gives a summary of the argument, and Chapter Thirteen, section 2, contains the general conclusions on children's writing development from the Crediton project on which the book is based.

If you wish to read generally about the project, Chapter Five gives the models devised for the analysis of written work (repeated in the Appendix for easy reference); Chapter Six describes the project, and Chapter Twelve gives profiles of three writers, Jimmy, aged seven, Catherine, aged ten, and John, aged thirteen, who were among the children taking part. A more detailed analysis of the written work in terms of the models is given in Chapters Seven to Eleven.

If you wish to read about the background and theoretical justification of the work this is contained in the first part of the book. Thus Chapter One evaluates some current models of language, and Chapter Two some common modes of assessment. Chapter Three (Development — Language and Style) and Chapter Four (Personal Development) outline the thinking on which the models set forth in Chapter Five are based. Readers may find that on Personal Development less difficult than that on Language and Style which is necessarily concerned, at the present state of our knowledge, with fairly abstract theoretical considerations. Chapter Thirteen, section 3, sums up the general implications of the book.

A final, somewhat old-fashioned approach, which may nevertheless have something to commend it, is to start at the beginning of the book, and to read on until you come to the end.

2 What this book is about

This book is about the development in written language of children 7–14 years old, and how we are to judge this. It suggests that the usual criteria of judgement are too narrow, and offers some wider ones for consideration.

All teachers have a responsibility for the personal development of their pupils and this responsibility is felt especially by those concerned with language, language being a major means by which it takes place. Thus the literature abounds with terms like 'growth', 'development', 'maturity'. These terms, however, are notoriously ill-defined. And yet there are clearly differences between the language of (say) a two year old, a five year old, and a ten year old. Development obviously takes place, but does not take place obviously.

With a view to obtaining a clearer picture of the language features of pupils at particular ages, post-graduate studies have been carried out at the Language in Education Centre of the University School of Education at Exeter, the initiating paper being that of A. and E. Wilkinson (1978). The work has been extended by Carlin (1978), Marshall (1978), Taylor (1979), Witcombe (1979). The most recent project, The Crediton Project, is the focus of this book. A team from the Centre worked in collaboration with teachers mainly in Crediton, Devon (U.K.), using a simple research design.

Four different compositions — narrative, autobiographical, explanatory, and argumentative — were requested from groups of children at seven, ten and thirteen respectively, in the context of their normal lessons. The same four subjects were given to each group so that the compositions could be more easily compared.

The question arises how these compositions are to be assessed. Commonly used 'linguistic' criteria as in many marking schemes, are often very limiting, and do not take into account the child as a developing being. Thus the Project was concerned to look at just this: at the nature of the thought, the feeling, the moral stance, as well as at the style, manifested in the writing.

Hence four 'models' were devised to serve as systems of analysis — in the fields of cognition, affect, morals, and style. For the second and fourth of these there was scarcely any previous work to go on.

> *Cognitive.* The basis of this model is a movement from an undifferentiated world to a world organized by mind, from a world of instances to a world related by generalities and abstractions.

> *Affective.* Development is seen as being in three movements — one towards a greater awareness of self, a second towards a greater awareness of neighbour as self, a third towards an inter-engagement of reality and imagination.

Moral. 'Anomy' or lawlessness gives way to 'heteronomy' or rule by fear of punishment, which in turn gives way to 'socionomy' or rule by a sense of reciprocity with others which finally leads to the emergence of 'autonomy' or self-rule.

Stylistic. Development is seen as choices in relation to a norm of the simple, literal, affirmative sentence which characterizes children's early writing. Features, such as structure, cohesion, verbal competence, syntax, reader awareness, sense of appropriateness, undergo modification.

These models are not intended to be used as day to day marking schemes; but to heighten levels of awareness. Their detail enables them to pay due regard to the varieties of activity going on in the process of writing. In one sense they are assessment instruments, but only in the sense that assessment is an essential part of education — we need to make assessments of development to help further development. So far assessment instruments of this kind, based on a broad view of personal development, have been conspicuously lacking.

Chapter One

Models of English

1.1 Introduction

We all act on assumptions of which we are imperfectly aware. As teachers we act on assumptions about the nature of the learner, the nature of learning, the ends of the learning process, and so on. These bodies of assumption or 'models' necessarily influence our teaching; and if they are unexamined will affect our behaviour more powerfully and irrationally, give us less opportunity for choice, than if we are aware of them.

In this chapter we shall examine two kinds of models: first general models which lie behind the different emphases discernible in the teaching of English; and second models of development in language. One reason for bringing these two together is that we believe a proper model for the teaching of English must essentially be based on a theory of human development. A second reason is that any criteria of assessment (and assessment is one of our principal concerns in this book) can only be devised in terms of the ends such assessment is serving. If we wish a reader of this book to join our choir it is no use weighing him despite the large size of many operatic principals; only if he elicits our aid in slimming is that a relevant measuring device. Our scheme of analysis outlined in Chapter Five is only appropriate if a certain philosophy about the teaching of English is accepted.

1.2 Models of English Teaching

In *Growth Through English* John Dixon discerned three major 'models or images of English that have been widely accepted in schools on both sides of the Atlantic. . . . The first centred on *skills*: it fitted an era when initial literacy was the prime demand'. The second stressed the *cultural heritage*, the need for a civilising and socially unifying content. The third (and current) model focuses on *personal growth*: on the need to re-examine the 'learning processes and the meaning to the individual of what he is doing in English lessons'. (Dixon, 1975, pp. 1—2).

It is not necessary to make more than brief comment on the first two models.

1.2.1 Skills

In the *skills* model English is regarded as a series of activities each of which can be practised and improved by means of exercises separate from one another and from a context. It has a long history. *The Self Educator* in *English Composition* (1901) by G.H. Thornton, M.A., is divided into thirty lessons on such topics as Vocabulary; the Sentence (Order of Words, Kinds of Simple Sentences, Compound and Complex Sentences, Loose and Periodic Sentences); Punctuation; Metaphors and Similes; Direct and Reported Speech; Verbosity, Pleonasm, Tautology, Common Errors, Paraphrasing, and so on. Exercises are given in each lesson and the correct versions supplied at the end of the book. 'At last the blind god succeeded in making a bull's eye of Cairns' heart', should read 'At last Cairns fell in love'. 'Such a 'skills' approach is of course still popular. Just as Mr. Thornton had his sentence-combining —

> Combine the following sets of simple sentences into complex sentences; first with a restrictive relative clause, and second with a copulative relative clause in each case —

so the Canadian Council for Teachers of English Conference on *Learning to Write* held in Ottawa in 1979 had, in an otherwise impeccable programme, its 'Sentence Combining Day'.

The skills model has value. By working on spelling, punctuation, paragraphing, direct and reported speech, forms of address in letters, arrangement in composition, one can certainly make improvements in performance. Obviously a certain amount of direct skills learning is necessary. What is questionable is the adequacy of a skills model as a philosophy of English teaching, basically because it concentrates on mechanics and techniques of expression rather than on the nature and quality of what is expressed. Unfortunately external examinations, such as the 'O' level in the UK, tend to support such a model because it has features which can be marked with a certain ease and objectivity — spelling, punctuation, grammar, are either 'right' or 'wrong'. There is therefore a risk that they will be over emphasized as against more ambiguous features such as style or imagination.

1.2.2 Cultural Heritage

The *cultural heritage* model also has a long history. It really goes back to the Greek view of literature as a moral and spiritual influence. The HMSO Report, *The Teaching of English in England* (1921) speaks of the 'preliminary training of the child in the language which is to be his means of communication for all the common purposes of life, and the scientific study of language', and then with an undisguised enthusiasm goes on to say:

> It remains for us to consider the actual and possible position of English in the highest sense, that is a channel of formative culture for all English people, and the medium of the creative art by which all writers of distinction, whether poets, historians, philosophers or men of science, have secured for us the power of realising some part of their own experience of life. (p. 12)

The Report is deliberately advocating a strong liberal element in what we would call a skill-centred English curriculum:

> The idea of a liberal education is either ignored or struggles feebly for the right of existence; and even where it still lives, there is a singular depreciation of the value of English literature for such a purpose. (p. 12)

Historically the heritage model provided a very necessary content to the English curriculum, though it tended to remain isolated. The provision of two quite distinct external examinations at 'O' level in the UK symbolizes the separateness of the two—language and literature.

This model has virtues. It transmits the culture, it is a means of receiving the insights of intelligent, shrewd, far-sighted people; it presents interpretations of life to which one may relate one's own experiences, where one may gain in awareness and self-knowledge. It presents modes and styles of writing for inspection and possible use. This model also has its limitations. It tends to transmit high culture, the 'classics'. It tends to assume (even though this is not necessary) a passive recipient to whom culture is *given*; that the most valuable experience is the second-order second-hand experience; that other forms of art, e.g. film, television, are *per se* inferior (though obviously the 1921 Report was not concerned with these). Most important of all it gives no cognizance to the value of the pupils' own day to day, minute by minute experience, to the validity of their own world, to their own roles as unique persons, as creative entities (in this model it is *others* who create).

1.2.3 Personal Growth

The *personal growth* model is to be seen in context of the child-centred (perhaps we should say person-oriented) emphasis on education since the war. The most dramatic statement we have come across occurs in Vicars

Bell's book, *On Learning the English Tongue*, which was published in 1953:

> But I think that it is necessary to remind myself now of the basic truth that all education and all learning must partake of the nature of *Growth*:
>
> BE LIKE ME — NOW!
>
> We should all of us repudiate the suggestion that our teaching methods were based upon that injunction. We should all of us aver, with our hands on our hearts, that our motto is:
>
> BE LIKE YOURSELF — NOW AND ALWAYS
>
> In the teaching of English, it is even more important to act upon this principle than it is in the teaching of any other subject. For we must always regard language as a means whereby the child may honestly, sincerely, and unaffectedly express his *own* opinions, his *own* feelings, and — thereby his own inviolable and unique self so far as he has discovered it at a particular moment in time.
>
> (Bell, 1953, p. 21)

This is splendid, and a little ominous: splendid because it is a statement about human value, ominous because of its assertion of individuality without any mention of other individuals. Peer Gynt took an onion and began to inspect it, searching for his true self. When he had taken off layer after layer, and got to the centre, he found there was nothing there.

In 1965 a notable international seminar on English teaching was held at Dartmouth, Connecticut. Bell's words are interesting as an early statement of the *personal growth* model, including even the metaphor 'growth' which Dixon's book was to give such currency to as a result of the Dartmouth Seminar.

Basically the assumption of this model is that the individual learner should be the focus. He develops in no small measure through language: by language he is enabled to understand his world. Dixon is concerned that the individual should establish his unique world view, a structure which for the time being gives him security and confidence, and at the same time a certain self-knowledge:

> In ordering and composing situations that in some way symbolise life as we know it, we bring order and composure to our inner selves. When a pupil is steeped in language in operation we expect, as he matures, a conceptualisation of his earlier awareness of language, and with this perhaps new insight into himself (as creator of his own world. (p. 13)

The *personal growth* model places the development of the individual in the centre, and is concerned to further the way he processes his experiences, particularly through words. He will need to use words to express his feelings, to understand, to interpret. In these processes the words and structures 'come', or are sought out, not provided externally; the 'skills' are acquired almost incidentally, though not accidentally, in a context where their need is felt, though not necessarily perceived consciously.

1.2.4 Context

The model presented by the Dartmouth Seminar was seen in subsequent years to have limitations which were not, and probably could not have been, discerned at the time. Writing in 1975 Dixon acknowledged that the Seminar had left unexplored the language and roles which relate us to others —

> the roles we take on when we use language to inform, convince, persuade, report, invite, order, request, instruct. . . . It's a very large body of language to neglect. (p. 123)

In 1973 in its evidence to the Bullock Committee the National Association for the Teaching of English was emphasizing the social aspect of the individual, as the title *Language in Context*, suggests. The opening statement attempts to bring together both the *heritage* and the *personal growth* models.

> To learn about English is a way of becoming humanised. On the one hand it is a way of finding out about one's commonalty with others, for we hold a language in common with others, and its potentialities for transmitting culture, as well as for helping us to understand one another. On the other hand, it is a way of discovering one's own uniqueness, by trying out one's identity, by exploring one's own nature. (1.1)

The paper's basic argument is that we need to think about the teaching and learning of the individual, in relation to other individuals and in relation to social situations. Thus the paper describes what it calls the 'horizontal context':

> It comprises the social and familial background of the child, particularly his relationship with parents: it comprises the educational system, the school itself, and its hidden curriculum; and more specifically the overt curriculum. Aspects of language itself, speaking, listening, writing and reading, must be seen in context of one another. The neglect of oracy and the frequent isolated treatment of reading are too notorious to need further comment at this point. (1.3.2)

This passage reflects the increasing awareness in the late sixties and seventies of the socially related aspects of language in race, sex, class, and region; of the importance of audience and of interaction.

There is also a 'vertical context' — the 'growth' of the individual:

> The other, the vertical dimension, we see in terms of the development of the child and the proper sequencing of our demands upon and expectations of him.

> Development in human beings is not a progress to a pre-ordained conclusion as
> with the rose or romping molly, but is brought about by interaction with people,
> ideas, events, in many but specific environments. (1.3.3)

The model offered by the NATE paper thus accepts fully the importance of individual development, whilst giving more emphasis to the aspects of inter-relationship. It regards the child as a communicating being, with emphasis both on the communicating and the being.

1.2.5 Comment

Ideally all the models should be underpinned by a theory of development; for the last two this must be a theory of the development of the human personality. No complete theory has been offered, though there have been some interesting moves in that direction, two of which we shall now examine. Moffett's is the more general, seeing language as serving an essential part in a decentring process in the human personality. Britton concentrates more specifically on language as having a relationship to cognitive growth.

1.3 Some Views of Development in English

1.3.1 James Moffett (1968), *Teaching the Universe of Discourse*

> The most sensible strategy for determining a proper learning order in English, it
> seems to me, is to look for the main lines of child development, and to assimilate
> to them, when fitting, the various formulations that scholars make about language
> and literature. (p. 14)

Moffett is aware that what we call 'development' may be imposed on children: we should know more 'if textbooks had not prevented teachers finding out the facts that the textbooks were guessing at'. Nevertheless he does not despair of finding out 'what children cannot read and write at various stages of their growth' (p. 54). He sees the sequence of psychological development in children as being principally conceived with the increasing degrees of abstraction:

> The concept that I believe will most likely permit us to think at once about
> mental development and the structure of discourse is the concept of abstraction
> which can apply equally well to thought and to language. (p. 18)

Two aspects of abstraction are commented upon — one is the arranging of the mind's materials in hierarchies: 'dog' is of a lower order than 'international trade'. The other is perceptual selectivity. In order to make abstractions the mind must select. For instance, we have *perceptions* of the real

world which we select (wheels, body, shape — a pig on the roof is not relevant) to give us 'car'. *Memories* (not necessarily the actual objects, car, lorry,
bicycle) combine to give us 'vehicles'. (We select these and exclude other
objects such as a policeman); selecting vehicles, aircraft, shipping together
with notions of movement and so on forms the *generalization* 'transport'. The
achievement of a high level of abstraction in thinking does not mean that we
abandon lower levels. Each new challenge may cause us to repeat the cycle:

> Not only do we grow slowly through the whole abstractive range during our
> period of maturation, but at any time of life we are constantly processing new
> experiences up through the cycle of sensation, memories, generalisations, and
> theories. (p. 25)

The processing is by three principles of organization: *chronology*, where the
temporal sequence is important, as in a simple story; *analogy*, where various
generalizations take place, as in a scientific account; and *tautology*, where
speculations and hypotheses based on generalizations take place. (It should
be said that the terminology seems quite unnecessarily obscure: 'tautology' is
high level theorizing, but the word has associations of redundancy and stating
the obvious).

Moffett sees the hierarchy of abstractions as being manifested in:

> Recording, the drama of what is happening
> Reporting, the narrative of what happened
> Generalising, the exposition of what happens
> Theorising, the argumentation of what will, what may happen. (p. 47)

Examples of *recording* Moffett gives are a personal journal and correspondence; of *reporting*, a memoir and fiction; *generalizing* is represented by
history and science; he specifically lists a biology textbook, a government
manual of procedures, Montaigne's *Essay on Friendship*, and Pope's *Essay
on Man*; *theorizing* is to be seen in metaphysics — *Summa Theologica*, and
a *Critique of Reason* — 'sustained logical combining of some prior generalizations used as premises' (p. 46). Of course one cannot equate a particular
type of work completely with a particular level of thinking 'for something
at every level is found at every other level'. (p. 48)

> Associated with abstracting is 'decentering'. 'The primary dimension of growth
> seems to be a movement from the centre of the self outward'. (p. 59)

As specific characteristics of decentring, Moffett lists the following:

1. From the implicit, embodied idea, to the explicitly formulated idea.
2. From addressing the small known audience like oneself to addressing a distant,
   unknown, and different audience.

3. From talking about present objects and actions to talking about things past
   and potential.
4. From projecting emotion into the there-then to focusing it into the here-now.
5. From stereotyping to originality, from groups into individuality. (p. 57)

We may gloss these characteristics as follows. No. 1 is the movement from
context-bound 'restricted code' language to context-free 'elaborated code'
language. No. 2 is the movement from formulating one's own thoughts in
order to clarify them ('reflexion') on one hand to writing them down for
persons not present or even alive at the time ('publication') on the other.
No. 3: in gossip one is often talking about things immediately or recently
present. In autobiography distancing and objectifying are likely to take place:
'writing about one's life of a long time ago is very much like writing about
another person' (p. 43). No. 4 is the opposite process to 3 and, Moffett
suggests, is characteristic of fiction. We begin with the symbols of myths and
fairy stories and then move to more explicit understandings: 'gradually we
withdraw projection as we become willing to recognize the personal meaning
symbolized in our myths and able to objectify inner experience to the point
of treating it objectively'. In No. 5 Moffett is saying that a unique statement
is a hard-won thing: young children 'do not make up stories easily without
stimulants and prompters, and when they do, the stories are seldom original'
(p. 56).

Moffett sees growth predominantly as a cognitive matter. And cognitive
developments have linguistic correlates about which he is properly tentative:

> This can only be a hypothesis of course, but I think that shifting, say from
> narrative discourse to that of explicit generalization necessarily entails shifts in
> language and rhetoric and thus tends to bring successively to the fore different
> language structures and compositional issues . . . The kinds of paragraph structure
> one tends to use shift. And generally, the increasing complexities of sentence
> structure described as embeddings by transformational grammar, accompany
> the increasing cognitive ability to interelate and subordinate clauses and
> propositions. What will further the normal growth of sentence elaboration is
> practice in language tasks that are at bottom intellectual.

The relation between thought and language is not necessarily an obvious one.
Not all metaphysics is written in sentences which are complex. It is often the
mark of mature exposition to move from a complicated grammar to a simple
one. It does however seem to be true that whilst children are developing
linguistically their structures do become more complex, though this varies
very much from situation to situation.

Moffett does not define the cognitive categories beyond the five we have
listed, nor is his purpose to go into detail about the linguistic ones. The hints

about other kinds of growth given us in the 'decentring' dimension are not followed up. But this does not mean his work is not significant; quite the contrary. In its suggestions and evocations it points onwards.

1.3.2 James Britton *et al.* (1975), *The Development of Writing Abilities 11–16*.

The aim of this Schools Council Research Project

> was to undertake a developmental study of the processes by which the written language of young children becomes differentiated, during the years eleven to eighteen, into kinds of written discourse appropriate to different purposes . . . (p. 50)

The research team found the traditional rhetorical categories — narrative, description, exposition, and argument — unsatisfactory. The tradition was prescriptive and showed 'little inclination to observe the writing process; its concern is with how people should write, rather than with how they do' (p. 4). It is very seldom that one finds a sustained piece of description; so often it occurs as incidental to, for instance, a narrative. Again, a description of a landscape or a person may use a completely different type of language from a description of a jet engine. And again, a 'description' may be an 'argument' — to persuade us to buy a car for instance. The whole situation is hopelessly confused. The research team concluded:

> . . . we must be concerned with what people actively write when they are performing, as far as we can judge, at least competently. We must base our model, in other words, on mature adult competence, if we are to trace stages in development towards that competence. (p. 5)

Instead of the conventional categories the Britton team devised a scheme by which each piece of writing could be classified in terms of the predominant function it performed.

One category is the *Expressive*. This is utterance that 'stays close to the speaker' and hence is fully comprehensible only to 'one who knows the speaker and shares his context. It is a verbalization of the speaker's immediate preoccupation and mood of the moment' (p. 82). Examples of written expressive writing would be diary entries and personal letters. Another category is the *Transactional* — the 'language to get things done' — to record facts, exchange opinions, construct theories, conduct campaigns. Examples would be reference books, scientific treatises, political speeches. And another category is the *Poetic*. Here language is used as an art medium. 'A piece of poetic writing is a verbal construct, an "object" made out of language'. It exists *'for its own sake,* and not as a means of achieving something else' (p. 91). Examples are not only poems, but plays, novels, songs.

The Expressive is the seed-bed out of which the other two can grow. On the one hand we as adults frame our tentative draft of new ideas as expressive; on the other young children seem naturally at home in it and seem to move towards the other modes through it.

> This, at all events, provides us with a major hypothesis regarding the development of writing ability in school; that what children write in the early stages should be a form of written down expressive speech, and what they read should also be, generally speaking, expressive. As their writing and reading progress side by side, they will move from this starting point into the three broadly differentiated kinds of writing — our major categories — and in favourable circumstances, their mode of doing so will be by a kind of shuttling between their speech resources on the one hand and the written forms they meet on the other. Thus in developmental terms, the expressive is a kind of matrix from which differentiated forms of mature writing are developed.

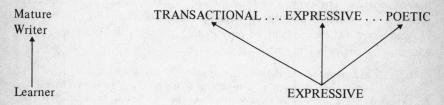

Mature Writer

TRANSACTIONAL . . . EXPRESSIVE . . . POETIC

Learner

EXPRESSIVE

The expressive as a matrix for the development of other forms of writing (pp. 82–3).

The Expressive category is not susceptible of subdivision, and the research team failed to make any subdivision of the Poetic which could be meaningful in classifying writing in schools. The Transactional, however, they subdivide into informative on the one hand, and conative on the other.

The debt to Moffett is acknowledged in the concept of the informative. His categories are extended and defined. The informative divides into *record*; *report*; *generalized narrative* or *descriptive information*; *analogic, low level of generalization*; *analogic*; *analogic-tautological (speculative)*; *tautologic*. The conative divides into *regulative*; and *persuasive*. Not all the terms are immediately self-explanatory, and a golden opportunity to improve on Moffett's confusing terminology is lost. The important category is the informative, and the stages of this are on a cognitive dimension — they are related to the abilities of the writers to think — to record the concrete on the lowest level, and progressively to generalize abstract, speculate, theorize at the highest level. In fact, the unity of types of discourse in the informative category seems to lie in cognition rather than in 'getting things done' — it is difficult to see for instance a history book as getting things done, or having a similarity with a stop sign, which enables them to be grouped together.

In this project then we are offered a model to examine the development of thought insofar as it is manifest in written language. It cannot be regarded as a comprehensive descriptive tool in that other aspects of development — for instance, the social, emotional, and moral — are not included. Nor is stylistic development considered, which might be considered essential for a scheme which includes the Poetic as a major category.

The members of the Writing Research Unit were disappointed at the evidence obtained in their attempts to validate the model. They examined 2,122 pieces of writing from secondary schools in a variety of subjects. Most pieces were transactional, and increasingly so as the writers moved up the school, but even so there was minimal development into the abstract levels of the informative. The expressive function which the Unit saw as so important accounts for a mere 6 per cent of writing in year one, declining to 4 per cent by year seven, where it occurred only in English and R.E. There was also a dramatic fall off in poetic writing in year seven.

> If, as we had predicted, the development of writing abilities showed itself as a growing range of kinds of writing shaped by thinking processes we should have expected to find in the sample a great range of expressive writing in the early years in all subjects, and an increase in later years of analogic, speculated and theoretical writing, as well as persuasive and poetic — all these compensating for a reduction in the expressive; and at the same time a proportion of expressive writing maintained and developing into its maturer forms and purposes. (p. 197)

There is a fundamental problem here that was touched on by Moffett. How can one talk of 'development' unrelated to the social and situational demands made on the learner? It is clear that there was little expressive writing in the sample because the schools did not require it; that there was a good deal of lower-level transactional, because pupils were encouraged to report, record, generalize; that there was little higher level because they were not encouraged to speculate, hypothesize, in writing; that there was little poetic writing in the seventh year because they were not asked for poems and stories in the crucial external-examination year. We can only begin to look at a development within the writer when we give him an opportunity to carry out these various tasks and see how far he succeeds. Even so we have to accept that we are defining development in terms of the tasks we set; and there is no way out of this dilemma.

1.4 Summary

In this chapter we have argued:

1. That teaching and assessment are based on the assumptions or 'models' underlying them; we cannot operate without a theory of some kind whether aware of it or not.
2. That there are various models of English teaching in the most complete of which the learner is regarded as a communicating being.
3. That such a model needs to be supported by a theory of human development which is only now beginning to be formulated.

Chapter Two

The Assessment of Written English

2.1 Introduction

In the previous chapter we argued that methods of assessment are essentially related to underlying assumptions, such as what constitutes 'good English'. Public examinations tend to reward the formal qualities of written work, the 'skills', partly because they can be marked objectively. Such examinations influence the curriculum by being taught towards.

In this chapter we will look at various methods of assessment. It is useful to bear in mind what one may call the archetypal assessment − a single composition in a fixed-time examination, marked by a detailed marking scheme with a heavy loading on spelling, punctuation and grammar. Candidates for training colleges in 1885, for instance, were examined in this way (subject choice from Truthfulness, Poetry, the Queen) (Daniel 1898, p. 899). It is interesting to see how much this model has influenced practice right down to the present day.

2.2 Analytical Marking

The traditional method of marking English compositions which have been set for examinations has been by analytical marking: that is to say the marker has a series of headings with the number of marks he should assign to each. Thus one scheme quoted by Hartog and Rhodes in their study of examinations is as follows:

	Marks
1. Quantity, quality and control of ideas	50
2. Vocabulary	15
3. Grammar and punctuation	15
4. Structure of sentences	10
5. Spelling	5
6. Handwriting	5
	100

This was used for a Special Place (entrance to secondary school at eleven) examination. Another from a similar examination has the following categories (seven marks to each): vocabulary, accuracy, craftsmanship, consistency, completeness, substance, quality. It is often very difficult for the marker to know what to reward under each heading. What is the difference for instance in the first schedule between 'grammar' and 'structure of sentences'? In the second is 'craftsmanship' style, and anyway how does it exist separate from (say) 'accuracy' and 'completeness'? How far does 'quality' in the second schedule, which gets a maximum of seven marks equate with 'quantity, quality and control of ideas' which gets a maximum of fifty marks? There are many other problems, not least that the questions: what is the writer trying to do? and what functions does this writing serve? are not asked. The schedule is meant to apply to all types of writing, yet 'quantity of ideas', which might be appropriate in an argument, seems far less so in a fast moving narrative; certainly a very different definition of the phrase is required.

Hartog and Rhodes (1935) were concerned with the 'reliability' of examinations, (the consistency between examiners, and their consistency with themselves on separate occasions) and their 'validity' (how far they were measuring what they purported to measure — ability in English composition rather than mechanical accuracy only, for instance). Their investigations found considerable unreliability; code marking and impression marking 'produce, on the average, the same degree of discrimination between the different candidates — the same spread of marks' (p. 29) — but the reliabilities were relatively low, i.e. subsequent markings tended to produce different results. Further work of a sub-committee chaired by Hartog produced a report *The Marking of English Essays* (1944). In an attempt to improve the consistency and validity of the examinations (eleven plus, and School Certificate — sixteen plus) they asked that revised categories should be used in their experiments.

Particularly they were concerned that the purpose of a piece of writing with a particular audience in view was not taken into account.

> In previous work on the subject by the Director of the Enquiry it was pointed out that in real life a person does not just 'write' — he writes for a given *audience* with a given *object* in view, which may be to explain, to persuade, to convey an order, to amuse, to imagine, or indeed to fulfil any other purpose or combination of purposes. The word 'sense' in this investigation has been used to express the measure in which the object of a composition clearly defined in some cases, to be guessed from internal evidence in others, has (in the opinion of the examiners) been attained.

(Stevens, 1970, p. 12)

A modified code was therefore used: sense; spelling; punctuation (including formal paragraphing); power of expression (felicities of vocabulary, and sentence structure); and general impression. Perhaps 'sense' is an unfortunate term for what we now regard as the major concepts of 'audience' and 'function'. It is to Hartog's great credit that he had been proclaiming to an unhearing profession the importance of these concepts since before 1907 when his *The Writing of English* was published. The writer, he says,

> is not merely writing vaguely, as our schoolboys write essays on lofty themes for the world in general; he is writing for a particular audience with a particular object in view.
>
> Hartog, 1907, (p. 61)

The new schedule did not produce greater reliability than had the old one compared with impression marking, an overall judgement from a reading through. The report felt that this may have been due to the markers, with the best will in the world, having been unable to free themselves from their older habits.

2.3 Impression Marking

The importance of an 'overall' impressionistic 'holistic' judgement was increasingly recognized in the thirties and forties. Whilst advocating a simplified code (content 12, structure 7 for mechanical accuracy) Schonell, writing in 1950, formulates instructions for its use very carefully:

> It is not suggested that in using the following schedule examiners should laboriously give three separate marks for the three aspects of composition, but they should be conscious of the three aspects and their relative values in making their final assessment, that is they should mark by general impression guided by the schedule. (1950, p. 186)

Wiseman's work (1949) confirmed that there was little difference between the reliability of general impression and analytical marking. He suggested also that impression marking was more valid, though he gave no evidence beyond his experience of marking school essays analytically and finding that 'the obvious "best" essay is not at the top of the list' (1949, p. 205). His research demonstrated that by using four independent impression markers for eleven plus compositions no more time and effort was required than for one analytical marking and that the results had a high degree of reliability.

Interestingly Wiseman asked his markers not to 'give a mark to the composition as a piece of English'. This was a diagnostic not an attainment test — to assess the ability of the candidate to profit by a secondary education: 'you are judging children, not essays'. The markers were not to look for errors but 'for excellences to reward'. Sentence structure was to be regarded as a 'sign of ability to deal with complex ideas'. If at all possible the markers were to distinguish between the writing resulting from good teaching and that which results from intelligence and originality. This might have been difficult to do. But the point of Wiseman's general advice is still clear — behind the language is a person.

Britton (1963) found that the composition of fifteen year olds could be assessed as reliably by a combination of impression marks by three examiners and a mark for mechanical accuracy as the writing of eleven year olds could by Wiseman's original method. There were some indications that such an assessment was more valid than analytical marking by individuals, but these fell short of conviction. The advice given to markers once again is 'Look for excellences rather than penalise deficiencies' (p. 23). But that there will be different kinds of excellence in different linguistic tasks is not sufficiently explicit, any more than in Wiseman's work, though it could be said to be hinted at in 'Reward the writer who is involved enough to write in a direct expressive way, and detailed enough to show a point of view by direct comment or by implication'.

2.4 What Constitutes 'Impression'?

In making a judgement from a total 'gestalt' which is more that the sum of the parts some parts must nevertheless carry more weight than others. Obviously these will vary from individual to individual and from group to group. But it seems interesting to know what criteria judges are using, as this will be some indication of their internal model of what constitutes good written English. Actually what criteria they are *really* using would be difficult to establish. The most we can consider is what they say they are using or what they appear to be using.

On these we are not without evidence. There is for instance the study by Diederich (1974). He took 300 pages by freshmen at three colleges and 'had them all graded by sixty distinguished readers in six occupational fields' (p. 5). He does not say how distinguished is 'distinguished' but clearly they were people of some education: ten college English teachers, ten social science teachers, ten natural science teachers, ten writers and editors, ten lawyers and ten business executives. They were each asked to sort the papers into nine piles in order of general merit. It certainly appeared they were distinguished by their variousness for the median correlation turned out to be 0.31 which does not indicate very close agreement. However what is interesting for our purposes is the analysis Diederich made of the comments on what they liked and disliked which he had asked them to write on the papers.

The largest cluster of readers were most influenced by *ideas* expressed — their 'richness, soundness, clarity, development and relevance to the topic and the writer's purpose'. The next largest commented upon *errors* in usage, sentence structure, punctuation, and spelling. The next group were concerned with organization and analysis. Another group commented on wording and phrasing. The smallest group was concerned with personal qualities, the 'flavor', the way the passage was 'sincere', revealed personality. Perhaps predictably there was a predominance of English teachers in the group concerned with errors, of businessmen in that concerned with organization, and of writers and editors in that concerned with personality.

There is a problem in trying to apply the same criteria to a variety of different writing tasks; personality obviously should not come through in an instruction manual for instance. And unfortunately we are not told what the writing tasks were, though insofar as we can judge from the report at least some of the judges were aware of the need to assess in relation to the 'topic and the writer's purpose'. It is very difficult to know from the information given what would be rewarded under 'ideas'. But the big stress on errors in mechanical and grammatical matters seems significant. So does the fact that it was the smallest group which emphasized personality; in any large group of readers, says Diederich, these 'would be recognised as devotees of creative writing' (p. 8).

Another piece of evidence on the criteria teachers use to evaluate composition is *Assessing Composition*, a discussion pamphlet prepared by members of the London Association for the Teaching of English (LATE, 1965). It presents twenty-eight imaginative compositions by fifteen year old pupils arranged in order of merit from the most inadequate to the best, and follows these by a commentary which explains the order.

An impressionistic analysis of this commentary suggests that the basis of judgement is how far an 'experience' is 'realized' and 'explored' on the one hand, and how far there is 'language control' on the other. Take comments on two essays:

> Although inadequate in amount and uncontrolled in spelling and punctuation this piece shows an imaginative realization of a human situation and some exploration of that experience. (No. 1). The experience in this piece of writing is both vividly imagined and well controlled (No. 26).

We find these two themes returned to again and again. In the first category we find: 'attempts to explore another person's emotions', 'attempted to explore an experience', 'backed by real school experience', 'recreate an experience', 'exploration of personal experience', 'entered imaginatively into a terrifying experience', 'external to the meaning or experience of the title'. In the second category we find: 'adequately structured', 'structure and language control very weak', 'advance in technical control', 'control of even this low level of language structure fails', 'control of sentence structure and punctuation poor', 'some competent control of language', 'all adequately structured'.

A straight comparison between these criteria and those of Diederich's sample is not possible because of the way each is reported but one would suspect that the LATE group would find themselves in his final category as 'devotees of creative writing'. Their stress on 'experience' does not seem to coincide with the emphasis of his main group on 'ideas' but rather with his 'sincerity', 'flavor', and 'personal feeling'.

The LATE group has the great advantage of not trying to devise criteria for all types of writing. It can thus present quite a simple model of writing. It is not mainly audience-oriented but self-analytical. The two words 'experience' and 'control' chime antiphonally through the comments. Experience is to be presented as real or at least as imaginatively realized by means of a language which shapes and 'controls'; which may be less in 'error' than 'inadequate' to the task.

A completely different model is implied by the examiners' reports for the General Certificate of Education in the analysis of Knight (1977).

> A few examples from the recurring phrases of commendation and reproof will indicate the consensus: 'ability in vocabulary'; 'good correct style'; 'everyday slipshod speech patterns'; 'good standard of written English'; 'cogent, succinct and accurate writing'; 'graces of fancy or style'; 'distinction in content or style'; 'proper and exact use of the English language'; 'neat conclusion'. These phrases keep each other easy company; but they do not all come from the same report. (p. 25)

Such language, argues Knight, implies a global view of language ability, that there is one way to write, judged by the same standards, irrespective of the purposes of the writing. This view is a classical one as commonly understood; the model seems to be that of the eighteenth century essayists. He quotes tellingly, first from Johnson and then from the report of an examining board:

> Language is the dress of thought
>
> (Johnson)

> ... old wine is particularly welcome if it is in new bottles
>
> (A.E.B., 1975)

But the most damning quotation is one from an A.E.B. report of 1974:

> Inexperienced writers with nothing to say find it harder than professionals to disguise their work with elegant variations or redundant examples and not only the content but the style deteriorates.

The implications that one ought to be able to get by on style with nothing to say is a disturbing one.

Whatever the function of style for the eighteenth century authors the aping of this style in itself, Knight says, unrelated to the experience it is to convey can only result in confusion, insincerity and failure.

2.5 The Need for a Variety of Writing Tasks

2.5.1 Language and Situation

One of the major problems in the assessment of writing has been that so often it has been thought that an adequate judgement of a person's writing ability could be made on a single piece of composition. Thus attention focused on the way of marking this.

However it has been increasingly realized in recent years that our linguistic competence is very much related to the situation in which we find ourselves. The model which has become a point of reference is that of Roman Jakobson (1966).

CONTEXT

ADDRESSER   MESSAGE   ADDRESSEE
————

CONTACT

CODE

The Addresser sends a message to the Addressee. In other terms for every language act there is an audience, even if this is the addresser himself. The London Writing Research Unit have developed this concept in recent years. As far as pupils in school are concerned they discern the main relationships as *child to self; child to teacher* (trusted adult, teacher-learner dialogue, pupil to teacher — a personal but professional relationship, pupil to examiner); *pupil to wider audience* (expert to known layman, child to peer group, group member to working group); *unknown audience* (writer to his readers), (Britton *et al,* 1975, ch. 8). The 'context' is the 'referent' the subject of the exchange, what is being talked of or written of. The 'code' is the written or spoken language or a variety of the two. 'Contact' is 'a physical channel and psychological connection'—two people in a room able to hear each other and willing to listen, for example. Thus a salesman (addresser) communicates with a customer (addressee) on the subject of cars (context) in spoken English (code) over the phone (contact). Each factor will influence the outcome: the attitude of the salesman, his relationship with his customer, their knowledge of cars, his command of language, the fact that one talks by phone somewhat differently than face to face. Change the situation and we will change the nature of the language. If the customer is the salesman's doctor and the scene is set in his surgery the linguistic performances of both are likely to be different.

The implication of this situational relativity for the assessment of language and of writing in particular is that we need performances in a variety of situations before we can begin to form a fairly satisfactory view of the writing of an individual.

2.5.2 F. J. Schonell, *Backwardness in Basic Subjects* (1948)
Schonell recognized that one composition was inadequate as evidence of judgement. He thus advocated and used four:

> Narrative-descriptive – 'Home'.
> Imaginative – 'If you had wings and could fly what would you do?'
> Explanatory or expository – 'How to play – (a game or sport)'
> Story reproduction – 'Urashima, the fisher boy'.

He used a representative sample of 1,300 children from 7—14, and a marking scheme based on impression, guided by a schedule: Content (12); Structure (7); Mechanical Accuracy (6). By this means he was able to choose compositions in each area which would serve as a 'median sample' for each age group. Harpin (1976, pp. 65—7) places median compositions on the same topic alongside Schonell's. He comments 'In punctuation and the use of paragraphs particularly, the two sets show clear differences, which may reflect a contrast in teaching priorities.'

2.5.3 The National Assessment of Educational Progress (USA)
This is a national project in the United States designed to furnish information 'regarding the educational achievements of children, youth and young adults'. Information is sought in such areas as Art, Careers, Citizenship, Literature, Mathematics, Music, Reading, Science, Social Studies, and Writing. Interestingly the goals designated must be acceptable to 'scholars in the discipline', 'educators and teachers' and 'thoughtful lay citizens'.

It is the writing with which we are concerned here. The Educational Testing Service (ETS) of Princeton worked with representative panels to produce writing objectives.

The panel recognized that ability in writing could not be measured by one specific task. They saw their objectives as threefold — to demonstrate the ability to reveal personal feelings; to demonstrate the ability to write in response to a wide range of societal demands and obligations; and to appreciate the value of writing. The writing objectives are set out as follows:

I Demonstrates ability in writing to reveal personal feelings and ideas.
  A. Through free expression
  B. Through the use of conventional modes of discourse

II Demonstrates ability to write in response to a wide range of societal demands and obligations. Ability is defined to include correctness in usage, punctuation, spelling, and form or convention as appropriate to particular writing tasks, e.g. manuscripts, letters.
  A. Social
    1. Personal
    2. Organizational
    3. Community
  B. Business/Vocational
  C. Scholastic

III Indicates the importance attached to writing skills.
  A. Recognises the necessity of writing for a variety of needs (as in I and II)
  B. Writes to fulfil those needs.
  C. Gets satisfaction, even enjoyment, from having written something well.

The first set of tasks elicit free expression. IA form is not crucial — jottings, journal, note, verse, perhaps with the self as reader. In IB some more conventional form might be expected with another person as reader — a letter to the editor or public official. But there are no hard and fast distinctions. IIA1 is also instanced by an informal letter, with attention paid to accuracy of information and tone and style of communication. IIA2–3 will be often done in more formal circumstances and 'will require a greater degree of correctness because it will be viewed as representative of someone or some organization in addition to the writer himself'. IIB includes all business correspondence. IIC, scholastic, covers writing that is usually done in connection with some kind of school work — 'such as a book report or examination essay response' (p. 11). Under III the importance of motivation and attitude is stressed, and measured by multiple-choice or short answer tests: writing ability is not being assessed here.

The above information is drawn from the NAEP document of Writing Objectives for the 1973–74 assessment. It is interesting that there is no specific statement of the criteria by which the compositions are to be judged. The only thing the panel seems sure of is the mechanics. Significantly aim II above does not define 'societal demands' except to say with immediate haste that the spelling and punctuation should be correct. And so often, judging from the examples given, these 'societal demands' are conceived in terms of the ability to write letters — from grandchild to 'Gammy' on the one hand to the unscrupulous rabble-rousing one to the 'Citizens of Winchester', or the grumble to the Evergleam Appliance Centre on the other. (There are specimens given.) Perhaps this is what life is about, but it all seems rather sad.

2.5.4 The Assessment of Performance Unit (APU) (UK)

This unit was set up in the UK with a similar aim to the NAEP in the United States — to monitor national standards in key areas of education. There are six panels, one of which is concerned with assessing language ability. This panel concerned itself first with reading and writing. The information which follows is from the 1978 working paper, *Language Performance*. This is the last available publication, and we recognize it may not represent the panel's final views.

The document focuses on important concerns. On the nature of the writing tasks it says:

> Writing is a highly complex activity and no test would be adequate that measured only a narrow segment of its spectrum.   (APU, 1978, p. 2)

On the nature of assessment it says:

> While the whole APU monitoring exercise has been deliberately designed to minimise any 'backwash' on the curriculum, it must be accepted that assessment procedures may transmit messages to teachers about curriculum priorities. Accordingly, it is essential for the APU to produce national forms of assessment that do justice to the intuitive model of writing acted on by most teachers. It must produce forms of assessment that will study a wide variety of writing produced by children in response to different demands and addressed to different kinds of readers.   (APU, 1978, p. 2)

It is not possible to produce written tasks for this purpose which contain all the variables of, for instance, topic, function, audience, situation: inevitably one has to compromise and go for what one considers the most important. The Unit has produced seven tasks for eleven year olds, and eight for fifteen year olds. No pupil does all tasks, but that is a statistical device for 'light sampling' which need not concern us here. It is sufficient that ideally these tasks would arguably give a fair indication of the writing ability of any one person.

Tasks for 11 Year Olds

11.1   Personal response to pictures, music, short quotations from poems or prose, or similar stimuli.
11.2   An autobiographical narrative or anecdote.
11.3   A fictional story.
11.4   A description or account in which the pupil is invited to reflect upon what is described and express no feelings about it.
11.5   An account of something the pupil has learned or read about.
11.6   A verifiable description or account in which the pupil is required to represent faithfully what he has observed.
11.7   An account of how the pupil plans to carry out a task, scheme, or project of some kind.

Tasks for 15 Year Olds

15.1   Personal response to pictures, music, short quotations from poems, or prose, or similar stimuli.
15.2   An autobiographical narrative or anecdote in which the pupil is able to reflect upon the experience recounted.
15.3   A fictional story.
15.4   An objective description or account of a process which the pupil can write from the confidence of personal authority.
15.5   Discussion of an issue of the pupils' own choosing in which he is required to present a point of view and persuade the reader to it.
15.6   An account of how a problem is to be solved or a task to be performed sometimes with the additional requirement of producing notes or a flow chart from which the account is then developed.
15.7   Discussion of an issue for which the pupil has had himself to produce data and evidence, explore the various arguments, and present his own conclusions.
15.8   Discussion of an issue for which evidence and data are provided and the pupil is required to take account of opposing viewpoints.

The tasks were devised on four dimensions: narrative/descriptive or reflective/analytical; control by writer or tester (treatment fairly free or closely prescribed); first-hand or second-hand subject matter; literary or functional. On the whole in the tasks for the older pupils there is more emphasis on an ability to reflect, on being able to operate in dimensions laid down by others; on being able to cope not just with personal experience, but with ideas and processes drawn from a variety of sources. Significantly the concept of 'audience' is not included as a dimension — perhaps because in an 'examination' it is difficult to control, perhaps because its specific influence may have been overestimated in writing — it is in origin a spoken language concept.

The tasks chosen are refreshing in their formulation. The instructions to markers, 'Criteria for Assessing Writing' are less so. These are: orthographic conventions; grammatical conventions; style; structure; and content. Each category carries a possible grade of 3. Under the first spelling and punctuation are considered, under the second grammatical errors resulting from mispunctuation, as well as morphological faults ('he done it') are included. The third, 'style', is a notoriously difficult category; here it is equated with 'appropriateness' rather than, for instance, effectiveness. Structure 'relates to the manner in which what is said in the essay as a whole is ordered or sequenced'. Content is defined, not very helpfully, as 'concerning the subject matter of the essay or written task', and will vary with the task. And in fact the writer rather gives up on advice — in some cases it might be appropriate to consider the extent to which the pupil responds with some degree of imagination or originality — 'while recognizing it is neither possible, nor perhaps desirable, to attempt to specify precisely what is meant by these criteria'.

Any panel trying to suggest manageable all-purpose criteria for national use will inevitably have to be general. This is just the trouble; their assessment procedures 'transmit messages to teachers' as they themselves say. What is likely to be transmitted now is encouragement for those who have always felt spelling, punctuation and grammar are the main concerns of the English teacher (they are placed first in the document); and a genuflection towards structure, style and content, the last two left as vaguely defined as they ever were. Structure is fundamental — we organize our world. Style is fundamental — it is by style not language that we communicate. Content is fundamental — it is in some measure what the people are who make writings for our reading. It will be our purpose in this book to attempt to look more closely at concepts such as these.

2.6 Comment

We have looked at assessments which have been devised for various purposes, which their nature reflects. A public examination tends to look for 'skills' because it can have no contact with the writers, and these have seemed the easiest things to mark objectively. Even so impression marking is probably more valid, in that a total judgement is made. However, little seems to have been discovered about what impression markers are rewarding: in the studies we have examined there seems little consistency. Our investigations suggest that experienced classroom teachers are assessing on a far wider range of criteria than conventional marking schemes would lead us to expect. It does seem that the criteria of assessment for written work need exploration and reformulation.

2.7 Summary

In this chapter we have looked at various schemes for assessing written English.

1. We have said that impression marking has advantages over analytical marking.
2. We have looked at some of the criteria which might be involved in an assessment by impression.
3. We have emphasized the need for a variety of writing tasks by which to assess an individual's writing ability.
4. We have suggested that existing criteria for the assessment of writing need reformulation.

Chapter Three

Development — Language and Style

3.1 Introduction

In Chapter One we claimed that coherent theory of human development must underlie the teaching of language. In Chapter Two we argued that the criteria for the assessment of language are too restricted at present because they do not relate to or imperfectly relate to such a theory.

In this chapter and the next we look at some of the considerations on which this theory of human development would be based. Because we wish to give as complete as possible a picture of human development as manifest in language, we shall not merely confine ourselves to 'linguistic' features of writing. Rather do the following suggest themselves:

1. Linguistic
2. Stylistic
3. Cognitive
4. Affective
5. Moral

We are not arguing that there is always a close relationship between these aspects of development in the individual. It is manifestly untrue that someone fluent in language is *necessarily* effective in style; that someone highly developed intellectually is so emotionally and morally, or can write half a page of decent English. It is however convenient to consider the verbal — linguistic and stylistic — in this chapter, and the personal — cognitive, affective, moral — in the next. Definitions of these terms where necessary will be given in the appropriate sections.

3.2 Linguistic Development

For over seventy years research workers have attempted to measure the language development of children objectively — by classifying and counting certain language features. This has clearly not been done with the insights modern linguistics could have brought to it. Many of the studies are by psychologists, concerned with diagnosis; many by educationalists interested in measuring attainment. For our purposes the result of all this is not very significant, and we have not used such 'linguistic' measures in our researches. Nevertheless because the work is so great in amount, and is so often quoted, it is necessary to give some account of it here, and to offer some explanation about why we did not take up a similar line of enquiry.

We may summarize the language features commonly looked for as follows. *Quantity*: the number of words, of phrases, of sentences, the mean sentence length. *Variety*: the number of different words, the variety of parts of speech (adjectives and adverbs are taken to indicate greater 'maturity' than nouns and verbs). These last two measures are calculated in relation to the total words used; obviously there is much more likelihood of variety in ten sentences than in two. This is how what is called the type-token ratio is calculated — the number of word types under study (e.g. adjectives) being expressed as a ratio of the total number of words, for every fifty or a hundred words. Again the number of unusual words has been regarded as significant (for instance words not occurring in basic vocabulary lists such as Thorndike's, 1944), as has also the variety of sentence used (question, statement, exclamation, etc.). *Complexity*: the basic sentence pattern is sometimes not easy to define, particularly in spoken language. Thus similar concepts have been suggested, such as 'phonological' or 'communicative units' (Loban, 1963) or T-units, the minimal unit that can be punctuated as a sentence whether the writer has punctuated it that way or not (Hunt, 1965: T-unit = minimal terminal unit). With some workable definition of the unit one can look at complexities. The degree of subordination or embedding of phrases and clauses is widely employed. Thus Loban (1963) used a 'weighed index of subordination' giving one point for each dependent clause, and a similar type of weighting for other subordinate features: two points for any dependent clause modifying or within another dependent clause; two points for any dependent clause containing a verbal construct such as an infinitive, gerund or participle; and three points for any dependent clause modifying a dependent clause modifying a dependent clause. The grammar used in analysis has on the whole tended to be traditional, but there have been studies using transformational grammar (Loban 1963, Harpin 1973).

Loban's name has been mentioned. He directed by far the most substantial study carried out on these lines by taking kindergarten children and following their language development over thirteen years. He started with 338 students and 211 remained at the end (Loban, 1963 and 1976). Oral interviews recorded, written compositions, reading tests, IQ tests, tests on the use of connectives, teacher's ratings, provided the main data. The basic unit of analysis was the 'communication unit' — each independent grammatical predication, or each effectively complete answer to a question.

Certain specific features of language were selected and followed over the whole range. The first three dealt with fluency in speech and writing, and the remaining five with the 'use of syntactical strategies'. Loban carried out an analysis in which such features were related to age. The study was unlucky in the sense that it took so long that it was overtaken by other research, sometimes using instruments that Loban had originally devised; so that by the time of final publication in 1976 its findings were a matter of common expectation. But it was Loban's achievement that he developed this line of research to its limit.

The study by Harpin *et al.* demonstrates the kind of work possible in this tradition. Concerned with writing development in the junior school, it used the following measures: sentence length, clause length, subordination index, Loban subordination scale, use of simple sentences, use of complex sentences, use of 'uncommon' subordinate clauses (all except adverbial clauses of time and noun clause objects), the incidence of non-finite constructions in the main clause, general index of personal pronoun use, the proportion of first person and of third person uses, the proportion of personal pronoun uses other than as subject.

If we may generalize from the results of numerous studies (for summaries of the research see e.g. McCarthy, 1954, Carroll, 1968, Harpin, 1973) it seems that in pre-school children language maturity is marked by greater number of words, greater mean sentence length, greater variety of words and parts of speech, greater use of unusual words, use of varied sentence types, greater complexity of structure, and superior coherence. However, we have to be cautious in considering these findings. Early researchers do not seem to have been sufficiently aware of the importance for its linguistic content of the situation in which the language was produced. Harpin *et al.* (1973) with junior school children find that their results agree with those of other research workers (p. 132) on the importance only of sentence length, clause length, and to a less extent on index of subordination. They point out that the most important source of variability in all measures is the kind of writing required.

As far as this line of enquiry is concerned — describing the development of written language in conventional 'linguistic' terms — investigation seems to have gone as far as it can. The results are not surprising: on the whole older children write more, have a wider vocabulary, and use more complex sentences than younger children. These things are worth knowing. But it seems that we shall have to redefine our linguistic instruments if anything more significant is to be revealed. 'Count' measures are inevitably crude because they cannot account for meaning, and development lies essentially in the meanings that can be offered.

For completeness it should be added that the growth of linguistics from c. 1960 onwards, together with the advent of the tape recorder, gave impetus to the examination of the language of *pre-school* children, under the stimulus of Chomsky's work *Aspects of the Theory of Syntax*, 1965, particularly. McNeil produced a notable description in *The Acquisition of Language* (1970). The child was seen to move from holophrases to phrase structures (with an apparently pivot-open class grammar unlike adult systems) to the transformational rules and rules of accidence. Meaning was not considered except incidentally. After 1970, however, with the writings of such workers as Brown, Bruner and Wells, the behaviour of the child and its meaning has been seen as prior to the language.

After the age of four and a half years Crystal discerns what, in his nomenclature, is a seventh stage which he characterizes thus: 'In short what the child has to learn after the age of five is that there are layers in the interpretation of a sentence that are not immediately apparent from the perceived form of the sentence. Sentences do not always mean what they seem to mean' (1976, p. 49). The work of Carol Chomsky (1969) demonstrates this. For five year olds, Bill does the shovelling in 'John promised Bill to shovel the driveway' on analogy with 'John told Bill to shovel the driveway'. It is only by the age of ten years that nearly all of them understand the two constructions.

Study of the acquisition of further syntax seems to be rare. Yerrill (1976) examines a number of parenthetical, appositional and related items in various adult spoken and written texts to establish categories which he applied to the spoken and written language of nine—eighteen year olds. Constructions such as non-embedded, participal, and relative clauses, and appositions, as well as parentheses proper, are included. He concludes that syntactic development, as evidenced by such items, continues into the later secondary stage, and it is the written rather than the spoken word that plays the important part in this development. But a good deal more work would have to be done in a variety of situations to see if this thesis could be sustained. The parentheses in spoken language (asides, *sotto voce* explanations, reciprocal devices) are not necessarily of the same kind as in the written language. But that such syntactic development does take place in the written language seems sufficiently demonstrated.

3.3 Stylistic Development

Whereas, as we have seen, there are many measures, at least of a certain kind, of linguistic development, there are at the moment none whatsoever of the development of style in the writings of children.

'Development of style' is usually discussed in two contexts — one is the historical, as in Robert Adolph's *The Rise of Modern English Prose Style* (1968) (readers looking for an evaluation of Saul Bellow or John Fowles will be disappointed — 'modern' means up to the later seventeenth century). The other is literary, referring to a particular author. Shakespeare is seen as moving from his derivative early period with formal heroic couplets, as in the Henry VI plays, to his unique 'mature' style with its tension between the meaning and the form. But it is not discussed in terms of the progress of pupils from childhood towards adulthood. Indeed at first sight this seems a hazardous undertaking. And yet so much is talked about style, in discussing English composition, so many marking schemes reward it, that it seems the attempt should properly be made, exploratory though it must inevitably be.

3.3.1 Definitions of Style

Crystal and Davy (1969, pp. 9—10) distinguish four commonly employed senses of 'style' — the language habits of a person, of groups of people, the effectiveness of a mode of expression, and the idea of style as 'good' writing.

The first is what in the spoken language could be called idiolect; it represents the particular features by which we learn to recognize a speaker or writer. The 'style' of Browning, the 'style' of Pope, refers to certain characteristics they individually possess. The second is what is sometimes called dialect — consisting of a regional, class or occupational usage. Rather more closely defined is what is sometimes called 'variety' or 'register' — the group of associated lexical and structural items which tend to occur in association with a particular purpose and a particular subject matter — in a court of law, a football commentary, a church service, and so on.

The third connotation of style is effectiveness — the fulfilling of a particular purpose. 'In every work regard the writer's end' as Pope says (*Essay in Criticism*, line 255). This has tended to become associated with a 'plain' and 'unadorned' style.

This fourfold classification gives us some hints of the way that development in style could be viewed. An individual could move of himself towards greater articulateness. He could operate in more registers. He could express more complex things effectively. He could work towards elegancies of style in the way that Dylan Thomas did, so that sometimes there is only style.

Nevertheless none of this gets us very far — we need to be able to look at the development of style in a much more detailed way. To do this a linguistic model is helpful.

3.3.2 The Norm and the Deviation
Enkvist (1964, p. 12) makes a distinction between statements on style which are objectively verifiable, and those that are subjectively impressionistic. Amongst the former, he mentions

> Style as a shell surrounding a pre-existing core of thought or expression; as the choice between alternative expressions; as a set of individual characteristics; as deviation from a norm; as a set of collective characteristics.

Three of these statements coincide with those of Crystal and Davy as discussed above — style as 'shell' is their 'style as ornament'; as a 'set of individual characteristics' is their 'language habits of a person'; as a 'set of collective characteristics' is their 'language of a group'. The one which does not, because it goes into the degree of detail that Crystal and Davy's definitions were not concerned with, is 'style as deviation from a norm'. This and 'the choice between alternative expressions' interest us especially.

Enkvist takes up the idea of the norm and defines style as follows:

> The style of the text is a function of the aggregate of the ratios between the frequencies of its phonological, grammatical and lexical items, and the frequencies of corresponding items in a contextually related norm. (p. 28)

Thus, with Pope, decasyllabic rhymed couplets occur frequently in satire as indeed they do in much Augustan satiric verse which we could regard as a norm. But many other items, such as the marked contrast between 'vulgar' and 'polite' terms, actually might not occur so frequently in the norm, and thus give the style its distinction. Speaking of norms Enkvist writes:

> For the stylistic analysis of one of Pope's poems, for instance, norms with varying contextual relationships include English eighteenth century poetry, the copies of Pope's work, all poems written in English in rhymed pentameter couplets, or, for greater contrast as well as comparison, the poetry of Wordsworth. Contextually distant norms would be e.g. Gray's *Anatomy* or the London Telephone Directory of 1960 (p. 29).

A further example is from Swift. In his *A Modest Proposal*, he writes of the condition of the poor in Ireland:

> But I am not in the least pain about the matter, because it is very well known that they are every day dying and rotting by cold and famine and filth and vermin as fast as can be reasonably expected.

Here Swift is setting up a complex of features which distinguishes this sentence from the norms he has provided already in the text and also from other norms associated with rational and human persons. The surprise element embodied in the contrast between the neutral 'not in the least pain about the matter' and the evocative 'rotting', 'filth', 'vermin', and the compounding of this contrast with the word 'reasonably' to suggest that any rational man would expect the poor to die thus, provides a shock for the reader which demands that he reviews the meaning of what has come before. The placing of the phrase 'everyday' between the auxiliary and the verb rather than after it causes a disfunction which adds emphasis to the rest of the sentence, which in itself defies norms which have already been set up in the text. Both the cumulative use of a succession of co-ordinating conjunctions and the pounding rhythms, indicated by the words selected, give to this sentence a power which isolates it from the rest of the surrounding text. In this way Swift defies inattention in the reader and demands more than a superficial reading, which the measured and temperate syntax of the immediately preceding sentences might have induced. In linguistic terms McIntosh (1961, p. 33) expresses something of the stylistic choices open to the writer:

> Normal collocations, normal grammar
> Unusual collocations, normal grammar
> Normal collocations, unusual grammar
> Unusual collocations, unusual grammar

This then is the view of style where language is regarded as in relationship to a norm. It implies the other view of style we noted in Enkvist's list — as choice — for any writer is choosing how far he will deviate from the understood norms; and after that more particularly he has a choice between a variety of linguistic items. Milic (1969) in his introductory essay to his examples of style writes:

> Style is made possible by the availability of variant forms with synonymous context and is realised by a choice among these variant forms . . . but the writer's choice is not really free: it is limited by the resources of his idiolect (his active repertory of lexicon and syntax) and by the way in which this idiolect functions below the surface of his consciousness.

He discusses four sorts of choice which are available to the writer. These are: addition, omission, transposition, and substitution. Addition includes such things as the insertion of adjectives before nouns, intensifiers before adjectives and adverbs, the doubling of items as in 'assume and suppose', 'hale and hearty', parenthetical asides, parallelism and seriation. Omission involves the deliberate omission of connectives or the leaving out of parts of a structure, as in ellipsis. Transposition employs inversion, rhetorical effects such as the periodic sentence (where the grammatical structure cannot be identified for certain until the end), and the placing of adverbs such as 'however' and 'therefore' almost anywhere in the sentence. Substitution may be lexical as in the choice of individual words with roughly the same meaning, as in 'stay' or 'remain', 'paternal' or 'family'. It may also be syntactic as in the choice between active/passive, nominal/verbal, attributive/phrasal modifiers, participle/infinitive. Milic proposes a method of stylistic analysis which involves the stripping away of all the expressive elements. The method is reminiscent of the transformational grammatical analysis of language to discern the deep structures. It will tell us nothing about the overall effectiveness of the text, but a good deal about the means of expressing meaning that the writer uses.

The two related notions of 'norm' and 'choice' outlined here will now be discussed in relation to children's writing.

3.3.3 Norm as Sentence

These notions of norm and sentence seem useful when we come to look at development, for *norm* gives us the idea of a starting point, some form of language which exists early, from which we see changes made by *choice* as the writer evolves. On this we suggest that it is possible to build a theory of development which is chronological, corresponding in rough terms with the development of children. It may or may not apply to other kinds of stylistic development — the changes in the adult Shakespeare's language for instance. The argument is based on what seems to us to be the special place held by the narrative in written English.

Briefly the argument is as follows:

The *norm* of all language is the sentence.
Because of the form of the sentence the basis of writing is the narrative.
Development is to be discerned in choice, in the deviation from the norm of the sentence, and by enlargement of the narrative.

'The norm of all language is the sentence'. Chomsky argues that there are only a few basic sentence patterns in language, and that the human infant has the innate ability to recognize these and to learn to use them himself. Often these patterns are not presented to him as 'well-formed sentences', yet he is able to select from 'natural speech', with all its 'numerous false starts, deviations from the rules, changes of plan in mid course, and so on . . . the underlying system of rules' that he has to master (1965, p. 4). These rules enable him to produce, in English, the following four types of sentence:

S V O   John loves Janet
S V (intransitive)   John loves
S V be complement   John is in love
S V copulative complement   John seems confused

These sentences make one of two statements — about action, or about existence. The first two above tell what John *does*: the second two what John *is*. All sentences basically do one of these two things.

The reason that the sentence is like this is very simple. It is because the world is made up of people and things. These people and things have characteristics. And further they may perform actions, which must essentially be performed in time. Thus there is a time sequence implied in 'John loves Janet' in that both must exist prior to the act of loving. The order of words in English does not reflect this, though the meaning does. (There are of course some languages with the pattern SOV so that the two people are named prior to the action). At any rate, we need sentences to say people and things exist, and sentences to say that they carry out actions. Child-rearing practices reflect the nature of the language in this way. Without any linguistic training mothers nevertheless require their children to name people and objects —what is usually the first 'word' is a name — Mum — shaped from the stream of babble; and they require them to describe actions — what are you/is he (she) doing, etc.

To anticipate our argument a little it is by variations on these basic sentence patterns for particular purposes that we create 'styles'.

3.3.4 Sentence into Story
In his *The Child's Concept of Story* Arthur Applebee looks at the structure of children's stories using terms drawn from Vygotsky. He sees between two and five a movement: heaps, sequences, primitive narratives, unfocused chains, focused chains, narratives. 'Heaps' are ideas recorded as they occur with few sentence links. What is interesting in the examples Applebee gives is that the individual items are recorded as 'well formed sentences' even when the linkage is poor or non-existent. This is from a child of two years, eleven months (Eliot M.)

> The daddy works in a bank. And Mommy cooks the breakfast. Then we get up and get dressed. And the baby eats breakfast and honey. We go to the school and we get dressed like that. I put coat on and I go in the car. And the lion in the cage. The bear went so fast and he's going to bring the bear back, in the cage. (1978, p. 59)

Applebee sees story as moving from dissociated items to the items being linked together 'on the basis of an attribute shared with the common centre or core of the story' (p. 60). A coherence can be seen in for example Lucetta D., three years four months:

> A little girl drawed her mummy
> Then the mummy got mad at her and she cried.
> She lost her mummy's cookies. She got mad at
> her again. And she drawed her mummy again.
> And her mummy got mad at her again. And her
> daddy got home. That was Judy.

In these examples and in many others we could quote our attention is constantly drawn to the structure of the simple sentence. These are spoken, but the feature is even more in evidence in children's early writing — they necessarily regress because of the taxing cognitive and mechanical load imposed upon them.

The difference between the two examples quoted lies, as we have said, in the 'centring', but also in the modifications of the sentence in the latter. First there is the linking of the two ideas causally in the second sentence, which presages a formal result clause. Second there is the 'stylistic' use of repetition of the drawing incident and the mother's ire. And third there is the beginning in very conventional form of providing greater information than the basic sentence gives — the *little* girl'. Fourth, although emotion cannot be conveyed, and metaphorical language is out of the question, yet anger is at least stated.

There are hints then here about how we might draw up a model of the development of style, based on 'norm and choice'. The sentence as we see it in the early compositions of young children has the following characteristics:

> It is narrative or descriptive
> It is affirmative
> It is literal and factual
> It is self-oriented

These characteristics mark a norm. The choices lie in deviations from it. The narrative/descriptive characteristics appear in this example by Daren, aged 7, The Last Day of the War:

> It was 10 days from the end of the war
> the bombing had stopped. A girl
> went into a building then a bomb fell
> through the ceiling. Just then two boys
> came down the street they came in the
> saw the girl.

The first two sentences describe: the others further the action. There is a sense in which all discourse is basically narrative or descriptive, because this is what sentences do, narrate and describe. Take a sentence chosen more or less at random from Spencer (Enkvist *et al*, 1964, p. vii).

> It is true that modern linguistics achieved what autonomy it possessed by turning its back, at least for a time, upon the historical and comparative preoccupations of traditional philosophy, focusing much of its attention on the task of describing exotic languages, many of them with no written history.

The narrative structure of this will emerge as being similar to

> Now the king turned his back on the traditions of his country and spent his time engrossed in books.

Or again the descriptive structure appears in

> (the English speaking student) is 'rarely however, able to analyse and classify those differences' (p. xi)

in comparison with

> The king's subjects were unable to understand this.

This is not to argue that for instance argumentative discourse is the 'same' as narrative or descriptive, but that the sentence with its two functions does in fact provide a norm against which development can be seen in terms of choice. In one sense narrative/descriptive can be seen as a training ground for more abstract forms of discourse. As we have seen in Applebee's work the thinking problems in more abstract structuring are involved in the stories of quite young children.

The fact that the basic sentence is a statement enables all kinds of variations to be made. Milic (above, 3.5) argues that choices are in terms of addition, omission, transposition, substitution. Addition could be of many kinds — the placing of further sentences next to a single sentence: the addition of words within the sentence — adjectives, adverbs, subordinate clauses and phrases. One example of omission would be if Daren's sentence

> Just then two boys came down the street
> they came in they saw the girl

were written as

> Just then the two boys came down the street,
> came in and saw the girl

Transposition would include all kinds of rhetorical effects of inversion, repetition, and so on. But it would also include re-ordering in extended writing, so that such devices as beginning *in medias res*, flashbacks, etc., are included. Substitution would include Chomsky-type transformations:

The girl was seen by the two boys

and the choice between individual words

The child was seen by the two boys

The literal nature of the statements of young children is no accident. The fact that these statements are in fact so literal may come as a surprise; we hear so much of the 'imaginations' of young children. But much of this imagination is literal in the child's terms. The child who thinks his father can put the sun out like a light is not imaginative, but restricted because of his egocentric viewpoint. The child who thinks the sun is an orange is just confused. To create metaphors requires the ability to perceive objects as distinct and having a relationship, yet not to confuse one object with another. This is a task beyond young children. Not only are the statements literal; they tend to be factual. The ability to express affect *in words* is not easily come by. In the spoken language the emotion is carried by the paralinguistics (tone of voice, speed, etc.) and so anyway there is little need to express it otherwise. When the child comes to write he is faced with cognitive and mechanical problems which he did not have in the spoken language, and so even more tends to write simple factual sentences.

These problems also explain to some extent the self-oriented nature of young children's writing. So intent is the writer on the task of writing individual words that the only audience he has is himself as he goes from word to word. But there is also an explanation in terms of the child's subjectivity, a sense of audience requires an ability to project which is beyond him at this stage. Just as when he talks he talks from a background of shared experience with people he will know very well, so that there is no need to be explicit, so when he writes he will tend to do the same — the utterance will be context-bound with clues for the uninitiated absent.

3.3.5 The Development of Style in Children's Writing
We may sum up the argument of the previous section as follows:

That style is the result of a series of choices made to diverge or not to diverge from the norm represented by the sentence

It may be expressed in tabulated form as follows:

SENTENCE	CHOICE
Sentence as affirmative statement is	added to
	omitted from
	transposed
	substituted for
Sentence as narrative/description is	re-ordered
	abstracted
Sentence as literal/factual is	made metaphorical
	made affective
Sentence self-oriented is	made other-oriented

So far so good, but in fact there must be some principle of choice. Choice can only be exercised in terms of the meaning one wishes to convey, and convey effectively ('the best words in the best order') and so we must add a fifth statement:

Sentence as meaning is	made effective

We can now add to our definition, that

Style is the result of a series of choices made to diverge or not to diverge from the norm represented by the sentence. The choices are made to the end of effective communication.

Let us consider what these statements imply for a developmental model of children's writing.

Sentence as affirmative statement. Choices imply that vocabulary will become more extensive and more apt, that syntax will become more complex, more varied, that sentences will become longer, and that they will be associated with more sentences, so that the discourse becomes longer. There is clear evidence that this happens from the count measures of language which have been used in so many pieces of research.

The king sat in his counting house
The king counted out his money.

Neither of these will do for the effect the writer intends. Addition will not help ('The fat king sat comfortably in his cosy counting house'.) But omission will

The king sat in his counting house
Counting out his money

Transposition will not ('Did thinking sit . . .), nor will substitution ('counting out his lolly'). The effect is best achieved by a singing rhythm, minimum information, good rhymes, no disruption in idea till the last line ('pecked off her nose'). Maturity of style implies, not that one writes more, and uses more complex devices, but that one can choose between them in terms of effectiveness.

Sentence as narrative and description. In this nursery rhyme the first four lines are largely descriptions, the last one narrative

> The queen sat in the parlour, eating bread and honey,
> The maid was in the garden hanging out the clothes,
> When up came a blackbird and pecked off her nose.

The effect is achieved by surprise. Had the blackbird been introduced earlier, waiting in a tree, the effect would have been achieved by suspense. Either way the action is chronological. If however the next line went on

> The blackbird long had waited to do this horrid deed,
> And fed him on a diet, of almond tarts and mead,

then we should have a non-chronological principle of organization introduced, one of retrospection to explain the main events. There are two re-ordering processes. They are a matter of overall structure.

There is also a development of narrative description, not only into more complex narrative description, but also into more abstract writing. Consider:

> The king sits in his counting house
> The government sits in parliament
> Government legislates

or

> If the maid hangs out clothes
> She will get her nose pecked off

> If a certain course of action is embarked upon
> Then terrible consequences follow

In psychological terms the process is one of moving from concrete to formal thinking. In stylistic terms we can still see the description and narrative respectively in the two groups.

Sentence as literal/factual. One line of extension is towards literal/factual discourse expressing more complex ideas, though the more extended the discourse becomes the more it is likely to contain metaphor at various levels, some completely dead, others much less so (see for instance the passage quoted above (3.3.4) from Spencer, where modern linguistics is 'turning its back' and 'focussing much of its attention'). Another line of extension is metaphorical and affective.

As we have mentioned one of the problems in writing is to communicate emotions which were formerly carried by the paralinguistics. We may illustrate from Alasdair Aston's anthology of children's writing for the ILEA, *Hey Mister Butterfly* (1978). Olive Barnes is seven:

> Spring
> I love the strong wind
> I love the spring when birds start
> to build their nests
> And the daffodils are growing
> I love the light of the sunlight upon me

Here we have the affirmative sentence. The effect is built up by repetition (an aspect of 'transposition'). It has gone beyond the description of the external world and is attempting to describe the internal world of feeling. The resources available do not go beyond statements, to which the reader contributes the emotion. In 'Spaghetti' by Natasha Bartlett, aged eight, a comparison is made:

> A long piece of spaghetti
> bolognaise,
> A long piece of string

This is the beginning of metaphor, but only the beginning because string and spaghetti are so similar (we refer to a string of spaghetti). On the other hand an older girl, Rochelle Beman, aged eleven, in 'The Park' compares things not apparently alike (dandelions and park lights), yet with considerable felicity:

> I'm glad that I live near a park
> for in winter, after dark,
> the park lights shine,
> as bright and still as dandelions
> on a hill.

In a writer aged seventeen there are features to be noticed which are not present earlier. The poem 'Love', by Henryk Borowski is based on the simple sentence:

> Love is
> Running, excitedly,
> Through the chilly evening,
> Dialling a number
>
> Love is
> Dialling the number
> And making a mistake

Love is
Dialling a number
And dropping the coin
On to the floor

Love is . . .
Receiving a cold line
Colder than the line
On which the word is carried

The love is now
Colder than the air around you
Colder than your
Nose or toes,
Colder than the
frozen tears
On your face

The whole poem is a sustained metaphor in which the telephone and its failures symbolize the failures in communication between lovers, and within that metaphorical framework arises another series of metaphors based on 'cold', stemming from 'receiving a cold line'. The word 'cold' ('colder') occurs five times driving home the emotion, culminating in 'frozen' tears. We are not of course suggesting that all this is the only possible movement in the metaphorical/affective dimension, far from it. But the poem demonstrates very aptly what may happen to the simple affirmative descriptive sentence in all three of the categories we have discussed so far.

Sentence, self oriented. For reasons which we have already touched on the young child's outlook is egocentric. One way that this affects the sentence is that it may not contain sufficient information for the reader to fully understand it without sharing the child's forms of reference. There is a gradual move to do this, so that the language becomes less context-bound, more context-free. Thus stylistic choices for effectiveness may require considerable 'additions'. Associated with this is a growing sense of appropriateness in language, an awareness of the social/linguistic conventions of language use for which we use the term 'register' or 'variety'; or from another viewpoint 'genre'. This is not to say that children do not gain very early some sense of this. Pre-school children are well able to role-play adults, sometimes giving them gruff voices and severe disciplinary phrases. But register is complex and takes time and experience to acquire. The first major problem for children is to differentiate between spoken and written English when they come to write. Further differentiation needs to be acquired between modes of spoken and modes of written English. This is not a matter which need detain us here as it is fully considered in the work of Britton *et al.* (1975)

in terms of movements from a 'seed bed' of expressive language (pp. 82—3).

Sentence as meaning. Stylistic devices are all subordinate to the effectiveness of the communication, which has some relationship to the intentions of the writer though not necessarily to his conscious intentions. We can only go so far, though this is quite far, in considering style in terms of 'norms' and 'choice'. Over and above this we need to know how well the writing succeeds in getting across its message to us. It is more than the sum of its parts. Nevertheless, there is clearly a relationship between the choices a writer makes and his effectiveness as a writer.

The concept of choice is in fact basic to our view of stylistic maturity. It is not even the effectiveness of a writer on a particular occasion — the young children we quoted were all 'effective'. It is the resources at his command on which he can draw, his repertoire — they must be adequate to express complex thoughts and emotions as well as simple ones. If he can do this in a simple way so much the better, but that is a matter of his choice.

3.4 Summary

We have attempted to build up a theory of the development of style on which a system of analysis for children's writing can be based. We have proceeded as follows:

1. Some definitions of style have been looked at: style as the language habits of a person; a group of people; the effectiveness of a mode of expression; style as 'good writing'.
2. The idea of certain writers — of style as choices in relation to a norm — has been discussed.
3. The norm proposed as that suitable for discussing style in children's writing is the sentence. All sentences are seen as basically narrative, and thus the narrative is the basis of all writing.
4. The choices which may be made in relation to this norm have been considered with particular examples from children's writing: choices of syntax and vocabulary; choices of structure and level of abstraction; choices of metaphor and affect; choices of audience; overall choices in terms of writer's intentions.

Chapter Four

Personal Development

In Chapter Three we considered the development of language and style in the individual. In this chapter we want to look at some ideas on aspects of his more personal development — his thinking, or 'cognition', his emotions and feelings, or 'affect', and his morality. The material of these two chapters thus serves as a theoretical basis for the criteria of analysis for children's written work which we set out in Chapter Five.

4.1 Cognitive Development

4.1.1 Piaget

The classical account of cognitive growth is Piaget's. Cognition, he argues, is a way of organizing one's experience. Perceptions of items are related to or differentiated from perception of other items so building up internally a schema. This is not so much added to but modified and adjusted as new items are received into it. He uses the term 'operations' by which he means actions carried out in the mind — ordering, combining, separating, re-ordering, and so on. In the early stages the child will display no more than rules for simple operations such as the ability to make concepts. Later on he will develop and use rules for generalizing and deducing, for instance.

Piaget's four stages of development are well known. In the *sensori–motor* period, 0–2 years, the child's physical sensations build up for him a picture of the world — he sees objects, touches them, tastes them and thus registers them. Piaget argues that one of the main things he learns is the permanence of objects — that they do not disappear just because one ceases to perceive them. In the *pre-operational* stage, 18 months–7 years, he learns symbolization, particularly the symbol system of language, but also modes of play and drawing for example. He uses language to organize and classify the particular instances but cannot carry out the 'operations' of relating instances. Thus in Piaget's famous 'conservation' experiment a child recognizes a quantity of liquid in a thin jar. Because he judges on one dimension only, e.g. height, he cannot recognize that there is the same amount of liquid when it is poured into a shallow wide jar. He cannot relate this observation of the first jar to his observation of the second. In the *concrete operational* stage, 7–11, the child will have mastered conservation because he can deal with two variables (in this case width and height). The logic of cause and effect becomes established as do the concepts of time and space. He can classify and order serially. *Formal operational thinking*, 11–16, enables the adolescent to go beyond classification and seriation based on the 'real' to an ability to work from postulates or hypotheses, to entertain a world of possibilities.

> Finally, in formal thought, there is a renewal in the direction of thinking between reality and possibility in the subject's method of approach. Possibility no longer appears merely as an extension of an empirical situation or of action actually performed. Instead it is reality that is now secondary to possibility. . . . In other words, formal thinking is essentially hypothetico-deductive. By this we mean that deduction no longer refers to perceived realities, but to hypothetical statements.
>
> (Piaget and Inhelder 1969, p. 251)

This suggests that the capacity to theorize and speculate is a later cognitive stage than that to describe and explain, since describing and explaining are operations on real events or phenomena. Formal operational thinking may involve the capacity to reason on the basis of verbal statements:

> Edith is fairer than Susan. Edith is darker than Lily. Who is the fairest?

Children of ten years find this difficult, yet would have no trouble if it were simply a matter of arranging dolls in serial order. If a child can argue a case in writing a speech he is operating in some sense hypothetico-deductively, though at what level depends on the complexity of his argument. We should not expect this development to emerge until adolescence.

4.1.2 Thought and Written Language

Piaget's hierarchy of cognition is a point of reference but work on its implications in practical situations has not been as useful as the classroom teacher has a right to expect. We shall look at three of the studies which have a bearing on the relationship of thought to written language, drawing on the work of three notable psychologists, one British (Peel), and the other two American (Bloom and Bruner).

(i) B.S. Bloom *et al., Taxonomy of Educational Objectives* (1956) (cognitive domain).

In devising a taxonomy or system of classification in the cognitive domain,

Bloom and his collaborators are very much in the Piagetan tradition. They define cognition to include activities such as remembering and recalling knowledge, thinking, problem-solving and creating. The Taxonomy contains six major classes: knowledge, comprehension, application, analysis, synthesis, and evaluation. They maintain that the major thread running through the Taxonomy 'appears to be a scale of consciousness or awareness' (p. 19); that is, the further up the hierarchy of cognitive functions a child or learner is within a given educational context, the more conscious he is of his own thinking — he can subject it to examination.

The tasks Bloom devises for testing students at each level of the Taxonomy indicate a movement from knowledge of specific information to what the learner can do with the information — use it in a different context, judge its adequacy and so on. All facets of the hierarchy above 'knowledge' emphasize 'the mental processes of organizing and recognizing material to achieve a particular purpose. The materials may be given or remembered' (p. 204). Within the level 'knowledge' the sub-classifications range from particular details or 'knowledge of specifics' to 'knowledge of theories and structures', a movement from concrete to abstract.

Relevant to language competence, the behavioural objectives found under 'knowledge' are 'familiarity with a large range of words and their common range of meanings' (p. 64), 'familiarity with the forms and conventions of the major types of work, e.g. verse, plays', and 'a knowledge of the rules of punctuation' (p. 70). It is not until 'synthesis', which Bloom regards as level five of the Taxonomy, that we find objectives like 'ability to write creatively a story, essay or verse for personal pleasure' and 'ability to tell a personal experience effectively' (p. 169). There is insufficient definition here — very young children can relate personal experiences 'effectively'.

The hierarchy of the Taxonomy suggests that 'knowledge' must be acquired before tests involving 'synthesis' can be attempted, which implies that the child must have a knowledge of punctuation rules and a large vocabulary before he can attempt a personal story. Another limitation is the inadequate theory of language which is expressed. Notions like 'correct form and usage in speech and writing' predate current linguistic theory, in which usage is dependent on a complex web of factors (see 2.5.1 above). Bloom says (p. 168) 'The nature of the audience to whom the student addresses himself or his work is often crucial in determining what he does', but goes on, 'in some cases it is likely that the student need not take into account any special audience; he carries out the task according to certain minimum standards that will be applied by those who evaluate his work' (p. 409). On none of the writing tasks mentioned at the level of synthesis does he specify the audience. Again, Bloom places the traditional writing categories: transaction, description, argument and exposition, at the same level of cognitive skill — synthesis. Later theorists such as Moffett (1968) argue that the essay, for instance, calling as it does for generalization, probably makes greater cognitive demands on the writer than the story, a chronological sequencing of events in the past.

Bloom's Taxonomy, the cognitive domain, is dated 1956 and cannot really be expected to contain insights which later scholarship has provided. We are in agreement that sustained writing is a complex form of cognitive functioning, embracing both knowledge and synthesis, and Bloom describes cognitive advance as being from recalling information to using it to explain and evaluate. We do however need a finer instrument for assessing the level of cognitive functioning in different types of written discourse than his taxonomy provides.

(ii) E.A. Peel, *The Nature of Adolescent Judgment*, (1971)

Peel extends the work of Piaget and Inhelder in looking at the judgements adolescents make of written materials. Although he is concerned with their reading and interpretation rather than their writing abilities his work is relevant to our interests in bringing out the spread of cognitive abilities demonstrated in this age group. He maintains that the hallmark of formal operational thinking is 'a growing awareness of possibilities' by which he means ideas, theories, hypotheses, opinions, values, causes and analogies and comparisons with previous experience' (p. 15).

The aim of his study is to investigate the understanding and judgement of adolescents by calling for judgements which may be set on a 'describer-explainer scale'. He defines describer-thinking as 'an account of the phenomenon and a relating of its parts without reference to other ideas, analogies, similarities and antecedents or contiguous circumstances', whereas explainer-thinking 'refers a phenomenon causally to previous phenomena and independent generalizations' (p. 26). A child of eleven, when given a problem calling for a judgement will categorically answer 'yes' or 'no' and simply repeat part of the information given as part of the reason for his answer. This is describer-thinking. Full explainer-thinking is evidenced in the replies of the older students; they do not give quick assessments, their answers are not context-bound, but evoke possibilities, go beyond the information given, drawing on generalizations and hypotheses from their own experience to explain their stance.

One of the problems Peel devised presents an aerial photograph of a town in the Canadian wheat belt. Children of 11–14 years were asked: 'Why has this small town grown up there, where the road and railway cross each other?' Younger pupils reply: 'Because the land is flat and they build houses on flat land usually'. At 12½–14 years the replies change to context dominated ones: 'Because you can get the wheat there by railway and road and seeing how the railway goes straight through, it can pick up all the wheat from the farms'. Such answers are dominated by concrete pictorial evidence, with little sign of the child envisaging other possible factors. By 14½ years responses are possibility-invoking:

> Because it is used as a central place to store food and to have it shipped off. It would be used as a central starting point and it provides a shopping centre. Also anything for the farmer can be gathered here, and collected by the farmer later. (p. 22)

This suggests that between 11 and 14½ years there is a marked advance towards hypothetico-deductive reasoning.

Peel's findings indicate that formulations of hypotheses to explain problems correlated markedly with age and mental ability. He maintains that the average thinker up to the age of 13–14 'will not produce more than one or two hypotheses'. Another general result was the apparent incapacity of the younger adolescent thinker to deal with more than one piece of evidence at a time (p. 153). Development in early adolescence is a move away from an *ad hoc* logic to a hypothetico-deductive one. If the movement is discernible in children's written responses to specific questions then we may assume that it will be evidenced also in children's writing in response to more general questions, particularly those which draw on the child's first hand experience. Peel notes that these types of problems given generate different results, and that social problem passages are judged with greater maturity than others (p. 56).

(iii) J.S. Bruner, *The Course of Cognitive Growth*, (1964)

Whereas Piaget, and subsequently Bloom and Peel, give us a general direction to pursue in the development of thinking from the concrete to the formal stage, Bruner's theory of cognitive growth focuses more directly on the part language plays in the process. Bruner is concerned with the development from iconic forms of representation to symbolic ones. He argues that thinking by, for instance, mental pictures is essentially of a much lower level than thinking by means of language:

> In children between four and twelve language comes to play an increasingly powerful role as an implement of knowing ... Translation of experience into symbolic form, with its attendant means of achieving remote reference, trans-

formation and combination opens up realms of intellectual possibility that are orders of magnitude beyond the most powerful image forming system. (1972, p. 165)

This suggests that the interpretative system by which we organize experience can be changed by representing old experiences to ourselves anew, 'recoding' them in different terms, and that language is one of the chief means of 'recoding'. In a later paper (1975) Bruner extends this idea by drawing a distinction between communicative competence and analytical competence. Drawing on current socio-linguistic theory, he defines communicative competence as the ability to make utterances that are appropriate to the context, and he links this with Piaget's notion of decentring since such competence involves both the need to recognize context and the need to recognize the intentions of the speakers in the dialogue. But he maintains that such competence has little effect on the thought of the users; the use of language in ordinary discourse allows us

> to go no further than Piaget's concrete operational stage in which one deals with concrete events in a logic that is *ad hoc*, and not one based on propositions related to each other by a principle of logical necessity (p. 70).

On the other hand analytical competence is akin to formal operations for:

> It involves the prolonged operations of thought processes exclusively on linguistic representations, on propositional problem solving appropriate not to direct experience with objects and events but with ensembles of propositions (p. 72)

It is debatable whether analytical competence develops effectively in the spoken mode alone. The shift from spoken to written representation would seem to aid the emergence of analytical competence, for the very act of writing enables the writer to subject his thought processes to examination. Writing, too, calls for more developed capacities to decentre than speech. The writer has not immediate feedback; he needs a developed sense of internalized audience at once more abstract, more remote. He is carrying on a monologue, unlike the speaker, so his attention is drawn to the inference and inter-relatedness of his propositions in writing which spoken discourse does not offer.

Further, spoken utterances are in a sense context-bound: 'The most general specification of such language use is its movement towards context-free elaboration' (p. 70). It seems that the written forms of the language constitute *par excellence* the means by which such context-free elaboration is achieved as the child grows. In asking a child to write, rather than to reply to us in person, we are asking him to reformulate experience for himself, transform it, into a form in which his propositions are open to examination. In doing so we are moving him towards analytical competence. The child's early attempts at writing are often close to speech in intention; he may give insufficient information to be fully intelligible. His capacities for analytical competence may not emerge until adolescence. Bruner's distinction certainly confirms the notion that some writing tasks may only call for communicative competence—telling a story about events and people would, by his definition, amount to a concrete-operational use of the written mode. Theorizing about a problem would on the other hand call for analytical competence on the part of the writer.

4.2 Affective Development

The term 'affect' ('affective') is often applied to aspects of the human personality seen as distinct from logical reasoning. We are using it here to describe the emotional, interpersonal, and imaginative aspects of man's nature.

Whereas with cognition there seems to be at least some consensus about development this is by no means the case with affect. Instead of attempting the impossible task of trying to reconcile the findings of a vast literature, we have preferred to make a statement based on our own reading and observation, with all the limitations this implies. For our purpose it will be convenient to consider development in terms of the Self; Others — beings who interact with self; and Reality — the external world, as we conceive it, of phenomena and circumstance. These three provide a context.

It is not possible to take a normative view of emotional maturity — to say that all mature individuals must exhibit certain characteristics. This will be related to the value system of the particular society, as well as varying with individuals. Where self-control is regarded as a virtue self-expression might be regarded with suspicion. The Southern Italian is able to express aggression verbally; he might be thought of as immature by the laconic self-contained Scot, whom in turn he might think of as underdeveloped. Again dignified acceptance of what cannot be changed is often advocated. A traditional prayer reads:

> God grant me the courage to change the things I can change,
> the serenity to accept those I cannot
> and the wisdom to know the difference.

But Dylan Thomas cries out to his dying father:

Do not go gentle into that good night.
Rage, rage against the dying of the light.

All we can do therefore is to record some of the aspects of behaviour which seem to be intended in Anglo-Saxon society whenever terms like 'maturity' are used.

4.2.1 Self

The general movement in the growth of Self is from dependence to autonomy; from convention to uniqueness; from unconsciousness to awareness; from subjectivity to objectivity. These are not states which are attained to finally: one does not arrive, one is continually arriving.

The human infant is completely dependent on others for his most trivial needs. In moving towards autonomy he is learning to cope with his own needs; to be responsible for himself, to have confidence in himself, to feel secure, to make choices, to have purpose. He learns a sense of his own worth. Independence in emotional terms is of course different from independence in physical terms. The truly independent person emotionally is the psychopath who is unable to make warm continuing emotional relationships with others; maturity implies the ability to form such relationships and thus be vulnerable to separation and death.

The progress from convention toward uniqueness is preceded by a socializing process whereby the infant is welcomed into the family and community, and is necessarily equipped with its rules and values, behaviour, perceptions. In this way it is inevitably provided with stock judgements and responses. The process of formulating the question 'What do *I* really think and feel?' and beginning to search for answers, is seen as an essential part of growing up.

A third movement is from unconsciousness towards awareness. At first life is undifferentiated — things happen, people behave. Gradually the person becomes aware that things happen for a reason, that people behave from motives. He realizes that this applies to himself and that apparent motives are not necessarily the real motives: self-knowledge begins to emerge. And this is associated with a fourth movement — the decentring we have already spoken about in connection with cognitive judgements. The infant is in essence egocentric, judging everything from the immediate effects on him; there is a gradual process towards objectivity, towards being able to see things in context. As Shotter says:

To be counted an autonomous individual in social life, we must be solely responsible for our own actions. If when so acting we want to be said to be

acting reasonably, in a way intelligible to our fellows, we must attempt in acting
to make our actions intelligible to ourselves in *their* terms; that is, we must
attempt to assess the value of our performances in relation to interests other
than our own immediate and idiosyncratic ones.

(Shotter 1974, pp. 218–219)

4.2.2 Others

In talking of the Self and in using such terms as 'self-development' or 'self-
fulfilment' as is commonly done, there is a danger of considering individuals
in isolation. It is thus helpful to look at a statement of their *needs*. Kellmer
Pringle (1974, p. 148) writes:

There are four basic emotional needs which have to be met from the very beginning of life to enable a child to grow from helpless infancy to mature adulthood. These are the need for love and security; for new experiences; for praise
and recognition; and for responsibility. Their relative importance changes of
course, during the different stages of growth as do ways in which they are met.

In the young child all four of these arise from the presence of others,
particularly his parents in the environment. It might seem that they are
conferring love, praise, widening experience, opportunity to be responsible.
But this is in fact a superficial view. These things arise in interaction between
the child and his parents. Even a young baby will respond at the approach of
his mother by turning his head, wriggling and gurgling. This delights her and
she in her turn replies with coos and handling, to which the baby appropriately responds. Blind babies however go rigid and silent because they are listen-
ing; and this apparent lack of response in the baby to his mother causes her
difficulties because she feels the baby rejects her. She may be unable to
confer the necessary love; and may even reject the baby.

Part of the growth of Self is an increasing sense of Others. The Infant
relates by a process of interaction to people in his environment, but his
judgement of them is primarily as servicing agencies. What they think and feel
he has no concept of. On the other hand a sensitive adult will have acquired
the ability to empathize with those he comes into contact with, know what
it feels like to be in the other person's shoes, though if he is sensitive he will
appreciate that he constantly fails to do this, as well as often succeeds. All
kinds of factors intervene — distance, appearance, race, accent, age, dress,
occupation may suggest a stereotype which handicaps judgement. The process
is not one that accompanies growing up only; it is one that takes place in our
increasing understanding of individuals we come into contact with daily and
whom we meet as new acquaintances. It is a process of moving from external
judgement to a judgement from the viewpoint of the other. This is related to
a good self-image; a person loving himself is secure enough to love others. It
was Christ who spoke of 'loving thy neighbour as thyself'.

4.2.3 **Reality**

By 'Reality' we mean the external world of phenomena; and the facts of a social or personal situation. As an example of the first — the mountain refused to come to Mahomet, so Mahomet very wisely went to the mountain. As examples of the second: if a person has no money he cannot buy a Rolls Royce; if he can't play an instrument, he cannot join the Boston Symphony Orchestra, however good his ability in interior decorating — and so on. The first situation cannot possibly change — there is no way in which the mountain could walk to Mahomet. The second conceivably could in that the ambitious motorist *could* earn enough money to buy the car of his dreams; the interior decorator could take up the flute, practise till perfect, and then be begged to join the orchestra. But both are highly unlikely; for the exceptional individual they might happen, but for the majority of people, outside the super-tax class, or with no musical sense, they are clearly impossible. Wisdom in this case lies in knowing when to stop yearning and to focus on some more accessible goals.

Clearly someone who does not accept the facts of the external world such as that mountains don't walk about, that water drowns, that fire burns, is unlikely to survive long in his non-acceptance. Such individuals are rare outside institutions. In the personal and social world however things are different. On the one hand there are the problems of living — housing, food, heating, schooling, work; on the other the problems of personal relationships.

Jerome Bruner's concepts of 'coping' and 'defending' are relevant here. Coping is a process by which we 'respect the requirements of the problems we encounter, while respecting our integrity' whilst defending is a strategy 'whose objective is avoiding or escaping from problems for which we believe there is no solution that does not violate our integrity of functioning' (Jones, 1968, p. 227). One way in which people 'cope' is by imaginative means. For our purposes we distinguish on the one hand 'fantasy' and on the other 'imagination'.

In our terms 'fantasy' comprises dreams, day-dreams, oral or written stories or episodes involving wish fulfilment. These interpret life in the dreamer's favour. Fairy stories in which good triumphs over evil, are of this kind, so are dreams of what one would do if one won the pools. What characterizes fantasies is that the interpretation of life which they offer is ultimately of no benefit in living life because it is based on a very limited assessment of the situation, though this is not to deny their value as escape and refreshment devices. The good do not in fact always live happily ever after, the pools win is very rare (and often disastrous to the winner).

By imagination, on the other hand, we mean an interpretation of complex phenomena which offers insight into motives and relationships in such a way as to increase the awareness of the interpreter, or those to whom he is interpreting. They are thus put into a position to make choices or at least to apply the insights to their own situations; the activity is 'life enhancing'. Thus a dramatist, a novelist, a sculptor, an artist may be offering imaginative interpretation, often by a parallel symbol or 'objective correlative'.

Infants inhabit a world of fantasy in that their construction of the world only selects very limited evidence. They acquire a real sense of physical objects early — the bed exists and is soft, the floor exists and is hard if you fall, but their wider interpretations are based on limited logic and limited experience. Parents, as in the famous comic postcard, delight in telling stories of their children whose defective logic leads them to explain a pile of milk-bottles as a cow's nest. Imaginative play however is often of a different order. Here children playing the parts of adults, particularly in family situations, are often beginning to internalize roles which will be useful to them later on. As far as speech and writing are concerned small scale or isolated imaginative insights are produced by quite young children. The growth of the imagination lies in the direction of the depth, breadth, scale and control shown in, for instance, *King Lear* or *War and Peace*.

4.2.4 The Education of the Affect

It is not possible in this book to consider the general matter of an education in cognition, in morals or in style. However, on the education of the affect so much has been written which is difficult or confusing that it seems important to try to clarify one or two of the issues.

The question is often asked: 'How do we educate the affective aspects of the personality?' Thus attention is being paid to the education of the emotions. But confusion appears to reign:

> In the presence of so many widely different aims and criteria the ordinary teacher is apt to be perplexed about the purposes of emotional education. Is the basic aim to control emotions, to nourish them, to refine them, or to provide therapeutic release for inhibited feelings? Or should it be to help children to achieve depth and sincerity of emotion, to develop self-awareness, and to make them more considerate for the feelings of others.
>
> (Yarlott, 1972, p. 3)

An obvious answer to these questions appears to be 'Yes', 'Why not?' All these aims appear to be worthy; and are by no means self-contradictory — one might need 'self-control' on one occasion and 'release for inhibited feelings' on another. A good deal depends however on the outcomes one wishes to achieve; the stoics thought that man should display neither joy nor sorrow in the face of good or bad fortune.

One question therefore is about the aims of emotional education. A second question is about its possibility. It does not help that no-one will admit to knowing what an emotion is. A recent book (1978) by Strongman is gloomily discouraging: 'at present emotion defies definition' (p. 2). Fortunately even if people cannot define them, they at least know they have them. Davitz (1969) assumed that emotions are phenomena which people experience, and collected data on the words which they use to describe their emotional states. Ultimately he drew up a list of fifty terms, ranging from admiration, affection, amusement, anger, through fear, friendliness, frustration, to shame, solemnity, surprise.

No emotion is feeling alone: it involves a cognitive element in that it involves appraisal of a situation. One feels admiration *for*, affection *towards*, amusement *at*, anger *against* some person, group or circumstance because one has evaluated them, not necessarily deliberately:

> In other words emotions are basically forms of cognition. It is because of this central feature which they possess that I think there is any amount of scope for educating the emotions.
>
> (Peters, 1972, p. 467)

The evaluation may, for example, be wrong, or incomplete, or too simple. Anger against someone may be completely unjustified, or it may be modified when one understands his motivation. On the other hand it may be completely justified in the light of further knowledge.

The quotation from Peters may seem to suggest that we have just arrived at the point where it is possible to educate the emotions. Emotional education is in fact part of the child-rearing practice of any community; this has always been so, and is a commonplace in developmental psychology.

> Parental efforts at child rearing are certainly the most potent influences in shaping the child's social, cognitive and emotional behaviour.
>
> (Singer and Singer, 1969, p. 274)

Thus Becker (1964) summarizes research on the results of child rearing on a warmth-hostility (coldness) and a restrictive-permissiveness dimension. It is clear that various emotions or reactions are fostered by certain differing types of parental discipline. Thus low aggression, guilt, shame, occur with a warm-restrictive regime; desire for dominance, friendliness, as well as creativity and independence with a warm-permissive regime. Coldness, whether restrictive or permissive produces anger, aggression, resentment – in the first case the aggression turns towards self, in the form of self-contempt, in the second towards others.

Accordingly when the educationalist comes to consider the 'education of the emotions' he has to consider it in the whole context of child rearing and socialization practices, including those of the school and its teaching techniques. Within the curriculum a certain group of subjects are seen as having a special role in emotional education (see for instance Witkin 1976, Ross 1978) — subjects such as English, drama, art, music, particularly, in the opportunities for creative work which they offer. Witkin (1976) uses the term 'feeling form' for the outcome of creative activity (though it's not just feeling). He talks of the way in which this process educates feeling. He speaks of the difference between kicking in a window and painting a picture. In the first case

> The impulse is released and burned up in the behaviour but the behaviour
> does not reciprocate it. The behaviour is not a means of recalling the disturbance
> and thereby of assimilating into Being . . . When the individual paints a picture or
> composes a piece of music, however, his use of the expressive medium recipro-
> cates his impulse in the sense of being that which recalls it. (p. 33)

Breaking the window gets rid of the impulse. Painting a picture keeps the impulse, explores it, makes use of it, perhaps enables one to understand something permanently about one's own aggression. In what real sense one can be said to 'recall' the impulse it is difficult to say; no-one creates from one impulse, and the effect of creating a work of art is sometimes to trans-form original impulses beyond recognition. But the main point still stands. It is important since the distinction is not made in social terms between acceptable and unacceptable behaviour, but in terms of behaviour precipitat-ing growth and that not doing so.

Witkin defines 'personal development' as the 'child's progressive mastery of new and more complex levels of sensate experience' (p. 49). He defines the definition in terms of 'a parallel development of sensate experience to the one that prepares to logical thought' (p. 175) but stresses it is 'not the same order' (p. 177). He confesses however that at this stage he is not able to provide a 'proper developmental sequence' for 'classifying sensate experi-ence' (p. 180). The difficulty seems to be in the rigid separation of 'sensate' and 'cognitive' development. If 'emotions are basically forms of cognition' (Peters, p. 467) or at least involve cognition then it should be possible to devise a developmental scheme involving both. For example feeling is experi-enced as a disturbance which we categorize as an emotion of anger against someone. At the first level it may be repressed or translated into action — one may hit the person concerned. At a second level it is symbolized in verbal aggression, whether sheer abuse or the delicate thrust of a politician who pierces the heart but scarcely leaves a mark on the skin. On a third level it may be formulated as a hymn of hate or a campaign song. We are still concerned with a fairly simple emotion. At a fourth level the situation may be evaluated and other emotions may be seen to be involved; pity, fear and so on. A more complex response, a more complex creative outcome may result. A fifth level may concern the examination by the angry person of his own motivation, again to himself, or in a piece of writing, or other art form.

There are two problems with the model proposed by Witkin. The first is that of the three terms proposed above (4.2) as the context of human activity, Self, Others, and Reality, it only considers Self. Speaking of adolescents he says:

> Theirs is the problem of becoming subjective, of becoming persons. It is the problem of everyman threatened with suffocation by objects that include him as an object. It is the problem of insisting upon one-self. (p. 2)

However sympathetic we may be to the general sentiments, the simple equation in the first line of 'becoming subjective' with 'becoming persons' is disturbing. The second problem is the one just mentioned — the 'sensate' self seems to be regarded as developing without any reference to the cognitive self except that the stages are 'parallel'. But it is not necessary to argue that intellectual and emotional maturity are essential bedfellows (so often this is demonstrably not the case) to be able to argue that cognition is part of emotion, as we have done above.

We have found the most useful model yet produced in that of Harrison (1979), which has a place for cognition and the Self/Other/Reality dimension. Harrison took all the pieces of writing done by a class in English during their 4th, 5th and (if they stayed on) 6th years at secondary school (14—15, 15—16, 16—17 years of age respectively) and with this as evidence devised five stages of growth.

   i. Expressive stage. What do I sense, feel, do, experience, in this world?

> In summary, the first, expressive stage is: directly responsive to the senses, naively communicative and eidetically expressively, context bound. Simple, immediate and unsifted recall of experience; strongly autobiographical basis to writing. Enthusiastic for simple events and sensations of a story in writing and reading.

  ii. Reflexive stage. What effects do these experiences have on me?

> In summary, the second, reflexive stage is: reflective, growing aware of own feelings, relating outside to self, exploring 'inwards'. Tending to exploit relationships, reading for own purposes in working out personal bearings.

 iii. Identifying stage. How do I identify with the people and things related to me?

> In summary, the third, identifying stage is, growing aware of the 'thatness' of the outside world, growing in empathy, aware of feelings and identity of the

other. Capable of some sustained and detached attention to own emotional involvement. A weighing towards 'cognitive' or towards 'affective' aspects may be noted, but a *blend* of these is assumed in the act of identifying. Learning practical skills in relating to people and problems. Tending most to value the person/problem/story for him/her/itself, valuing distinction and difference.

iv. Organizing stage. What values and aims and concerns do I hold on behalf of my world?

Growing sense of commitment on behalf of others, of the group, community, world; growth of sense of belonging, critical, supportive of, contributive to communal values. Comparative skills develop. Tending to synthesise, response to people with response to wide social and moral concerns.

v. Integrating stage. What values emerge from all my relationships, on what do I claim to found my beliefs?

Having established a secure sense of self-hood the learner moves towards a disinterested and independent speculation and exploration, towards a sense of meaning, a 'world view', blossom of spiritual/religious life; developing sense of integrated response, of harmony in relationships.

To fully explain the part of many of the statements in Harrison's summaries we have to go in detail into his arguments and evidence which is not possible here. The quotations however will be sufficient to indicate the comprehensive nature of this approach, with which we have great sympathy. We have a similar concern with the individual, and with the language which at once manifests and helps to create his individuality.

4.2.5 Writing and the Education of the Affect

The act of writing is itself a commitment. Speech vanishes as soon as uttered, but writing does not go away on its own. Writing enables one to organize experience, to structure the world. One is in control of events in a story, of figures in a landscape description, of argument in an exposition. One has extended control for one is not interrupted by another party.

Writing is a means of discovering one's own uniqueness. A common process is the working through of the conventional responses in early draft until one arrives at what one really thinks and feels which has in fact been modified in the process of writing. In Stratta, Dixon and Wilkinson (1974) the writing of a teacher through successive drafts arriving at a three-fold 'uniqueness' (self, expression, form) is discussed. Some poets go through numerous drafts before arriving at what they consider acceptable. For one of Dylan Thomas's poems on his father there are sixty pages of drafts extant, and the poem was unfinished at his death.

Writing enables one to examine one's own feelings. This is the function for instance of many shortish poems. The point is clear so that much illustration is superfluous. However a quotation from 'Make me feel it' by Marge Piercy is particularly apposite because it has as its theme the frustration of not feeling:

> I need an old friend to drop dead so I may weep
> I need a good fighter to be murdered by the CIA so I may care
> The old sores are covered with scartissue.
>
> *Living in the Open*; Poems by Marge Piercy (p. 7)

Hourd (1949) demonstrates the uses of writing on Lawrence's 'Snake', to help a young girl to come to terms with early sexual pressures.

In moving from context-bound to context-free utterances writing essentially requires some objectification of experience, context-free utterance has to contain the information, however this is defined, to make it meaningful to someone other than the writer. The experience must be reformulated and considered (we have already spoken about Bruner's views on the way that this process helps to develop 'analytical competence' (see 4.1.2). Thus in describing a lamprey to his classmates Kevin says:

> and so he put him/in with him/and he was about this long/and he ate him up

His written version of the incident from his diary explains much more to the uninitiated:

> We caut a long worm in the cannal it was yellow it ate all the sticklebacks.
> My littel brother put it in the tank the worm ete him up
>
> Wilkinson in Torbe and Protherough (1976, p. 160)

Further, whereas much speech tends to be subjective, there are quite specific modes of writing which require objectivity — propositional writing, reports, instructions, etc. Necessarily the writer must distance himself from the material.

The way writing widens one's sympathies is of course related to the particular writing task. Poems like 'Timothy Winter' by Charles Causley or Dylan Thomas's 'The Hunchback in the Park' or 'The Chimney Sweep' by William Blake are attempts to discover the uniqueness of other human beings. Any story writer has to come to terms with 'people' other than himself as he uses them as characters. The novelist and dramatist face the problem in its most demanding form as they make their dramatis personae convincing and not just projections of themselves.

Finally, writing is obviously a key medium for the expression of fantasy, for the coming to terms with experience, for its interpretation in imaginative terms. An example of writing in realistic terms would be the book *Silence Falls* by the British Member of Parliament, Jack Ashley, who tells of his experience after going deaf as the result of an operation.

An example of imaginative treatment of experiences arising from a different disability is the novel *Down All the Days* by Christy Brown. As an athetoid who could scarcely move or talk he was often regarded as though he did not exist. He was thus able to observe the most curious goings on between members of his family, and other people, which he transformed into a fascinating novel of Irish life.

4.3 Moral Development

By 'morality' we understand a set of culturally prescribed rules for social action which have been internalized by the individual. They are internalized only if they are obeyed by inner motivation, and not because of external threats or sanctions. There can be a discrepancy between what we feel we 'ought' to do, and what we actually do in specific situations.

The work of the cognitive-developmental psychologists is most relevant to our interests, particularly that of Piaget (1932), and Kolberg (1963, 1964). The most obvious characteristic of these theorists is their use of some type of stage concept, some notion of age-linked sequential re-organization in the development of man's attitudes. In early childhood 'anomy' or lawlessness gives way to 'heteronomy' or rule by fear of punishment or hope of reward, which in turn gives way to 'socionomy' or rule by a sense of reciprocity with others, which finally leads to the emergence of 'autonomy' or self-rule.

Despite the different emphases and some disagreement about the number of stages a child passes through as he becomes a principled moral thinker, there is general agreement that the development of moral thought parallels and is related to general cognitive development — from the pre-operational phase and anomy, to the concrete operational phase, heteronomy—socionomy, and on to the formal operational phase and autonomy. As Piaget (1932) succinctly put it 'logic is the morality of thought, morality is the logic of action' (p. 404). The development in moral judgement is seen as the process of decentring in thinking. The general direction is from 'The good that I want' (lawlessness), through awareness of society's expectations, to the capacity to question rules in terms of articulated principles. Socrates, Christ, Sir Thomas Moore, as represented in Bolt's *A Man for all Seasons*, all stood outside the accepted morality of their time and judged it.

Although there is evidence of a relationship between moral and cognitive development, the attainment of, for instance, the formal operational stage is a necessary but not sufficient condition for principled moral thought. The stereotype of the nuclear scientist disassociating himself from the moral implications of the use of the H-bomb is a familiar one. And again not all adult thinking is at the principled level all the time. A man with a new car who accepts the laws on speeding as being for the benefit of himself and others may nevertheless try it out on the pleasure principle. Stages of development are not discrete but cumulative — one may operate on a different level from one occasion to the next.

Kolberg (1963—64) developed a moral model from the analysis of responses of seventy-two boys aged 10, 13, 16, to a group of some ten dilemmas in which an individual is faced with a conflict between obedience to a moral rule and concern for others. His stage sequence was as follows:

Level 1.	*Premoral*
Type 1.	Punishment and obedience orientation.
Type 2.	Naive instrumental hedonism.
Level 2.	*Morality of conventional role conformity*
Type 3.	The 'goodboy' morality of maintaining good relations, approval of others.
Type 4.	Authority-maintaining morality.
Level 3.	*Morality of self-accepted moral principles*
Type 5.	Morality of contract, of individual rights and of democratically accepted law.
Type 6.	Morality of individual principles of conscience.

Kolberg found that individual children's judgement of his hypothetical moral dilemmas clustered with some consistency at a certain level on his six-point scale, but that some statements fell in categories one stage below and one stage above the dominant stage in the child's thinking.

It can be seen from Kolberg's general model that he originally omitted reference to anomy — 'the good is what I want', but in a later article (1976) he has added a level to include this, and is currently speculating about a level 7 or judgement by a coherent personally developed value system. In other words his six original levels are currently undergoing modification.

There is of course an essential reservation in the use of any model of this kind. There is no necessary relationship between the judgements people make upon deliberately constructed moral dilemmas and their own behaviour. A good deal will depend on the assessment they make of what is expected of them by the experiments of others. Devereux (1970) gave sixth grade children a Dilemmas Test. One group was told that their answers would only be seen by 'researchers and computers', another that they would be plotted on a big chart and displayed at a PTA for teachers and parents to see; another that the chart would only be shown to the group. The expectation — that adult conformity answers would occur under the 'adult conditions and peer-uniformity ones under peer conditions' was fulfilled (p. 121).

4.4 Summary

In this chapter we have considered personal development under the headings of cognitive, affective and moral development.

1. As far as cognitive development is concerned there is general agreement on a movement from simple recording to hypothetico-deductive thinking.
2. Affective development is seen in terms of changes in the individual's view of self, of others, and of external reality.
3. Moral development is seen in terms of changes from a morality of personal satisfaction at all costs to a principled, individually developed value system.

Chapter Five

Models for the Analysis of Writing

5.1 Introduction

It is clear from Chapters One and Two that we consider the criteria of judgement used for children's writing have been too narrow. Standardized examinations and objective tests tend to reward such skills as can easily be marked, and this affects the teaching accordingly. Attempts to assess by purely 'linguistic' criteria are equally restrictive; however much we refine these little progress seems possible; a Rolls Royce driven up a blind alley goes no further than a Mini. We have argued that judgements need to be based on a view of the development of the individual as a communicating being.

Thus in the Crediton Language Development Project, on which this book is based, four models of development — stylistic, cognitive, affective, and moral — were devised. These arose from an interaction between our perceptions of the written materials, teachers' judgements, and theoretical considerations. Details of the project are given in Chapter Six. In the present chapter we set out the general theoretical bases of the models, followed by the models themselves.

5.2 General Considerations

5.2.1 Cognition

The cognitive model reflects movement from concrete to abstract. The first two categories 'describing' and 'interpreting' we envisage as 'concrete operational' and the final two, 'generalizing' and 'speculatory' as moving towards 'formal operational' language use. Each category is divided into sub-sections, which progress from word/sentence to full discourse level, so that the model is an attempt to describe quite fully the cognitive moves which children make in writing. Certainly we would not expect sustained 'theorizing' from children aged seven—thirteen years but there is evidence (e.g. Tough, 1976) that even young children are able to give reasons, drawing inferences, making hypotheses at sentence level. They are able to generate and abstract, but with restrictions. As Moffett (1968, p. 29) notes:

> A child frequently over-abstracts; he cuts his world into a few simple categories that cover too much and discriminate too little. . . or he makes a generalisation that is too broad for the meagre experience it is based upon. He fails to qualify and quantify his statements.

Three of our coherence categories — reporting, classifying, and theorizing — are drawn from Moffett but as they stand do not have the degree of refinement which we need. The London Writing research (1975) extends them, but only seeks to make overall judgements with them. Once again this does not go far enough. We wish to be able to examine writing at the word/sentence level so that under each of our coherence categories functions are arranged hierarchically from word to discourse.

Describing we take to be basic. Even higher orders of discourse depend on us being able to say what is, to name items in the environment. Our first distinction, between labelling and naming, is at word level. Children frequently use large labels to carve up experience — 'man', 'lady', rather than naming them. The capacity to name is a move towards context-free language. But composition is not made up of separated details — links are necessary: some form of narrative is likely to appear:

> . . . the logic of lowest verbal abstractions is chronologic (narrative) because it conforms most closely to the temporal and spatial area in which phenomena occur.
>
> (Moffett, p. 34)

Narrative is the earliest form of coherence the child meets and it would not be surprising to find children using it exclusively at first in writing, moving up to the level we have called 'reporting' where there is integration of the parts.

In Moffett's ladder of abstraction 'generalizing' was seen to develop out of narrating. This seems too large a leap. The transition between description and generalization appears to be by way of offering concrete interpretations, causal explanation and deductive sequences which go beyond the reporting of the events themselves. Our interpretative category as a whole reflects the *ad hoc* logic of childhood at sentence to discourse level. Such capacities for explaining, assessing, inferring and deducing are seen as operating in a concrete way — the child can give reasons for the things he knows and observes; he reasons from events, not from propositions. This is the stage of transition between concrete and formal operation.

Our third major category, 'generalizing', parallels the movement from word to discourse in the 'describing' category. A writer cannot proceed with classification beyond a certain point without using genuine abstraction. Our first subsection, 'abstracting' is at word level. A child who describes a game in terms of 'what you do to him' is working at a concrete level, the one who talks about players and opponents is starting to use abstractions — but only starting. There are levels of abstraction. In our coherence category, 'classifying', more abstract terms are needed, and evaluating and summarizing at sentence level.

With the fourth category, 'speculating', the child may offer hypotheses which to the adult are simply irrelevant or inadequate, but the function this language is serving is speculative nevertheless. Full theorizing — arguing from propositions in a hypothetico-deductive way — we would not expect to emerge at full discourse level even among the thirteen year olds in our project. Yet part of this style of thinking is the capacity to raise possibilities, to ask exploratory questions, just as projecting a loosely linked set of hypotheses helps us to go beyond the information given. And these are the capacities we may expect some of the older children in the sample to demonstrate.

Barnes (1976) and Peel (1972) make a case for the hypothetical mode in instructing children — they mention that all too often the teacher provides the hypotheses rather than encouraging them to generate their own. What may look like an incorrect generalization on the child's part may in fact be a hypothesis. It seems that whilst in written discourse we associate generalizing and theorizing with 'essay' and 'argument' the beginning of these skills first emerges in children's narrative at sentence level. Our model implies that young children are capable of doing more than describing at this level — we find evidence of generalizing modes and occasional hypotheses being offered by seven year olds. Of course the expectation is that reporting and deducing will be the basic means of catering for all but the thirteen year olds.

5.2.2 Affect

The cognitive model is in terms of mental operations, ways of thinking. As we saw in Chapter Four we are in no position to list a hierarchy of ways of feeling which would be a parallel to these. Our argument anyway has been that ways of feeling are not ultimately distinct from ways of thinking. We have therefore chosen to devise this model on the practicalities with which the emotions operate — as expressions of, as attitudes towards, as awareness about, as creations in terms of.

In Chapter Four (4.2) we discerned three dimensions of personal development — Self, Others, and Reality, and these are the general categories, implied in our model. There is no suggestion that these categories are hierarchical, though *within* each category there is some development.

Self
This is a complete category in itself.
Self: expresses emotions, becomes aware of these emotions; evaluates them, recognizes their springs and complexities; becomes more able to tolerate conflicting emotions, becomes aware of motives behind apparent motives. Self becomes aware of self-image and possible image in the eyes of others.

Others
Under this class we have two sections — the one is, quite simply, other people as manifested in the writing; the second is the reader of a piece of writing. Both illustrate the degree of egocentrism of the writer.

Other People
The movement in this class is concerned with the degree to which others are perceived as distinct identities. In young children's writing there is often no topic but the self: or others appear as servicing agencies. There is a process apparent in some writing of others manifesting themselves as individual, signalled in terms of the amount of information given about them, of what they say and do, and how this expresses what they think and feel. The more mature writer will display a considerable degree of empathy towards others, whether they are his characters or other people about whom he is writing.

The Reader
Young children beginning to write have so great a cognitive and physical problem that their effort tends to be concerned completely with the task in hand. Over the years there is likely to be a development of greater reader awareness. It is often argued that writing to an unknown or not well-envisaged audience will be poor in quality since it lacks focus. Certainly the imaginative leap into the mind of another so that one grasps what terms have meaning for him is a kind of empathy. It would seem that the task is always greater than with the spoken language for in most cases of the latter the addressee is immediately present. This category is similar to that of 'reader awareness' in the stylistic categories to be discussed later, but here we are concerned with the degree of empathy rather than with the nature of the register used.

Reality

Here we have two categories. 'Environment' is the individual's relationship with the physical and social world in a fairly obvious sense. 'Reality' is his coping with the human condition.

Environment

The physical world is frequently absent in the writing of young children because they do not have the capacity to fill in the scenery, or the realization that it might be an important part of context. With older children there is often inclusion of environmental details; of a specific response to, a celebration of the environment, perhaps in the form of focus on a particular detail, for its literal or metaphorical detail — 'heaven in a grain of sand' for instance.

Reality

An early stage of response seems to be one in which reality and fiction are not differentiated. As Applebee (1978) says, the earliest interpretation seems to be that a story is something that happens in the past, a *history* rather than a fictional construct. (p. 38)

There is then a recognition, comparatively early with some children, of the difference between the two. Carol, just over four, is in conversation with her mother:

What is this book *about*? she asked. 'Oh, a boy and a girl who go for a walk in England', I answered. She hunts round the pictures and puts her finger on the children, then, doubtfully, 'This book's not *real* England' 'It's about England, Carol'. Yes, but not real England, just paper England.

(Carol in Applebee, 1978, p. 39)

It should be noted though that some myths, strongly reinforced by adults, are believed for several years longer — that of Santa Claus for example. At any rate from this stage there is a movement towards accommodation with external reality which is never complete. It may be handled, literally, or in terms of fantasy, or in terms of imagination. Writing would seem to be particularly important here in that by its nature it gives opportunity for reflection and gestation.

5.2.3 Morals

This model is based on Kolberg's general description of the steps described in Chapter Three. We have collapsed Kolberg's steps I and II in a punishment/reward orientation, and we have added a stage seven for completeness. In addition, based on the work of Piaget (1932) we have isolated 'judgement by intentions' as a later development out of 'socionomy'. The reason for this is that we found evidence for it only at 13+ whereas other aspects of judgement in terms of convention appeared at 10+. The final model is only tentative; granted the age range of our sample we would not anyway expect to demonstrate all aspects of it. Levels M6 and M7 we would not expect to find on theoretical grounds from children of thirteen (see below).

In the empirical research into the development of moral thought we have found no studies in which the writing of children has been analysed for levels of moral thinking. Yet in the stories they write children come to terms with notions of good and evil, right and wrong. They read fiction in which the good are rewarded, the evil punished. They make implicit and explicit judgements which reveal moral values. Teachers also make moral judgements in recommending certain books as against others. It is a mistake to expect the child's judgement to be like that of the teacher; a knowledge of 'normal' moral development is therefore useful when children write stories or make moral judgements in which the judgements appear less principled than those of an adult.

5.2.4 Style
The present state of knowledge does not enable us to make a stage by stage description of the development of style, though it seems that there may be such a development. What we can do is to take certain features which we regard as significant, and look at the way they grow and change, and see how far they (or choices from them) cluster together at a particular age.

Of the five major sets of choices the individual makes in writing we have used four in the following model. The one omitted is that between literal/factual and metaphorical/affective, and the reason for this omission is that we have, of course, an affective model as a separate instrument.

It is quite impossible to look at all the detailed choices a writer makes in a work of this kind. Thus we have taken seven particular aspects of language which seem significant and attempted to indicate what might seem to be development in them. These are

   Syntax, verbal competence, (sentence as affirmative statement)
  · Structure/organization cohesion (sentence as narrative/description)
   Reader awareness/appropriateness (sentence as self-oriented)
   Effectiveness (sentence as meaning)

Here is a summary with the hypothesis proposed in each case.

Syntax. There will be a development from simple to complex, but the furthest point of development will lie in the control of appropriate structures in relation to semantic needs.

Verbal competence.   There will be in general a movement from limited concrete vocabulary, perhaps with imprecise and general meaning, to a vocabulary which has greater precision, and uses abstraction, and elaboration where necessary.

Structure/organization.   Concerned with the relationship of the separate elements of the whole organization. Development will be seen in terms of movement from perception of individual units to perception of the totality which they constitute.

Cohesion.   Cohesive devices are employed to maintain continuity between one part of the text and another. Just as grammar establishes the structural relativity within the clause or sentence, so cohesion established the semantic relations within the text. The better these are established the more accomplished the writing.

Reader awareness.   The degree to which the writer can put himself in the place of the reader — a decentring movement. The category includes such aspects as orientation, the degree of elaboration and explanation to give the necessary context and information.

Appropriateness.   There will be an increasing ability to adapt to the accepted style of discourse. Young children of ten write in oral modes, or mix spoken and written. At the other end of the scale a writer may be assured in a mode and for deliberate effect frustrate the reader's expectation by breaking the register.

Effectiveness.   This concerns the success of writing in communicating; in this sense it is the summation of the others. It is partly what Pope had in mind when he wrote, 'In every work regard the writer's end' (*Essay in Criticism*, line 255), but it is necessary to be aware of the intentionalist fallacy — that the quality of a work is necessarily what the writer intended to make it. There can of course be no single criterion of effectiveness. In a narrative it may be the interest and suspense sustained, in an autobiography the realization of the writer's feelings and motives, in a set of instructions the successful installation of a wall bracket, and so on.

5.3 Models

5.3.1 Cognitive Model

C1   *Describing*
C1.1   Labelling — the mere concept word e.g. 'There is *man* and . . .'
C1.2   Naming — the specific word e.g. 'Mr. and Mrs. *Jones* went to town'.

C1.3   Partial information — some concrete details given, but unorganized and unsustained, e.g. 'wene you get to near the red circle you would of de caught'.

C1.4   Recording — simple concrete statements about the here and now.

C1.5   Reporting — some linking between statements in a chronological/ spatial sequence, e.g. 'I went to school. Then I found my books had gone, so I went to the house tutor . . .' or 'There was an old house on the moor behind our village . . .'

C2   *Interpreting*

C2.1   Explaining — saying why something is so or how something is done, e.g. 'I was happy because it was my birthday', 'the card sorry means you can send one of the other players back . . .'

C2.2   Inferring — e.g. 'I think he's more sad than happy because he's alone', 'This wouldn't work because children wouldn't bother coming to school'.

C2.3   Deducing — links between statements, causal links e.g. 'teachers will be in short supply because there will be much broader choice of things to do. That teacher won't be able to cover all the subjects, so choice of subjects wouldn't work'.

C3   *Generalizing*

C3.1   Abstracting — using abstract terms as well as concrete ones e.g. 'People say children should go to school', 'The *players* move alternately, white beginning . . .'

C3.2   Summarizing — e.g. 'So you see Topcat won', 'The object of owning property is to collect rents from opponents stopping there', 'The first person to do that is the winner'.

C3.3   Overall Evaluation — e.g. 'So Topcat won by being more clever', 'The main object of the game is to meld seven cards of a kind'.

C3.4   Concluding — e.g. 'So he decided never to enter the race again', 'These seven points show just how ludicrious that suggestion really was'.

C3.5   Reflecting — generalizing with reference to external rules or principles e.g. 'This phase would generally have lasted several years'.

C3.6   Classifying — links between generalizations sustained in a classificatory system.

C4   *Speculating*

C4.1   Irrelevant (even if beautiful) hypothesis e.g. 'If we didn't come to school we would get sick and die', 'The elephant's trunk was stretched by a crocodile'.

C4.2   Relevant but inadequate hypothesis e.g. 'His trunk is to breathe better', 'if we didn't come to school the buses wouldn't come'.

C4.3   Adequate hypothesis — 'His trunk is for feeding with'.

C4.4   Exploring — asking tentative but relevant questions 'What would happen if . . .' e.g. 'But what would we do if we didn't come to school?'

C4.5   Projecting — a set of organized hypotheses about a possible future, loosely linked e.g. 'A far better system would be to give secondary school pupils a basic three years schooling . . .'. The writer goes beyond the information given, but cannot subject his thinking to critical scrutiny.

C4.6   Theorizing — sustained hypotheses in which links between one item and the next are hypothetico-deductive. Propositional logic rather than concrete reasoning as in C2.4.

5.3.2   Affective Model

A1   *Self*
The writer expresses his emotion and his awareness of the nature of his own feelings, or implies his emotion by describing action from which the reader can infer that the writer was in the grip of an emotion.

A1.1   The writer expresses or implies his own emotion, mechanically in some written work, explicitly in others, e.g. 'My feet were as wet as anything', 'I am afraid that day is a long, long, way away'.

A1.2   — not only expresses but evaluates emotion, e.g. 'The saddest day of my life', 'I did not like it indeed'.

A1.3   — shows awareness of self image, of how he appears or might appear, e.g. 'I looked like a fool'.

A1.4   — shows awareness of the springs and complexities of emotion, e.g. 'I got rather nevous about it and I couldn't find the way and went into another room and looked like a fool standing there asking where room one was'.

A1.5   — shows a general attitude or disposition, e.g. 'I long for the day when I can think about him without it hurting too much'.

A2   *Other people*
The writer shows an awareness of others both in relation to himself and as distinct identities.

A2.1   — records the mere existence of other people as having been present. This is the single dimension: others are present — acting, speaking — but no emotion is apparent by inference, e.g. 'The two boys went for

a walk with their mother and they got lost and they came to a fence
and that fence was electric and they was not lost . . .'.

A2.2   — begins to indicate the separateness of others by, e.g. giving their
        actual words or significant actions. 'I woke up, had my breakfast' is
        probably not significant; 'the old man smild' may well be.

A2.3   — the thoughts and feelings of others by quotation of actual words,
        perhaps as a dialogue, or by description of them, or actions indicating
        them. More perception called for than in the previous category though
        it might be fairly conventional.

A2.4   Analytical, interpretative comments on aspects of character and be-
        haviour; or insightful quotation or dialogue.

A2.5   Consistently realized presentation of another person by a variety of
        means, perhaps by assuming persona.

A2.6   Ability to see a person and his interactions in extended context (e.g.
        a character in a novel).

A3   *Reader*
        It is often argued that writing to an unknown or not well-envisaged
        reader will be poorer in quality since it lacks focus. Certainly the
        imaginative leap of the writer into the minds of others so as to grasp
        what terms have meaning for them must characterize effective com-
        munication.

A3.1   — reader not catered for. Writing context-bound, incomplete inform-
        ation, links missing.

A3.2   — the reader is a person or type of person to the writer. He may not
        be conscious of this, but rather attempts to fulfil expectations within
        the situation. He may do so partially but imperfectly.

A3.3   — the writer caters specifically for the reader, e.g. by relevant inform-
        ation, explanation (sometimes asides), shows an empathy with him,
        telling him what he needs to know to be able to imterpret what he is
        told.

A4   *Environment*
        The writer shows an awareness of physical or social surroundings, a
        sense of time and place. On the one hand the environment may be a
        source of special stimulus. On the other hand a 'restricted node' may
        not offer the necessary context. Getting the register right is a sign of
        awareness of social environment.

A4.1   — assumes the environment.

A4.2   — describes or explains the environment, barely adequately giving
        background details, or gives enough details to clarify the background.

A4.3   — responds to the environment in a way that shows it has been especially significant and stimulating.

A4.4   — chooses environmental items to achieve an effect, thus showing a higher degree of selectivity and evaluation than that suggested by A4.3.

A5   *Reality*
        This is concerned with how far a writer recognizes a distinction between the world of phenomena, and the world of imagination, between magical and logical thinking; with how far the writer's own preferences or beliefs can come to an accommodation with external reality; with how far the literal-metaphorical aspects of experience can be perceived in complexity.

A5.1   Confusion of the subjective and objective world. This seems to occur with young children who believe that stories are 'true'.

A5.2   — gives a literal account without evaluation.

A5.3   — interprets reality in terms of fantasy.

A5.4   — interprets reality literally but in terms of logical possibilities.

A5.5   — interprets reality imaginatively in terms of art, perhaps symbolically or metaphorically.

5.3.3   **Moral Model**
        Attitudes/judgements about self/others and events.

M1   Judging self/others by physical characteristics or consequences, e.g. 'She was ugly, so she was bad', 'He broke fiteen cups — naughty'. Judging events by pain-pleasure to the self, e.g. 'It was a bad day. I hurt my hand'. 'It was a good birthday. I got lots of presents.' 'A bad accident — the fence was smashed up.' Principle of self-gratification — 'anomy'.

M2   Judging self/others and events in terms of punishments/rewards. 'I won't do that, Mummy will hit me'. 'I'll tell Daddy on you and he will beat you up'. 'If I do the dishes, Mummy will give me a new bat'. Events judged as rewards/punishments, e.g. 'I must have been naughty last night, the fridge hit me'. Heteronomy.

M3   Judging self/others according to the status quo. Mother, father, teacher, policeman good by right of status; the wicked witch, the evil step-father bad by right of convention, e.g. 'I hated the Jerries, I used to call them stupid idiots'. Reciprocity restricted to the child's immediate circle, e.g. 'I won't do that — it will upset mummy'. Social approval/disapproval internalized in terms of whether behaviour upsets others or not. Stereotypic thinking. Events judged in terms of effects on other *people*. 'It was a bad accident. All the passengers were badly hurt'. Socionomy (internal).

M4   Judging self/others in terms of conventional norms/rules, e.g. 'It's wrong to steal. It is against the law'. Conformist orientation. Rules are applied literally on the principle of equity or fairness. 'It's not fair. We all did it, so John should be punished the same as us. We all broke the rule'. Socionomy (external).

M5   Judging self/others in terms of intention or motive, regardless of status or power, e.g. 'She didn't mean to drop those plates, so she shouldn't be punished'. 'Teacher was wrong, because she punished all of us instead of finding out who did it'.

M6   Judging self/others in terms of abstract concepts such as a universal respect for the individual rather than in terms of conventional norms of right/wrong conduct. The morality of individual conscience. Rules seen as arbitrary and changeable. Autonomy.

M7   Judgement of self/others in terms of a personally developed value *system.*

5.3.4   Stylistic Model

S1   *Syntax*
      This category is concerned with the relationship between grammatical units within the sentence. There is development from the simple to the complex sentence and from the use of restricted and unvaried means to the selection, as appropriate, from a wider range of more varied structures.

S1.1   *Simple sentences with few modifiers or compound sentences without subordinates.* The most common conjunctions are 'and', 'so', 'but' (often used in an additive rather than contrastive sense). Where subordinating conjunctions are used, there is not true subordination.

S1.2   *Short, complex sentences with some short modifying phrases.* Occasional use of adjectival clauses. Frequent use of adverbial clauses of time, place; clauses of cause and condition are used but not firmly established. Noun clause object very common.

S1.3   *Longer complex sentences employing adjectival clauses and most types of adverbial and noun clause.* Some re-arrangement of sentence units to stress meaning. More confident and elaborated use of modifiers. Some embedding.

S1.4   *Sentences become more varied and 'tighter' in structure.* Use of participal and infinitival expression embedded within the sentence. Clauses of concession and adversative constructions employed.

S1.5   *Greater control and facility with sentence structures.* Ability to adjust sentence structures according to the requirements of the subject field.

S2   *Verbal Competence*
        This category is concerned with the writer's capacity to express his meanings effectively, to define his terms adequately and communicate successfully an increasingly wide range of experience. There may be changes from the concrete to the abstract, and to a more diverse, discriminating and precise use of words; from the literal to the meta-phorical; from the stock to the individual statement.

S2.1   *Vocabulary limited.* Literal, not metaphorical, concrete, not abstract. A limited range of modifiers.

S2.2   *Increased range of vocabulary but still tied to the concrete and familiar.* Increased use of modifiers, temporal and causal initiators, adjectives. Circumlocution rather than precision in describing complex experiences.

S2.3   *Increase in number and range of words to express feeling and mental processes.* Many more modifiers related to the quality of experience: metaphor. Developing ability to use conventional language. More effective and precise use of initiating words and phrases. Experimenting with new words.

S2.4   *Ability to use abstract terms and express an abstract idea.* Use of general terms and superordinates: more extended use of metaphor.

S2.5   *Greater discrimination in choice of words.* Clearer definitions, greater precision in use of words. Ability to select the most effective word for the context: in control of choice.

S3   *Organization*
        This category is concerned with the relation between the separate sentences and the whole composition. There is development from a relatively uncontrolled and incoherent handling of material to a more controlled and coherent organization.

S3.1   *Little coherent structure.* Ideas are juxtaposed rather than related. There is little elaboration or integration.

S3.2   *Experience, ideas and observations are related to a single focus but without coherence between the parts.* In narrative structure takes the form of a cluster of events without focus. In discursive writing a 'primitive chain' structure is often adopted.

S3.3   *Sequence and structure are based on a simple linear or chronological pattern.* Elaborating detail where employed is not yet selected and organized with a clear aim. Introductory and concluding sentences are most common in narrative and least common in discursive writing. The connection between one fact and another is not always made clear.

S3.4 *More complex organization*, though the sum of the parts does not yet make a whole. Interruption of a straight-sequential pattern by, for instance, retrospection or anticipation. Other patterns such as a logical one emerge.

S3.5 *The relationship between the parts and the whole established.* Explanation and amplification handled more coherently. Appropriate sub-ordination of material within the paragraph. Introduction and conclusion employed with confidence.

S3.6 *Capacity to control ideas and organize structure by a variety of means.* Complex experiences or ideas often presented by balance or contrast. Image, symbol, the use of a predominant tone and atmosphere become unifying factors.

S4   *Cohesion*
Cohesive devices are employed to maintain continuity between one part of the text and another. Just as grammar established the structural relationship within clause or sentence, so cohesion establishes the semantic relationship within the text. There is development from the relatively unrelated to the fully related parts in a text.

S4.1 *Few cohesive devices employed effectively.* Pronouns where used, sometimes have no specific referent or are used imprecisely. Ellipsis, when employed, often shows no clear understanding of the referent, e.g. 'If they miss [the goal?] the other player has his [turn?] !' Little lexical cohesion. Most common conjunctions: 'and', 'so', 'then'.

S4.2 *Marked increase in cohesive devices.* Sequential and concluding conjunctions, e.g. 'afterwards', 'finally', 'eventually'.
Use of temporal conjunctions, e.g. 'when', 'first', 'first of all'.
Use of causal conjunctions, e.g. 'so', 'because'.
Use of 'but' in an adversative/contrastive way.
Some use of demonstratives as adverbs of place, e.g. 'here', 'there'.
Some substitution, e.g. 'one', 'other', 'some'.
Nominal substitution, e.g. 'one', 'the same' and verbal substitution, e.g. 'do so', 'be so'.
Appearance of low-level general terms, e.g. 'people', 'things'.

S4.3 *Greater awareness of textual coherence to clarify and define meaning.* Emphatic cohesive conjunctions, e.g. 'too', 'even', 'also'. Use of comparatives, e.g. 'identical', 'similar', 'more', 'less', and superlatives, e.g. 'the wealthiest'.

S4.4 *Development of logical coherence.* Use of superordinates. A wider range of adversatives employed, e.g. 'however', 'on the other hand', 'though'.

S4.5 *A wide range of cohesive devices employed.* E.g. Reiteration, synonyms, antonyms, parallelism, contrast, assonance, alliteration, echoic words, etc.

> The concept of cohesion is drawn from Halliday and Hassan (1976); 'If a speaker of English hears or reads a passage of the language which is more than one sentence in length, he can normally decide without difficulty whether it forms a unified whole or is just a collection of unrelated sentences . . . 'we can characterize any segment of text in terms of the number and kinds of ties which it displays . . . The concept of a tie makes it possible to analyse a text in terms of its cohesive properties . . . The different kinds of cohesive tie . . . are: reference, substitution, ellipsis, conjunction, and lexical cohesion'. (pp. 1, 3, 4).

S5 *Writer's awareness of the reader*
This category is concerned with the degree to which the writer can put himself in the place of the reader and see with his eyes. Initially a process of decentring, reader awareness includes such aspects as the writer's orientation to his reader, the degree of explanation and elaboration of detail to assist the reader and the relevance of that detail to the message communicated.
At first there is an implicit assumption of the reader's omniscience. Later the reader is assisted towards understanding by explicit means. Later still, in more sophisticated expressive and poetic writing, various devices are employed deliberately to control the reader by implicit means.

S5.1 *Writer assumes the reader's awareness of the context.* Few modifying or elaborating details to assist the reader in understanding the context. Verbal syncretism.

S5.2 *More elaboration of detail but without focus or reference.* Explanation and elaboration still have no clear objective or function or are seen egocentrically. Selection of detail seems arbitrary.

S5.3 *Detail related clearly to a theme or focus.* Marked increase in elaboration and explanation; more use of modifying expressions and emphatic devices including asides and parentheses.

S5.4 *Writer assuming a more confident stance to reader.* Increasing use of initiatory, anecdotes and evaluative comments. More information provided in a more coherent way.

S5.5 *Writer communicates with reader by sophisticated means.* Irony, parody sometimes employed to relate to reader implicitly. Fable, allegory, the use of image or symbol etc. indicate a relationship with the reader in less overt and obvious ways.

S6   *Appropriateness*

Appropriateness is the writer's ability to adapt his style or register to the field of discourse and to recognize and respond to the conventions of particular kinds of writing.

Development from the inappropriate use of writing conventions to appropriate — recognition of the stylistic conventions of particular subject fields and kinds of writing — is significant within this age span.

S6.1   *Writing close to speech.* Little awareness of writing conventions. Little awareness of stylistic differences according to subject field though in narrative conventional opening and closing sentences are often used.

S6.2   *Dawning awareness of writing models.* Modifying and elaborating expressions more appropriate to writing conventions. There are still inconsistencies in register, however. Second-hand writing. More varied opening and closing sentences used in narrative. In discursive writing an undeveloped and unelaborated discursive style is perceptible.

S6.3   *Appearance of 'literary' English and employment of 'literary' effects.* Re-arrangement of particular units within the sentence, experimentation with short, simple/longer, complex sentences for particular effects, some sentence patterning. In discursive writing a less personal style emerges.

S6.4   *Greater awareness of written conventions.* More varied means allow the writer to experiment in a variety of ways, e.g. in use of figures of speech — suspense, bathos, humour, control of effects. Appropriate use of lexical emphasis, lexical cohesion, initiating expressions.

S6.5   *Appropriate adjustment of register to requirements of subject field.* Ability to writer to assume a variety of roles and discriminate between the different demands of subject, audience and context.

S7   *Effectiveness*

The effectiveness of a written composition depends upon the writer's ability to respond appropriately to the demands of his subject and his readers. Objective criteria will never wholly supply the place of the personal judgement and personal response in assessing a piece of writing. The realization of an experience in writing, the unity and coherence of a composition ultimately depend upon an interaction between writer and reader in which the reader creates for himself from what the writer has offered.

In the discursive modes, the task of assessment is easier than for writing in the personal modes. In one, the duty to one's reader to enlighten and to persuade is paramount and the means employed must be subordinated to that end. The writer is not his own master; he must employ recognized, conventional, public means of communication. Within the personal modes, the writer is less under the constraints of a particular subject field. His means of communication will be unique, he will organize his experiences in terms of his own vision and his own style. The degree to which his reader understands him will depend partly upon a recognition of writing conventions but partly upon the writer's own unique handling of his material. Often the reader lags behind the writer's vision and has to become familiar with the writer's vision before he can truly appreciate it. The following scheme represents a tentative attempt to plot development in the four writing tasks which the pupils carried out:

SA   *Autobiography*

SA7.1 A string or chain of events related without proper emphasis or adequate contextualization. The writing is not shaped to assist the reader in determining its significance. The experience is unrealized.

SA7.2 A coherent composition with some elaboration and contextualization but without imaginative or emotional unity.

SA7.3 A coherent, if sometimes brief, composition in which there is adequate contextualization, explanation and a simple expression of feeling without the writer's being aware of the springs and complexities of his feeling. The recollected experience has been shaped but not examined.

SA7.4 An elaborated composition in which various literary effects are employed to heighten the narrative but without proper integration of the parts into a satisfying and imaginative whole.

SA7.5 A fully contextualized and elaborated composition in which the writer shows self awareness and reflective ability but is unable to distance the experience or transform the recollection into a total imaginative unity.

SA7.6 A satisfying composition in which the experience is fully realized; the feelings are explored and examined. A variety of means are employed to achieve the immediacy of the experience for the reader.

SN   *Narrative*

SN7.1 Little coherent narrative pattern. Events are described in a chain or cluster without adequate sequence or contextualization.

SN7.2 Unelaborated narrative pattern without any exploration of the nature of the events or experience described.

SN7.3 A narrative in which there is some elaboration, and some heightening of effects but the sum of the parts does not make a satisfying whole.

The writer's approach and handling of material is not consistent throughout.

SN7.4 A narrative which strives after particular effects rather than a unified vision. The writer experiments with a variety of literary devices and techniques, there is much 'second-hand' writing and no sustained emotional or imaginative involvement.

SN7.5 A fully realized and imaginatively satisfying narrative.

SE   *Explanation*

SE7.1 There is an inability to plan or organize material into a coherent account. Information is neither contextualized nor related to an overall design.

SE7.2 A coherent account but without sufficient information provided for the reader's understanding.

SE7.3 A coherent account with certain features elaborated without an understanding of the underlying principles. No precision in defining terms.

SE7.4 An over-elaborated account with some awareness of the underlying principles and broad structure but without classification or abstraction. Detail obscures the main design.

SE7.5 A coherent, austere account which shows an awareness of underlying principle and broad structure but has insufficient information for the reader's understanding.

SE7.6 A clear, coherent and fully elaborated account. Material handled confidently with adequate explanation and exemplification. Terms adequately and precisely defined.

SP   *Argument*

SP7.1 Statement, narrative, description or assertion rather than discussion or analysis. Little explanation or elaboration. Little organization of material.

SP7.2 Discursive style attempted but ideas are not developed or arguments sustained. Explanations are egocentric and argument primitive.

SP7.3 More elaborated discursive style with appropriate introduction and conclusion. Argument seen as a sort of 'chain'. There is an attempt to handle abstract ideas but without definition or analysis.

SP7.4 Discursive style established. Material is appropriately organized in paragraphs with topic sentences. Argument is sustained and handled with confidence but there is some limitation in the writer's awareness of the implications of his subject so that argument is often glib and other considerations unexplored.

Chapter Six

The Crediton Project

6.1 Project Design

The design of the project was to take groups of pupils at seven plus, at ten plus, and at thirteen plus, and to use their performances on the same four written tasks as evidence in constructing and applying the developmental models. Pupils below the age of seven were not used, as a minimum degree of writing competence was necessary.

No sophisticated matching procedures were used. We needed good average groups which were fairly compatible, and relied on the professional knowledge of the teachers concerned to provide these. We could in general assume fair homogeneity of background; we took a secondary school and one of its primary feeder schools in a community of considerable stability; the children in the one school often have brothers and sisters in the other. From these two schools about one hundred children were involved, with in addition a class of children from a similar secondary school to provide further information at the thirteen plus level.

To meet possible criticisms that the written tasks we set were imposed and 'unnatural', we tried to make them such as normally occur in English lessons. We decided to link them as closely as possible with the direct experience of the pupils, and to enlist the co-operation of the teachers so that they could become part of normal class work over a period of three months. This we felt would minimize the possible Hathorne effect in the sample (an improvement brought about by the sheer fact that the subjects know they are involved in a research project), and the negative effect of examination backwash on the children's understanding of the tasks themselves.

6.2 Criteria for the Selection of Writing Tasks

We wished to choose tasks which would give as broad a sample as possible of the pupils' range of writing abilities. The selection of such tasks is not simple..

On the one hand is the problem of the basic classification of tasks from which to choose; on the other the selection itself.

Harpin (1976, p. 38 ff.) discusses very usefully some of the possible ways of classifying 'composition'. He lists: by content, subject matter (the Dewey Decimal library classification system is an excellent example of this); by form (e.g. poetry, prose, essay, report); by audience (e.g. learned, popular); by writer-audience relationship (e.g. Moffett's spectrum of distance 1.3.1 above); by writer and task (creative, free, intensive, imaginative, practical, factual, recording); by function, purpose, intention (e.g. expressive, poetic, trans-actional, 1.3.2 above). It seemed most appropriate in view of our emphasis on the behaviour of the individual to use a function model; in other words we were interested, not so much in the form as in the individual performing in the form.

If we wish to build up a satisfactory description of the written language competence of any one person we need to take more than a single type of writing. Language performance is to some extent situation specific. As we have seen the APU for instance (above 2.5.4) suggests a spectrum of seven tasks for pupils at ten, and a similar more extended range for those at fifteen.

In our project it was important that the same tasks should be set at each level. Simply to take samples from pre-existing work would have presented us with the problem unsolved in the London research, that no direct com-parisons would be possible. Schonell's (1942) design did attempt to set the same tasks, not always satisfactorily. For instance, having fixed on 'story reproduction' he chose a story of general interest, but realized that it was too difficult for the younger children in his sample, and so produced a 'shortened version' with a 'limited number of ideas, simple development of action and clear, concise details and descriptions' (p. 314). This is not really holding the stimulus constant across age groups, the verbal sophistication of the story being an uncontrolled variable, even if the change was made for sound pedagogic reasons. We thought it was possible to avoid such pitfalls and yet to choose tasks which would represent certain significant aspects of written competence.

We selected tasks on the basis of function and of audience. It seemed sensible to choose two tasks which would lead to personal and to discursive writing and to postulate readers in the school situation and known directly to the children. The relationship between the writer, his situation or subject and his audience is of paramount importance. Writing to a close friend we can use an informal register which would be quite inappropriate were we writing letters of application for employment, or attempting to persuade an unknown audience of the integrity of our ideas. The main problem lies in convincing young writers that their writing is for someone real to them who is not simply wanting to assess their competence. The well-worn 'Write a letter to a friend' invitation fools nobody, least of all the child who knows that what he would write for a real friend is not for teacher's eyes.

We decided that in the project four audiences were possible; child to teacher as trusted adult; child to peer group; expert to known layman and child to wider public. These four audiences are real to the child in the classroom. 'Child to wider public' looks, on the surface, a 'pseudo audience', yet teachers of English do display children's writing in magazines, anthologies and on classroom display boards as a means of fostering childrens' pride in their writing. Sometimes the writing so displayed was meant for 'teacher as trusted adult' — the teacher making the display after the event. If, however, our teachers were to announce that the writing be for a display beforehand, we could say that the audience 'wider public' would be real to the child, 'wider public' including other children, teachers, parents and so on.

In postulating four audiences for the writing we were aware that the younger children might simply ignore the signals and write for 'self' or 'teacher as trusted adult' on all four tasks. Awareness of audience has to do with the child's capacity to decentre, to put himself in someone else's shoes. As Moffett says:

> Differentiating modes of discourse, registers of speech, kinds of audiences, is essentially a matter of decentring, of seeing alternatives, of standing in another's shoes, of knowing that one has private or local points of view. (p. 57)

Theoretically, then, we might expect that the younger children in the sample do not differentiate their writing in terms of audience/function in the way that thirteen year-olds are learning to do.

In the selection of writing tasks we specified prose in each case. We were lead to this by the problems encountered in the Harpin (1974) longitudinal research already discussed (see 2.5 above). Four witten tasks in the personal-discursive dimension were required, with the verbal preparation of the classes by the teachers varying from 'minimum' to 'maximum'. The 'creative' category drew idiosyncratic responses from some schools in the sample. Our specification of function and audience mentioned above was for the teachers to help us to specify as fully as possible the parameters of our sample and thus to avoid the problem encountered by Harpin where teachers made up their own tasks with little more briefing than the details mentioned above. Granted that the purpose of his research was to outline the child's actual acquisition of syntactic structures over two years, the preference for poetry as a response by some children led to odd findings on measures of syntactic maturity such as the Loban Index of Subordination. Further, Harpin reports that twice as many difficulties arose in creative writing situations as in factual ones. 'Where writing was to start from a picture, a poem or a brief story, the possibility existed of retelling a story or poem, describing a picture, a procedure inevitably producing, on the criterion adopted, factual writing' (p. 52). Harpin's work emphasizes that the strongest single determinant of the complexity of the syntax is the nature of the task set.

Our specification of prose seemed sensible from two considerations; we could assume that writing in poetic form could render some of our stylistic measures ineffective, and secondly, we wanted to keep a selection of visual stimuli for writing constant across age groups, but to avoid confusing children as to the type of writing required in response. Hence examples of childrens' writing in poetic form, as distinct from their performance in poetic function, were excluded from the sample at each age level.

6.3 The Selection of Topics

Our selection of four writing tasks had to take into consideration the problem of control by writer versus control by the teacher/researcher. Specifying four topics could have led to the researcher defining as fully as possible each topic and how it was to be dealt with, leaving little for the child writer to decide. The question of the child's sense of audience is begged when teacher or researcher controls content and function as well as form. We decided therefore that on at least one task the children should have complete control over content; on at least one the content would be controlled only in so far as the child's selection of one of three pictures acted as a constraint, or that on at least one task our topic was to be seen as only a starting point. The topics were ones which teachers of English commonly use on the simple expedient that children enjoy them.

The two tasks in the personal dimension with the writer in the role of the spectator — an autobiographical narrative and a fictional story — are common in the English curriculum. For the young child narrative is the most powerful tool for coming to terms with experience. Story-telling, whether spoken or written, is the young child's means of placing, ordering, shaping experience, and for many adults narrative or anecdotes serve this important function as well. Thus patients released from hospital may retell their experiences to a number of people, elaborating and re-editing, trying to understand; the experience of being depersonalized is not easily forgotten.

Story-telling is important for our psychological satisfaction, which is possibly why young children, worried about their competence in handling the written mode and inclined to shy away from writing, willingly engage in writing stories. Moffett suggests, in fact, that young children use narrative almost exclusively: 'whereas adults differentiate their thought into specialized kinds of discourse such as narrative, generalization and theory, children must for a long time make narrative do for all' (p. 49). In each of our tasks designed to elicit narrative we therefore decided to give a topic which was open. Thus for the autobiographical narrative we gave 'the happiest/saddest day of my life' (reformulated for the thirteen year olds as 'the best/worst experience I have ever had'). For the fictional story the stimulus was susceptible of interpretation — three pictures from which the children chose one, all of which depicted at least two people in a dramatic situation.

The trial run of these tasks gave us reason to expect that each would elicit responses along our affective/moral dimensions in particular, as well as some evidence for cognitive, stylistic and linguistic advances children make during the middle-school years. On the second task, the fictional narrative, we made a selection of five pictures and in consultation with our team of teachers we reduced these to three. Our final selection included a photograph of two small children looking at the view through a large mesh wire netting fence, beyond which seemed to be some hovels; a photograph of a teen-aged girl talking to an old man in profile against a brick wall; and a photograph of two young people with their backs to the viewer standing under a 'No Entry' sign at the entrance to a dark alleyway. (Copies of these photographs are to be found in Appendix B.) In the first and third photographs there was a transgression motif which would give us some measure of moral development, whilst all pictures could be expected to yield results on our affective model in that they were designed to tap a self/other dimension.

For our two tasks designed to elicit writing in the expressive to discursive function we had more difficulty. Teachers sometimes move children towards these tasks before they are ready for them, and so we decided that the topics given should be ones in which the child has confidence of his knowledge. Schonell's task, the 'How to play . . .' task, was chosen on the grounds that children have knowledge of the rules and processes in which they are, in a sense, expert. On this task the child picks the game he most likes to play and writes for someone who doesn't know the rules. Our final task was an argumentative one, again linked to the child's knowledge of school. The topic was 'Would it work if children came to school when they liked and could do what they liked there?' In deciding on it we were hoping to test the assumption that argumentative writing is too difficult for young children and properly takes its place in the secondary curriculum. If this is the case, and Moffett is right, we could expect the younger group to ignore the signals in the topic and to use narrative as a means of coming to terms with the issues.

6.4 The Writing Tasks

The writing tasks were as follows:

1. Autobiographical narrative.
Topic: (a) 'The happiest/saddest day of my life'. 7/10 year olds
      (b) 'The best/worst experience I have ever had'. 13 year olds
Reader: The teacher as trusted adult
Function: Personal statement
Content: Child's choice of content on the principle of memory selectivity

2. An account of a process from which the pupil can write with the confidence of a personal authority.
Topic: 'How to play . . . '
Reader: Layman; someone who doesn't know how to play . . .
Function: Discursive (explanatory)
Content: Child's choice of favourite game, his knowledge of rules and procedures

3. A Fictional Story.
Topic: Three visual stimuli, from which the child selects one picture with the instruction: 'Write a story for which your picture is one of the illustrations'
Reader: Wider public; that is, stories displayed in an anthology or on classroom display board
Function: Imaginative construct
Content: Child limited in terms of content by the picture chosen. Each contains at least one young person in a dramatic situation

4. Discussion of an issue close to the child's direct experience in which he is required to present a point of view and persuade the class to it.
Topic: 'Would it work if children came to school when they liked, and could do what they liked there?'
Reader: Peer group
Function: Discursive (argumentative)
Content: Pupils' own thinking stimulated by class discussion and based on personal experience.

It can be seen from the tasks that they represent an attempt to vary audience and function; that two call for writing in the role of the spectator and two in the role of participant. Our choice was intentional and related to the model of development which we were attempting to validate. Tasks one and three, in that they call for writing in which values and attitudes to events and people emerge, the 'I—you' relation as Moffett calls it, were intended to give evidence for our moral/affective dimensions; tasks two and four for our cognitive/stylistic dimensions. Stylistic measures can be applied to all.

6.5 Eliciting Written Responses

It can thus be seen that the tasks were designed in terms of audience, function, and closeness to the child's first-hand experience. Early research into writing development across the age range of our sample (Schonell, 1942; Ford, 1954) set written tasks to be completed under examination conditions and in terms of the traditional rhetorical categories, narration, description, argument and exposition. In order to overcome the possibility that the students in our sample would interpret their writing as 'for examiner' we asked our team of teachers to integrate the tasks into their normal classroom procedures, setting no time-limit and responding to student questions during writing time as they normally do. We also specified that the tasks be completed over a period of three months, to allow teachers to integrate them with their normal English curriculum. The central problem with setting tasks is that the child may see no reason for writing except that teacher/researcher wants it. Writing must fulfil students' purposes before it can fulfil the teacher's. In saying this we are not implying that children should write if and only if they chose the topic. As Mallett and Newsome (p. 166) say of their eight—thirteen year olds: 'In the early stages of learning to write, many children might never voluntarily take up a pen. But it does suggest that if teachers choose for pupils, they can only do so in a limited sense. They can choose the target area, or they can provide a set of starting points'.

In specifying reader and function on each task we were careful to allow students choice of context, so that the open topics could be seen as starting points. Sanders and Littleford (1975) claim that researchers must provide a full rhetorical context, that is, information about speaker, subject, audience and purpose in designing written tasks yet over specifying the task can leave little for the child-writer to decide. Odell, Cooper and Courts (1978, p. 10), point out that little attention has been given to the question of how to frame a writing task so as to obtain the best possible work from students and that there may be dangers in over specifying as well as in making tasks too vague. Our four tasks were designed as an intentional compromise between these two points of view.

6.6 Conclusion

Our decision to keep four written tasks constant across age groups and to assess student performance in terms of cognitive, affective, moral, and stylistic measures was necessary if we were to go further than the two Schools Council Research Projects and actually attempt to answer the basic question 'What are the characteristics of the writing of seven year olds and thirteen year olds?'. Furthermore, in collecting four pieces of writing from thirty children at each age-level we may be able to determine whether or not there are ages at which writers do not vary their writing according to their rhetorical purpose. Are there specific features of a ten year old's argumentative writing and a ten year old's personal writing which are significantly different, for instance.

If the question of what constitutes development in writing is to be answered, it is important that children at different age levels be presented with the same tasks: an autobiographical anecdote by a thirteen year old cannot be compared with an explanation of a process from an eleven year old: the tasks tap different types of linguistic, stylistic, cognitive, moral and affective considerations on the part of the writer. In this case the eleven year old would probably appear more mature on the cognitive dimension than the thirteen year old. The language acts, then, have to be directly comparable. Research in this area is needed. As Odell, Cooper and Courts (1978, p. 9—11) ask:

> When trying to accomplish a given rhetorical purpose, do older writers differ substantially from younger ones in their use of basic intellectual processes?

and further

> Are there holistic features that appear to be characteristic of say, the expressive writing of seventeen year olds and that rarely or never appear in the expressive writing of nine year olds? What exactly are those traits?

That these questions are currently being asked indicates that our research design may generate tentative answers in an area where little research to date has been attempted.

6.7 Summary

In this chapter we have described the research design of the Crediton Project. Four writing tasks, autobiographical, explanatory, narrative, and argumentative were given to each of three groups of children, aged seven, ten and thirteen respectively, in order to make a comparative study, keeping a main variable — the task — constant.

Chapter Seven

Cognition in Children's Writing — I (Explanation)

7.1 Introduction

The cognitive model described in Chapter Five can be applied to most forms of written discourse. Whether the writing is personal or impersonal in intention it is possible to demonstrate when a writer is summarizing, when he is deducing, when he is offering a hypothesis, within whatever form his discourse takes. If he does so in a piece which is basically narrative reporting in organization, then he is rated C1.5 on global coherence, the other moves at the sentence level being labelled specifically. However, the tasks we gave which produce the fullest demonstration of the cognitive model were the explanatory 'How to play . . .' and the argumentative 'Would it matter if children came to school when they liked and did what they liked there?' On each of these tasks we have selected some children from each age group 7+, 10+ and 13+ whose work is rated low, medium and high on our measures. Children's abilities with the written language vary markedly within chronological age-groupings. Some children at ten are still having difficulty reporting a simple sequence, others are moving towards classificatory thinking. Some thirteen year olds produce minimal explanations of game rules, others write in a fully classificatory fashion. Abilities within age groups differ markedly, yet we did not find any child in the 13+ age group who could not handle reporting a simple sequence, whilst we did find a proportion at 7+ unable to do so. This approach to analysis will give some information as to the range of capabilities within the age groups, as well as indications of developmental features in writing across age groups.

7.2 Explanatory Task

The range of games children in our sample chose to write about was enormous. Fifty-seven different games were described by a total of eighty-six children. In all age groups we found a preponderance of indoor games, from word games such as Hangman and Spill and Spell, at seven, to board games such as Draughts, Cluedo, Monopoly and Chess at 13+. (The sample was taken in the middle of a snow-bound winter.) Of the outdoor games mentioned, the seven year olds' favourites were Red Letter, Hopscotch and Hide and Seek masquerading under a variety of names from Sticky Glue to Fifty-Fifty. Only two children at 13+ mentioned these at all. The only game, in fact, in which we have examples from children in all age groups is football. Board games such as Frustration attracted the 7+ and 10+ but not the thirteen year olds. Draughts and Monopoly attracted the seven and thirteen year olds, but not the ten year olds. Card games appeared at ten. Such a variety makes it difficult to select representative samples from each age group.

One of the problems is that there is an enormous difference between the levels of representation of indoor and outdoor games for children. Some games, like Chasey or its variants are known 'enactively' to use Bruner's distinction — repetitive motor skills come into the means of knowing. To render into words what one knows by doing is difficult — one has to translate from enactive representation to symbolic representation in language. Bruner (1972) uses the example of trying to explain how to tie a shoe-lace, as indicative of the general problem. Many adults find it difficult to represent such an action in words to, for instance, their children, and also find it hard to 'decentre' enough to see the problem from the learner's point of view. To tie the lace facing the learner is to give him a mirror image of what he must do: rather one must face his direction so as to go through the motions he will have to duplicate. The child therefore has two problems to contend with in explaining games which are known enactively — he has to find appropriate words for actions which have become automatic, and he has to 'decentre' enough to present the sequence of actions in an order which makes sense to an outsider. The order in which he plays a game like Chasey is often not the best order in which to proceed from the learner's point of view. Indoor games may not present these problems in quite such acute form. They may well be learned from verbal representations, i.e. the rules, and the rules are often referred to in playing them (what is permitted in Monopoly for instance).

Problems also arise with board games and competitive indoor games which are played on grids or lined fields. Part of the game known to the child involves iconic representation — a visual image of the layout of the board, field, hopscotch grid. Not only does the child have to remember what he does, but how the game *looks*. Iconic representation must be translated into a form accessible to the learner of the game, either by means of a diagram or by means of words. Game rules like 'If you step on a line you are out' make no sense to a reader who has not been informed about how the lines are disposed. In order to describe a layout such as this the child needs to be able to give spatial markers — 'here', 'there', 'up', 'down', 'on top of', 'underneath', 'left', 'right'. Very few children at seven, ten and thirteen solved this problem by giving diagrammatic representations. At 7+ the diagrams were unlabelled, by 13+ the diagrams were named appropriately and of use to a reader. Most children, however, tried to describe such layouts in words, which presented difficulties or simply made the assumption that the reader would know, and therefore left out any such description.

For reasons such as these the 'How to Play' task is a difficult one for children, and classificatory approaches to game rules emerged in only seven children at 13+. The most common means children used to describe games was a simple chronology, within which occasional rules were either explained or summarized. The distinction between labelling and naming on our cognitive model was most apparent in the seven and ten year olds — many children at ten gave lists of names of positions in games to flesh out their accounts, as though naming the parts or the positions constituted an explanation. Lists of equipment also appeared. Those children who labelled, rather than named parts of games specifically, had great difficulty in giving a coherent account. To write a good account of a game requires that information be presented in an orderly fashion; hence the need of the writer to classify his information. He must select those rules which are crucial out of all the information about the game he has at his disposal. The question of the coherence of the child's account hinges on this difference. Non-selective information leads the child into specifying every concrete detail of the game with the occasional rule explained; selective informing leads the older child into classifying the information he has about equipment, rules of play, penalties under headings, and offering occasional concrete examples to illustrate the rules.

7.2.1 Explanation — seven year olds

The difficulties of organizing information for a reader were most apparent in the 7+ age group. Whereas most children can presumably specify a particular rule if asked by another child in an actual play situation, in writing an account of a game many young children are unsure of what their reader needs to know. Over one-third of our sample started their accounts with concrete descriptions of part of the equipment of the game; 'We all have three lines', 'you get a cup', without giving any indication of whether the games involved opponents or not. Such accounts frequently omitted any explanation of rules or summarizing moves about ways of winning at the end. To these children games are not perceived as competitive, but rather as instances of spontaneous behaviour — it is as though the young child, in playing with others, plays alongside another non-competitively, focusing on his own actions rather than on the game as a system. An example of one of the poorer seven year olds may make this clearer. Sally is trying to give an account of Tiddly Winks. She does not name the game at all and writes:

> We all have a number board and a cup in the middle of number board and you flick it in the cup if it land on the number board flick all the count.
>
> Sally M.

This account is highly confusing. She attaches names to the equipment needed for playing the game (C1.2) 'number board', 'cup', but fails to specify what 'it' is that 'you flick' — some sort of counter. The game has no overall aim, but is presumably played with others — hence her plural 'we all have . . .' She assumes that her reader knowns the name of the game, and her pronouns act as mere labels (C1.1). She does not elaborate enough of the context for a reader to be able to follow her instructions and gives no sense that the game can be won or lost. She cannot explain rules, though her starter 'if it land on the number board . . .' looks like a move in this direction which is incomplete. This is a typical example of C1.3 — partial information.

A more developed account of a game came from Peter, on Hopscotch. He tells us:

> To play hopscotch you can have 5 players or more to players the game all you need is a stone and when it lands on a number you have to jump over then if you step on a line you are out. So have another go.
>
> Peter G.

Peter gives us two explanations of parts of the game. He manages to specify the number of players required 'you can have 5 players or more' indicating that the game is competitive (C2.1). He uses appropriate names, like 'players' (C1.2) and names the game in his title 'hopscotch', yet there is some confusion — he labels 'numbers' and 'lines' (C1.1) without explaining these to his reader. The visual representation of the grid on which hopscotch is played is missing — we need to know what the numbers and lines are for and this he doesn't give, apart from 'you have to jump over'. That is, he focuses on what *he* does. His rule explanation (C2.1) 'If you step on a line you are out' is an advance on Sally who makes no attempt at explanation, but it is rather context-bound explanation granted the reader does not know how the lines are disposed. His concluding remark 'so have another go' is revealing — you can play hopscotch against yourself, not only against others. There is no sense here that *turns* must be taken at the game. Despite his opening explanation about numbers of players, his account centres on what he does, not on what others do in a system. He is operating at describer level, again at C1.3 — partial information, with the capacity to explain at a fairly low level.

One of the best accounts in this age-group came from Kathleen:

> *Kerplunk*
> This is how you play Kerplunk first of all you get this tube with holes in and then you fix it to the tray and then you put the skinny sticks in the holes and as soon as all the skinny sticks are in the holes you put in the marbles on top of the skinny sticks then each player takes a stick in turn the way to go round is clock-wize and the player to get the least marbles is the winner.
>
>   Kathleen M.

Kathleen, unlike Peter and Sally, has a clear idea that games are systems. Her concrete opening 'This is how you play Kerplunk' is characteristic of this age-group — about a third of them started with variants of this actual sentence. She gives us a chronological sequence of events 'first of all . . . then you put . . . as soon as . . .' (C1.5). She also gives us spatial markers 'you put the marbles *on top* of the skinny sticks' (C1.2). She names 'marbles', 'skinny sticks', labels other items of equipment — 'tube with holes'. She explains the process of the game 'each player takes a stick in turn' (C2.1) and makes no assumptions about the order in which turns are taken 'the way to go round is clockwise' — the beginnings here of the ability to use abstract concepts (C3.1). She can summarize the rule for the ending of the game (C3.2) 'the player to get the least marbles is the winner'. She elaborates the context fully for the reader. Overall, her account is chronologically/spatially organized — a clear example of reporting (C1.5).

The seven year olds' writing ranges in capacity from partial egocentric accounts of games to giving chronologically organized reports on what to do, with an occasional rule — explanation cited. Very few children at seven offer more than one rule explanation but about half of our sample manage this at least. Only a quarter of children could summarize rules for the endings of games (C3.2). No child at seven gave an overall purpose to the game at the outset — purposes of games are taken for granted at this age. The difficulty of giving both spatial and chronological details of games is apparent in this age group. Peter characteristically focuses on what one does and when in Hopscotch, omitting details of the spatial markers used in the game.

Generally then the seven year olds' accounts of games demonstrate that interest in the 'how' of events is beginning to emerge — nearly half of the children in the sample specify one rule explanation. Some explanations are partial and indicative of what Piaget calls childish anthropomorphism. One child offered this 'explanation' of the game Spotlight:

> When a car comes whis it lights on you have to hide behind a bush and if the
> can sees you you are out.
>
> Cathy K.

Here the child is attributing human motivation and intention to a mechanical
object. However, this was the only example of such egocentrism of explanation in twenty-nine scripts. The explanations offered are generally speaking
decentred ones, if they are there at all. It must be emphasized that over half
of children at this age offer no explanations — games simply start and end
with what people do to objects. Egocentrism in these children's accounts of
games manifested itself far more in the way the writers began their pieces,
that is in leaping into description without specifying how many people could
play the game. Over two-thirds of the pieces are ones in which the child
describes the game with self as the centre, failing to mention the presence of
opponents except incidentally.

Partial information in fact dominates the seven year olds' accounts of
games. Only one third of the pieces can be classified as 'reporting' — that is,
full chronological/spatial accounts of how games are played from beginning
to end. Most children can state how to start a game and end it, avoiding the
process in the middle. Most children have difficulties giving full reports — like
Peter they omit important information, focusing either on the enactive or the
iconic representations they have built up through direct experience. This task,
for the seven year olds, proves to be a particularly difficult one.

7.2.2 Explanation — ten year olds

In general, the problems of selecting and ordering appropriate information
persist in the ten-year-old group, though there are fewer partial accounts of
games. Whereas only a third of the seven year olds can be said to be reporting
full sequences, over three quarters of this age group give chronologically/
spatially organized accounts. There are vestiges of egocentrism; half the
children still assume that others will know how many people are required to
play games — this is particularly evident in accounts of board games. Whereas
the seven year olds focus on a series of actions with the occasional explanation of a rule, children at 10+ manage more rule explanations. Rules do not
arise incidentally for the ten year olds, but become a focus — they see games
as systems. Three quarters of ten year olds offered us rule explanations as
against less than half of the seven year olds. Generally speaking the ten year
olds' pieces are characterized by fuller describer thinking than the younger
children manage — they attempt to describe the boards on which games like

Cluedo, and Battleship are played as well as give in sequence the moves in
the game. Whereas it is not possible to describe any of the pieces overall as
demonstrating classificatory coherence (C3.6) the beginnings of classificatory
thinking emerge in some of the accounts.

We may quote Sandra's account as an example of writing in which we
discern less developed cognitive features:

> *How to Play Stay Alive*
> First of all you pick a coulur and put it on some round thing and you pull some
> long things and some time the Balls go down the hole and when your five Balls
> have gone down the person with some left is the winer. It is a very good game
> I sit and play and play with It is so good. the round things you put the balls on
> are white or orange the Balls are white, Black green and Blue.
>
> It is fun when the Balls full down the hole but they do not go down and till you
> pull the long white or orange things.
>
> Sandra M.

As an account of a game for an outsider who needs specific information this
is not very coherent, and the reason for this is mainly that Sandra cannot
name all the pieces of equipment needed to play the game. The 'things' she
labels (C1.1) appear to be crucial, as they are mentioned twice, but what are
they? The reader is left guessing — handles in some slot machine, perhaps?
Her opening 'First of all you pick a coulur' leads her into problems about
ordering her information; the colours of the balls used in the game are presented late 'the balls are white, Black, green and Blue' in a simple list. She can
summarize one rule for the ending of the game 'the person with some left
is the winner' (C3.2) and her initial description is based on a loose chronology
'first of all . . . when your five balls . . .' Sandra cannot elaborate fully for the
reader the content of the game. She does attempt assessment (C2.3) — 'It is
a very good game' — but she cannot explain the process by which the game is
played. She has difficulty organizing 'what you do' and 'what with' into a
coherent account. She is still operating at the level of partial information
(C1.3). Names of colours are not given any meaning — do the four colours
represent four players' tokens? Sandra's piece indicates the difficulties
children have in writing about board games — her only attempt at describing
the visual appearance of the board is the list of colour names.

An example of writing with more developed cognitive features is Andrew's
account of football:

> My favorite Game is football. It is well none all over the world. It is not just a
> kids Game it is a Gown up Game to. there are lots and lots of teams in Britain.
> There is Liverpool and Exeter City and York City and West Ham United and
> Many more team these team meat up and play against each over it. Ends like 3 v 1

and things like that. This is how you play. You have a field and up each end of
the pitch you have a goal. And the field has lines. thing you got to do is score in
the goals. I mean you have to kick a ball in the Net and Goal keeper got to you
from doing this. You elevan Players on each side if you are playing Proffesinill.
And Ill Tell you the Rules. If the ball goes off the pitch it is a throwing. And if
you kick some man you have a three kick. But you kick some in the Penelty. And
if you handell it you do same. I'll tell you the Bisians theres a Goal keeper and
Theres Defenders, midfielders, Strikers, Wingers, Right Back, Left Back, and
theres more too and that how you play football. and if you pracktise you may
play for a profeinel, one day.

Andrew B.

Andrew starts with a concrete personal statement and then goes on to give us
generalized information, reflecting for us on the state of the game. 'It is well
none all over the world. It is not just a kids game it is a Gown up game to.
There are lots and lots of teams in Britain' (C3.5). He then goes on to name
the teams 'There is Liverpool and Exeter City . . .' (C1.2). The problem with
this generalized and particularized information is that it is not really relevant
to an explanation of how to play the game. He is casting about, not sure
which details to select. This is also one of his difficulties when he comes to
the task proper. He explains the number of players 'you elevan Players on
each side if you are playing Proffesinill' (C2.1), indicating that football is a
team game, but he does this out of sequence — in the middle of a set of rule
explanations, rather than at the outset. He has difficulty ordering information
which is partly spatial, partly chronological. His description of the field 'you
have a field and up each end of the pitch you have a goal. And the field has
lines' lacks full spatial details. How are the 'lines' disposed? Part of the
problem is that he is labelling (C1.1) here, though he has names like 'pitch',
'goal' (C1.2) as well. He does, however, specify three rules: 'If the ball goes
off the pitch it is a throwing', 'if you kick some man you have a three kick',
'If you handell it you do same' (C2.1), though his explanations are not well-
articulated. The names for the different positions in a football team bulk out
the piece 'Theres Defenders, midfielders, Strikers, Wingers . . . and theres
more too' (C1.2). He concludes, not with how the game is won or lost, but
with a little hypothesis for the addressee 'if you pracktise you may play for a
profeinel one day' (C4.3) which is both relevant to his subject matter and
adequate. The main problem with Andrew's account is that it is not fully
coherent. He tries to do too much at once. His opening generalized narrative
and his ordered list of field positions for players at the end are the beginnings
of what will become classificatory thinking as he matures. His chief difficulty
is the selection of what is relevant to the task out of all the information he
has about the game. His thinking is still describer oriented (C1.5), though he
offers more rule explanations than the seven year olds.

An example of the cognitively more developed range of the ten year olds is Francesca's account of Cluedo, a board game. She writes:

> you have a board with rooms on it and in the rooms you put objects the objects are wrappon. you have three piles of cards a pile with the pictures of people on them you shuffle the people and take one out by don't look at it. you put it in the murder envelope. The second pile has got picture of the objects that you put in the rooms. you do the same as you did with the other pile you put another card in the envelope. The third pile of cards has got pictures of the rooms you put a room in the envolope. In the murder envolope you have how's the murder were it was done and what it was done by. Around the board is people. you throw the dice and you move your counter which is ment to be a person which is on card. You have to find out who is the murder. You go to rooms and aksed things to come in. The three piles of cards are shared out to the people play. You have to ask if anybody has a card with a picture of anything in the room. They show you and you mark it off on your piece of paper. If you have got three things not marked off they are the thing you say I know. If you are right about who is the murder and were it was done and with what you win. But if you are wrong to lose and the rest win.
>
> Francesca R.

Francesca's account is far more focused on explaining the moves in the game than is Andrew's. The information she has selected is relevant to the task. She does not, however, tell us what the board she describes represents — she assumes her reader knows this. How the board is set up and what the cards in the game are used for is made explicit. She fails to specify the number of players; other players are not mentioned until 'The three piles of cards are shared out to the people play'. However, in describing how the cards are shuffled and dealt she proceeds in a logical order. She explains what each pile of cards represents (C2.1) 'a pile with the pictures of people on them' 'the third pile of cards has got pictures of the rooms'. She then summarizes (C3.2) 'In the murder envelope you have how's the murder were it was done and what it was done by'. She explains what the intention of the game is 'You have to find out who is the murder', (C2.1). She can summarize the rule for winning the game 'if you are right about who is the murder and were it was done and with what you win' (C3.2). She names the pieces required in the game: 'dice', 'counters', 'board' (C1.2) and even explains what the tokens represent: 'You move your counter which is ment to be a person which is on card' (C2.1). In all she is attempting to describe the deductive process by which a player works out a solution to the murder game. Sometimes her explanations suffer 'If you have got three things not marked off they are the thing' from labelling (C1.1) 'thing' rather than naming, yet she has established the context that the 'things' are who the murderer is, where it was done and with what weapon prior to this. Whereas Francesca's account still follows the chronology of the game from start to finish (C1.5), she gives many more detailed explanations within the overall chronology than does Andrew, and is more selective of the information in terms of the task. She can also de-centre enough to give an alternative outcome to the game (C3.2) 'If you are wrong to lose and the rest win'. The chronology of her account is stronger than the account she gives of spatial markers — a fuller description of the board on which the game is played would help the reader. Yet she can handle explanation at a developed level. Her piece is a good example of explainer thinking.

Not all the ten year olds give such lengthy responses to the task, yet length of description appears to be no indication of quality. The more developed pupils often manage fairly brief explanations of games, and do so by organiz-ing their information more coherently. Board games and field games pro-duced problems for the ten year olds — possibly because they involve the child in having to select from a whole array of information that which is appropriate to someone not in the know. Card games prove easier for children to account for.

Generally, the ten year olds' accounts are much more explicit on the matter of rules than the seven year olds'. Three-quarters of the pieces offer rule explanations, over half of children can summarize rules for ending games, and nearly half specify the number of players. No children of 10+ give an overall evaluation of the purpose of the game. Statements like

'the object of the game is, you are given five crew cards'

look as though the writer is moving in the direction of stating a game's purpose, but what follows is a concrete explanation of some of the equip-ment used in the game. No child at 10+ gives a classificatory account of a game in full, though ordered lists of information rather than random ones do make an appearance in otherwise chronological accounts. Characteristic-ally the advance the ten year olds make over the seven year olds is in their capacity for full reporting rather than partial information. Only a quarter of pieces in this age-group can be classified as partial accounts.

7.2.3 Explanation — thirteen year olds

The major advance in the thirteen year olds' accounts of games is in the emergence of classificatory writing and the decline in partial information. Such classificatory pieces (C3.6) are characterized by accounts of games under headings like 'Equipment', 'Main Rules', 'The Playing Pitch' and one account of the card game Canasta began 'first I will define some of the terms used' under which the following headings appeared: 'The Meld', 'The Pack',

'Making the first meld', 'Making a Canasta'. In isolating such information in an ordered fashion the child is abstracting from all that he knows of the game that information which applies to the rule system, and in doing so he leaves simple chronology behind. That about a quarter of the writers organized their discourse in this fashion indicates the trend towards classificatory thinking in adolescence. Perhaps only two of the accounts at this age could be described as giving partial information.

Nevertheless, the bulk of the writing is still indicative that reporting sequences of concrete events dominates thinking. Classificatory writing emerges out of reporting, though there appears to be a transitional stage in between. The difference between the approaches may be explained as follows. Within a description of a game from start to finish some ordered lists of information are given, along with rule explanations leading to a summary of how to win. In full classificatory writing the child starts with a generalization about a particular set of rules, and moves back into interpretation and explanation to demonstrate how the rule works in practice in the game. Concrete details of moves in play are cited as instances of rule generalizations, rather than simply linked together in a chronological sequence. The bulk of the sample at 13+ operated in the former manner, giving very full chronological reports of games out of which arose interpretation and generalization.

Notable in this age group is the fading out of the problems associated with labelling versus naming at the word level. Children of thirteen have no trouble naming the pieces of equipment used in games precisely, so they establish context fully, unlike the children at 10+ who could not specify all names for parts of games and became incoherent as a result. What emerges at thirteen is the capacity to use abstract terms (C3.1) along with concrete names for objects. It is the rare child at 7+ or 10+ who can say of the way play proceeds 'the way to go round is *clockwise*'. At 13+ we see the emergence of abstraction at the word level: 'The player on the *left* of the dealer starts'; 'The ships can be placed on the board either *vertically* or *horizontally* but not diagonally'.

As well as increasingly abstracting at word level children at 13+ are beginning to generalize about the purpose of the game. A third of our sample at 13+ begin their accounts with overall evaluations (C3.3) like the following:

> The object of the game is to buy as many property's as possible and to make the opponint bankrupt.

> (Monopoly)

These evaluations enable the child not only to specify that games are competitive from the outset, but to give the audience a full context for the game rules which follow. An explicit statement of purpose indicates a movement towards context-free elaboration and is a completely decentred way of beginning. Alternatively many writers begin with concrete statements about the number of players. Hence, taking the presence of overall evaluations into account, the egocentrism noted in accounts at 7+ and 10+, where other players were not mentioned, has all but disappeared in this group.

An example of writing displaying less developed cognitive features, a full report in a chronological sequence, is Sally's account of non-stop cricket:

Non-Stop Cricket

You divide your players into two equal teams. You put up a wicket like ordinary cricket. (If you havent a wicket a post or stick will do). The team that are fielders first pick a bowler and a batstop (who stands behind the wicket) the rest of the players spread out. The batting team stand in a line. The first takes the bat and stands in front of the wicket. The batsman hits the ball and runs round the bowlers post and back to his wicket. The fielders have to retrieve the ball and get it back to the bowler as quickly as possible who tries to knock down the wicket before the batter reaches the wicket. The batter has to run every time the ball is bowled, even if he wasn't at the wicket when the ball was bowled. You can also get the batter out by catching the ball before it hits the ground or a wall. The Batting team count the number of runs and add them all together when the whole team is out. Then the teams swap over so the fielders are batting. They also add up their runs. When both teams are out the team with the most runs wins.

Sally R.

Sally's account represents a considerable advance over the ten year olds. She can name all the important elements of the game: 'fielders', 'backstop', 'batsman', 'bowler', and 'wicket' (C1.2), so her account is perfectly clear. She opens with a statement which indicates a capacity to use abstract terms as well as concrete ones 'you *divide* your players into two *equal* teams' (C3.1), thus indicating the competitive nature of the game from the outset. She proceeds in a chronological sequence, but unlike those of the younger children her spatial markers are also well organized 'and batstop' (who stands *behind* the wicket), 'the first takes the bat and stands *in front of* the wicket'. (C1.5). Although she proceeds in a chronological report from the starting moves to the ending of the game, she summarizes rules competently on the way (C3.2s); 'The batter has to run every time the ball is bowled'; 'The fielders have to retrieve the ball and get it back to the bowler . . .' She also explains how batters are got out (C2.1): 'the bowler . . . tries to knock down the wicket before the batter reaches the wicket'; 'You can also get the batter out by catching the ball before it hits the ground or a wall'. She ends her account with a rule summary of how to win (C3.2). 'the team with the most runs wins', after an explanation of the scoring system. Sally's account demonstrates that some children of 13+ are capable of full reporting, within which explanations and generalizations about rules arise. The problems encountered with younger children, of being unable to specify both the chronological sequence and the spatial markers of games are solved in Sally's account. Though there are elements of the capacity for abstracting and generalizing in her account, her generalizations about rules arise out of the chronological sequence — she does not start with rule generalizations in a system as our classificatory thinkers in this age group do.

An example of a transitional piece, which demonstrates elements of a classificatory account but lapses into chronology is Celia's account of Cluedo:

> To play Cluedo you have to have 2—6 players. The game is played by pieces and tokens being moved on a playing board, the board represents the ground floor of a Tudor house. The object of the game is to find out who committed the murder of Dr. Black, the owner of the house.
>
> The winner is the first player to say in one statement who committed the murder by which weapon it was done by and in which room the murder was committed.
>
> Each player takes one playing piece and moves that one for the rest of the game. Miss Scarlet always move first so you throw the dice and move the number of squares it says on the dice, you move towards any room on the board. The next player does the same. When a player reaches a room they make a suggestion of who they think the murder is done by, by what weapon, and in which room, the room is allways the one you are in. The player may move any weapon and any person into the room. Then they ask the person on the right if they have any of these things in their cards, if they have one they show you just one of them.
>
> When a player is satisfied that he knows what the three murder cards are he says it to the other players and then opens the black envelope and if he is correct he has won the game.
>
> Celia M.

Celia's account represents an advance on Sally's in one important respect — what she abstracts out of all she knows of the game in her opening. She starts with a general summary of the main thrust of the game, before going on to explain particular moves in it. All the important information has been selected out. She starts with an explanation of the number of players (C2.1), moves to a consideration of the board on which the game is played, and can say economically what it represents (C3.2). She then gives an overall evaluation of the game (C3.3) 'The object of the game is to find out who committed the murder of Dr. Black, the owner of the house'. She then summarizes the rule for winning, 'The winner is the first person to say in one statement who committed the murder . . .' (C3.2). The opening of her account is at a generalized level, giving an overview of the whole game — it is not chronological, the rule generalizations have been given systematically at the opening. This is a rudimentary form of classifying information for a reader, rather than remaining tied to the order of events as a game is played. However, after this clear opening, Celia's account then lapses back into chronology, and becomes confused. On the whole the rest of her account follows the process of the game from start to finish but she does omit important information. Unlike Francesca at 10+ she fails to mention the cards used in the game until late in her description of the series of moves and fails to make explicit what the cards represent. The 'black envelope' (C1.2), named in her final sentence, is totally unprepared for. In focusing on what players *do* in the sequence of moves she has failed to specify fully in advance all the equipment needed to play the game, so her ending is rather lame; it is an unexplained chronological sequence (C1.5):

> When a player is satisfied that he knows what the three murder cards are he says
> it to the other players and then opens the black envelope . . .

Presumably the 'three murder cards' were placed in the 'black envelope' at the outset of the game and represent the murderer, the weapon and the place of the crime, but this she has failed to make explicit. Celia's writing demonstrates that board games in particular still give difficulty to children of 13+. Giving full chronological and spatial details is hard, because the child has to draw on enactive and iconic ways of knowing and translate these into symbolic representation in words; so not surprisingly details are omitted in the struggle. The enactive game Sally reported so competently is less complex than the one Celia is attempting. Celia's chronological account is weaker than Sally's but her opening generalized information goes further than Sally in immediately classifying the overall purpose of the game and how to win it.

A sustained classificatory account typical of the better thirteen year olds is Antony's account of football, and the distinction we are making between reporting and classifying as the means of producing the overall coherence of the writing can be highlighted by comparing his account with that given by Andrew at 10+. Antony's writing is, for a start, completely focused — there is no information given, such as lists of teams in the league, which is irrelevant to the actual task set:

Football (Soccer)

Eleven-a-side

Equipment
To play soccer you need 24 players. Eleven on one team, against the other eleven on the other team. The extra two players act as substitutes. (Replace anybody who is injured or play badly etc.). The game lasts for 90 minutes, with extra time

(injury time) for any injuries or stoppages. There is a half-time after 45 minutes which lasts 10–15 minutes. The players come back on and resume play for another 45 minutes. There are two linesmen and a referee. The linesmen carry a flag and wave it about if he sees an incident or the ball has gone out of play. Out of play is when the ball has crossed the line. The linesmen generally help the referee in spotting fouls, offsides and off the ball incidents. The referee has a booklet and red and yellow cards. The yellow card is a booking. This means that he has broken the rules of play and it is considered a bad offence. The red card means a sending off. Meaning you can't come back on again or send a substitute to take his place. If you have been booked, and are about to be booked again, you automatically get sent off, as you have committed two bad offences and are not allowed a third chance. The two teams have to wear different coloured strips, as you may mistake there player for one of yours.

Each team has a player who plays in a certain position. A goal-keeper, who tries to stop the ball from going between two posts 8 yards apart and under a bar 8 feet up. There are full backs, the amount of fullback can differ. There are mid-field players, they can also differ. There are lastly the forwards, they can also differ. Here are some examples which exclude the goal-keeper: Three, Three, four. Three, four, three. Four, three, three. Two, Four, four. Four two Four. Four, Four. Two.

The pitch has certain markings. There is a goal line which stretches right across for a certain distance, forming the width of the pitch. The goals are situated on the goal line half way across. In front of the goals is a six yard area is the eighteen. yard area, with a little dome in the middle on the edge of the box. A few yards further on is the half-way line stretching across to form the width. In the middle is a large circle. This is where the game starts. On the other side of the line is the same markings to which I have just described. This forms the length of the pitch, when you have put the two halves together.

How to Play (Briefly!)

The players stand in their positions. The linesmen have taken up their positions on the touchline. The referee calls the two captains (There's a captain on each side to give directions). A coin is tossed. One of the captains shouts heads or tails, whoever wins takes a choice of either kick off or prefference to one end. If he asks for kick off, then the other team has choice of ends. The ball is placed on the spot and tapped *forward* to a player who runs on to it. From then on the aim is to keep possession and to score against the opposition. To score it has to pass the goal keeper, pass the posts and go under the bar, and over the line. If you win you score two points, if you draw you score one point and if you loose, no points. Once the game is on the go and the opposition have the ball and you want it, then you have to tackle them cleanly. If you don't then it's a free kick to them. If the foul is a bad one you may get booked. If it is in the eighteen yard area then it is a penalty. The person who has *been* fouled immediately has the ball, whether he had it before or not. If he is fouled inside the penalty area (the eighteen yard area) then it is a place kick. Everybody except the goal keeper, referee and kicker are allowed into the box until the ball is struck. If the ball hits the post then the kicker can't kick it again. Only the other 21 players can have access to the ball. When the ball goes out of play on the touch-line it is a throw in to the team who didn't touch it last. If the ball goes out of play on the goal line and a defender has kicked it out, then it is a corner and kicked into the penalty are for the attackers to score with, and defenders to clear with. If the ball was kicked out again by an attacker then it is a goal kick. Rather like a free kick except the kicker and referee has to be outside the penalty area. The goal keeper is allowed to handle it as long as he is within the penalty area. The goal keeper is allowed to handle it when it is in play. There is an offside rule, which has been changed, and I'n not quite sure what it is.

Antony B.

Antony starts by abstracting out of all he knows of the game the information the reader needs to know in advance before he can make sense of particular rules and does this under the subtitle 'Equipment'. He proceeds by summarizing, then giving specific examples to explain what the rules mean. He begins with the people involved in the game, gives us an explanation of the number of players and how they are disposed (C2.1). He then moves on to summarizing the rules for playing time, 'the game lasts for 45 minutes, with extra time for injuries or stoppages', (C3.2). He then moves into concrete explanation of the half time break, 'there is a half time after 45 minutes which lasts 10–15 minutes' (C2.1). He then goes on to discuss the functions of the referee and linesmen, 'The linesmen generally help the referee in spotting fouls, offsides and off the ball incidents' (C3.2). Concrete particulars, such as the dress of 'officials' follows. He explains fully the function of the penalty cards 'the yellow card is a booking. This means he has broken the rule of play . . . The red card means a sending off. Meaning you can't come back on again or send a substitute to take his place' (C2.1s).

His second paragraph gives general information about the functions of particular playing combinations. He does not simply name all the individual positions in play, as Andrew at 10+ did, but isolates the goal-keeper's function, then classifies the rest of the players into three groups 'There are full-backs . . . There are midfield players . . . There are lastly the forwards' (C3.6). Having specified that the number of such players is optional, 'these can differ', he goes on to give possible combinations of teams 'which exclude the goal-keeper: Three, Three four. Three four three . . .'. Again, the way he proceeds is from classifying his information to giving concrete examples to explain the classification. He moves on to giving the spatial markers of the pitch and here lapses back into describer behaviour, 'The goal is situated on the goal line half-way across. *In front of* the goal is a six yard area. *In front of* the six yard area is the eighteen yard area' (C1.5) but at least his description of the field is a full one. He describes how the lines on the field are disposed, unlike Andrew at 10+ who simply mentioned 'lines', and he names the areas

of the field appropriately 'The six yard area', 'the eighteen yard area' (C1.2).
This concrete detail he has isolated in advance, because explanations of the
rule system which follow depend on the reader understanding this terminology beforehand. Overall, Antony's introductory section, whilst containing
one describer sequence, is classificatory — it proceeds, not in a chronological
sequence but in a logical sequence of functions of all the components of
the game from the animate to the inanimate, from people to objects (C3.6).

His second section 'How to play (Briefly!)' begins with a description
of the toss-up which opens the game, but quickly leaves description behind in
favour of complex explanation of rules. He gives, at the end of this chronological sequence (C1.5) an overall evaluation of the purpose of the game
(C3.3) 'from then on the aim is to keep possession and to score against the
opposition. He explains how to score 'to score it has to pass the goal-keeper,
pass the posts and go under the bar, and over the line' (C2.1). When he
attempts to summarize scoring procedure he makes a mistake, giving the
scoring system for the league ladder rather than for a particular game: 'If you
win you score two points, if you draw you score one point and if you loose,
no points' He moves on to explain all the penalty rules for failure to 'tackle
cleanly' in order of severity: 'If you don't [tackle cleanly] then it's a free
kick to them. If the foul is a bad one you may get booked. If it is in the
eighteen yard area then it is a penalty'. These explanations (C2.1) are followed by a rule summary: 'The person who has been fouled immediately has
the ball, whether he had it before or not' (C3.2). This is followed by a full
explanation of how place kicks from the penalty area are taken by players
(C2.1). He moves from explanations of the rules governing fouling, to those
governing the ball being pushed out of play. He summarizes the different
rules governing the ball as it crosses goal line or touchline (C3.2) and explains
'if the ball goes out of play on the goal line and a *defender* has kicked it out
then it is a corner'. This means that the ball is placed in the corner 'and
kicked into the penalty area for the attackers to score with, and defenders
to clear with' (C2.1). He also gives the corollary of this rule, 'If the ball was
kicked out again by *an attacker* then it is a goal kick'. Antony's explanations
are not proceeding in a chronological fashion, but in a logical one — a ball
can go out of play at the instigation of an attacker or defender, so he explains
the rules for each in turn systematically. He is, again, organizing his rule
explanations into classes of events rather than simply listing them at random,
as did Andrew. His organization is classificatory (C3.6) rather than simple
reporting.

Antony's account of football demonstrates that at 13+ children can write
in the explanatory mode with a considerable degree of competence. Chron-

ological order of events is superceded by classificatory order — grouping game rules into classes emerges, and the writing is focused, the grasp of what is relevant information for a person not in the know is stronger at this age — expressive features such as 'I sit and play with it for hours it is so good' and 'My favourite game is football' which appeared at 10+ are seen as irrelevant to the task by thirteen year olds. Antony's account also reminds us that when the writer is placed in the role of an expert which is *real* to him, then he writes with confidence and can decentre enough to make his information fully explicit to a reader. It is not that describer behaviour disappears as the child moves towards classificatory coherence in his writing, but that the writing moves from generalization back to explanation and description. A generalization is only as true as the concrete details which support it.

7.3 Summary

The main dimensions of maturity or growth from seven to thirteen years on this task lie in a greater capacity for generalizing information and in a greater capacity for decentring. Describer thinking improves with age, as do capacities for interpreting and generalizing. The percentage of pieces at each age group which could be classified as full reporting, the coherence category for describer thinking, rose as expected from 31% at 7+ to 76% at 10+ to 70% at 13+. The plateau effect at 13+ is attributable to the fact that a further 23% of the writing was classificatory in coherence at this level. Similarly the number of pieces considered partial informing declined with age, from 69% at 7+ to 24% at 10+ to 7% at 13+. Capacities for interpreting also improved with age, at the sentence level at least. Explanations of rules in games rose from 45% at 7+ to 78% at 10+ to 93% at 13+; by this we mean that rule explanations appeared in that percentage of scripts at each age. We found, however, no pieces in the sample which could be classified as C2.4 'deducing' — the coherence category for interpreting, nor any pieces which could be classified as C4.6 'theorising', and this we would expect from the nature of the task. An explanation of how to play a game makes no demand for logical argument, but it does make demands for explaining at the sentence level and summarizing generally. Evidence for the other dimensions of the cognitive model will emerge in the discussion of the argumentative task — a task designed to elicit powers of logical argumentation in children.

Chapter Eight

Cognition in Children's Writing — II (Argument)

8.1 Introduction

The argumentative task was designed to elicit further information for our cognitive model than that provided by the explanatory task discussed in Chapter Seven. In writing about games of their own choice children were required to organize both generalized and particular concrete information in a coherent fashion, and whereas this is a test of the child's logical abilities, it is only indirectly so. The argumentative task, on the other hand, is a direct test of the child's capacity to justify an opinion in terms of reasons made explicit in writing. The topic given 'Would it work if children came to school when they liked and did what they liked there?' asks two questions. An adult, thinking hypothetico-deductively, may argue one or the other, supporting by sustained reasoning the child's choice of school subjects whilst rejecting optional school attendance, or vice versa. Children at 7+ and ten for the most part do not approach the topic given in this possibility-invoking way. Characteristically younger children fail to notice its two parts, and give a 'yes' or 'no' answer at the outset, followed by attempts at logical justification for their opinion, tied to the concrete situation of their own schools. Particularly at 10+ they often wound up in self-contradiction — the child would start with a definite assessment but in the process of writing come to a conclusion opposite to the assessment he made at the outset.

A classic difference between formal and concrete operational thought lies in the former being possibility-invoking whilst the latter is tied to the here and now. Our 'interpreting' category on the cognitive model, broken down as it is into 'explaining', 'inferring', 'assessing', and 'deducing' is designed to account for the concrete logic of childhood rather than the possibility-invoking logic of adulthood. Children do offer concrete reasons for their opinions and these concrete reasoning sequences we classify under our 'interpreting' category. The fuller, possibility-invoking statements of older children we classified either under 'generalizing' or 'speculating'. We would maintain that attempts at reasoning are a movement away from simple describer thinking, and must be rated as such, even if the child's attempts at interpretation are limited. Generally speaking, responses of the seven year olds to the question indicated that giving reasons, even at a concrete circumstantial level is difficult; less than a third of the pieces gave even one reason supporting opinion offered. The bulk of the writers interpreted the question, despite class discussion beforehand, as 'What would you do if you didn't come to school?' and gave incomplete accounts of their home activities. By 10+ three-quarters of the children gave reasons for their opinions whereas by 13+ all children did so.

8.2 The Argumentative Task

8.2.1 Argument — seven year olds

Children at 7+ found the argumentative task particularly difficult. Over half agreed that 'coming to school when they liked' was a good idea, and went on to describe what they would do if permitted to stay at home or if they 'came'. The grounds they offered for their opinions tended to be egocentric and based on the pleasure principle. Few children at 7+ could decentre enough to suggest that such a decision would have effects on others, such as parents, teachers, the school system as a whole. When they offered suggestions about changes to the school system they did not justify them logically, but simply listed their preferences. An example of a weaker response to the question came from Robert. He wrote

> No school on Friday and Thursday and Tuezday and Monday but Weday come for fut ball.
>
> Robert B.

Robert's response is a prelogical one. In the context of the question given he has decided by implication that the idea of coming to school when one likes is a good one, but he does not give an explicit assessment. Instead, he simply names (C1.2) the days of the week on which he would not come to school, and isolates his favourite day — 'come for fut ball'. Presumably, school is worth attending for this pleasurable activity. Robert is describing what he would do if given a choice, but his account goes no further than naming. He cannot give reasons for his preference.

An example of a more developed approach is Dan's:

> I think that we ought to be allowed to come to school when we like and we wouldn't get so cold in the mornings.
>
> Dan P.

Dan gives us a more elaborated assessment of his position on one of the two suggestions in the topic (C2.3). However, logical justification of his opinion is lacking. He offers one 'reason' for his preference — 'we wouldn't get so cold in the mornings', but is simply drawing on one concrete element of his situation at the time of writing — a snowbound winter. His thinking is tied to the here and now. Characteristically the middle range of children in the seven-year-old group responded, as does Dan, to one part or the other of the question, not to both. At best they assessed their position and offered one or two circumstantially restricted reasons for their opinion. A further example of the middle range of response is Sharon's account:

> I wish we could come when we like and go when we like because I don't like
> SRA and I don't like English work or Concept 7 to 9 because it is too easy for me
>   Sharon E.

Sharon's assessment of her position 'I wish we could come when we like and go when we like' (C2.3) is more context-bound than the one Dan offers — she assumes her reader knows the question refers to school, so does not elaborate the context fully in her opening sentence. She goes on to give highly ego-centric reasons for this opinion, naming her less-favoured school subjects on the way, 'SRA' and 'Concept 7 to 9' (C1.2). She offers reasons (C2.1) 'because it is too easy for me' but the reasons are circumstantial and restricted to her own concerns; the consequences for others in the school are not explored. Again, she focuses on one part of the question and her account is, overall, one of partial information (C1.3).

The most effective piece from a child at 7+ was Kate's argument in miniature. She writes:

> I think school should stay like it is. Because if we did not come to school we
> would not have anafe education to get a job then we would get no money and
> we would become tramps the we would diey but if we went to school we would
> get some education and we could go to college then we could get a very good job
> and get lots of money. So I think school is very good.
>   Kate B.

Kate's response to the question stands out in two respects. Firstly, she is not bound to the here and now of her particular school in attempting to argue her case. Secondly she assesses her position on the question at the outset (C2.3) 'I think school should stay like it is', and then raises a relevant hypothesis 'If we did not come to school we would not have anafe education to get a job' (C4.3). From this she deduces a consequence 'then we would get no money and we would become tramps and diey' (C2.4), which is logical if perhaps a little over pessimistic. She then gives the logical corollary of her initial deducing sequence 'If we went to school we would get some education and we could go to college then . . . we would get lots of money'. She concludes her argument with an overall evaluation, 'So I think school is very good' (C3.3). Her overall coherence is causal sequencing. Like the other children of this age she spells out the concrete consequences of her initial hypothesis — 'no money', 'become tramps and diey'. Here, her reasoning is concrete-deductive, rather than hypothetico-deductive. The argument Kate gives is very coherent in contrast to the responses of the other children of her age. Only one other child at this age was capable of spelling out the implications of a hypothesis in a similar fashion.

Generally, the demand for logical justification implicit in our task drew very little response from children at 7+. Two-thirds of pieces were rated at C1.3 — partial information. A further third actually offered circumstantial/ restricted reason for an articulated opinion on part of the issue contained in the question. Only one or two of the pieces such as Karen's were sustained deducing sequences, at a highly concrete level. Prelogical responses dominated the writing at seven years.

8.2.2 Argument — ten year olds

Whereas at 7+ over half of the children agreed either implicitly or explicitly that children should come to school when they liked, few ten year olds took this stance. Most children disagreed with one or other suggestion in the topic and could advance a variety of reasons, at a concrete level, for so doing. At seven, the reasons advanced for a preference were largely circumstantial and restricted to the child's immediate situation — others were not mentioned as having any bearing on the issue. The reasons advanced by ten year olds were more decentred than those of 7+; children explored what parents, teachers, bus drivers, and canteen ladies would suffer as a result of such a decision. Three-quarters started with an assessment of one or the other aspect of the question and could offer reasons at the statement level or inferences drawn from their experience of school. Sustained reasoning, however, proved to be a difficulty for them, and many pieces wound up in self-contradiction.

An example where the reasoning is not sustained is Sandra's account:

> To say I would like to do is come to school because of you can learn things out if I did not come to school I think that my mum and dad would say you are going to school if you like or do not like it.

> Sometime I feel like I do not what to come to school to work I just feel like staing at home but mum and dad said get to school sandra you are not staing at home to day sandra you are getting to school now sandra go on.

I think some times that we are better at School and that home.

Mum says sandra in a way you are much butter being at school.

But mum can I just today can I stay home. no sandra. please please Just to day
no no sandra. When you come home you can go to bed do I have to go to bed
yes Sandra.

When I got home I did have to go to bed but I thot that I was best to go to
School because I learn more at School and what I will at home like are mum's and
dad's can not give us exmahams so . . .

Sandra M.

Sandra's account it not a logical argument, by any stretch of the imagination. She is still bound by describer thinking. She oscillates between recording (C1.4) and reporting (C1.5) a narrative sequence. She assesses her position on the issue of coming to school 'I would like to come to school because of you can learn things' (C2.3) but this assessment is not well articulated. She then raises a hypothesis about parental reaction: should she please herself about attending school 'if I did not come to school I think that my mum and dad would say you are going to school if you like or do not like it' (C4.3). This is an adequate hypothesis relevant to the issue: parents reactions do matter. After this she moves into telling a story 'but mum and dad said get to school sandra you are not staing at home to day sandra you are getting to school now sandra go on' (C1.5). An argument, to Sandra, is assertion and counter assertion between parents and children; a far cry from arguing for a point of view. The narrative distance of the past tense reporting then lapses into recording — as she writes her way into her imagined argument with parents she records the voices in the conversation without placing them; it is as though the thought stream is undifferentiated (C1.4):

But mum can I just today can I stay home. no sandra please please Just to day
no no sandra. When you come home you can go to bed do I have to go to bed
yes Sandra

She then moves back into narrative reporting 'When I got home I did have to go to bed . . .' and returns full circle to the assessment she made at the opening (C2.3) 'I thot that I was best to go to School because I learn more at School' — none of which has been borne out by the narrative anecdote she has told. The reason she prefers school is to avoid parental anger and punishment, not that school is desirable in itself. Sandra, in fact, is still bound by describer thinking, although she makes two attempts at interpreting, both at the assessment level. She is a good example of a young child not yet distinguishing between types of discourse and as Moffett (1968, p.49) would maintain she 'makes narrative do for all'.

Other pieces, such as Barry's, attempt a more sustained argument. He writes:

> I think it would be quite a good idea. The only thing is they would always chose to play. They would never get a job and always be unemployed. If they could choose their subjects and didn't have any rests until after school it would be much better. (They would only have a dinner break). They could have a choice of subjects such as maths, English, astronomy, archeology. They could then have a period of time to do what subject you liked. If you did not go to school what would you do at home. Most parents would disagree with the idea of children not going to school. For nearly every child wouldn't come to school. I think it is good in some ways than others. I think parents would agree to it in some ways more than others. If the children told the teacher what they wanted to be then the teacher could tell them what qualifications they need. If parents agreed to this scheme then it might work.
>
> Barry T.

Barry begins with an assessment of his position on the issue 'I think it would be quite a good idea' (C2.3). He then draws an inference which in fact qualifies his initial assessment 'The only thing is they [children] would always choose to play' (C2.2). He spells out the logical consequences of this inference 'they would never get a job and always be unemployed' (C2.4). This argument sequence does not support the assessment he made at the outset — he is in fact arguing that optional school attendance wouldn't work. As he writes his way into the question he sees more of its implication and convinces himself of a different view, hence his overall evaluation later (C3.3) 'I think it is good in some ways than others'. He then goes on to tackle the issue of optional school subjects. He raises a hypothesis 'If they could choose their subjects and didn't have any rests until after school it would be much better' (C4.3), but he doesn't explain why he holds this view. He begins to explore alternatives to coming to school, raising an exploratory question 'If you did not go to school, what would you do at home' (C4.4). This leads him to drawing one generalization 'Most parents would disagree with the idea of children not going to school' (C3.1) which he goes on to explain (C2.1) 'for nearly every child wouldn't come to school'. He goes on to speculate on an alternative system of schooling at the end, offering tentative hypotheses 'If the children told the teacher what they wanted to be then the teacher could tell them what qualifications they need. If parents agreed to this system then it might work' (C4.3s). Barry is in fact finding it difficult to sustain an argument over his whole discourse. He has not sorted out in advance his opinions on each part of the question given, so that he oscillates between both issues, changing his mind as he writes on one of them. He can manage little bursts of sustained inference and bursts of hypothesizing but the structure of his whole discourse is rather loose. He is, however, writing at a decentred level — he generalizes about parents' attitudes, children's behaviour in the course of his writing, unlike Sandra who focuses on concrete particulars of her home situation. Barry can use argument as a form of discourse, but his grasp of logical sequencing is patchy. Like many of the children in this group he has difficulty being logically consistent.

The most consistent piece of logical argumentation at this age comes from Cheryl:

> No. It would not work because no-one would know anything because they didn't always come to school. There would be no teachers because nobody learnt anything so there would be no exams for the teachers to qualify to be teachers because no-one was clever enough to make exams. There would be nothing to do because nobody would be clever enough to make anything. There would be no factories or shops because nobody would be clever enough to make factory foods. Science and exploration into space would stop, for no one would be clever enough to man these things. There would be no medical care because nobody would make qualifications in medical care. As for doing the things you liked, well there would be no teachers to tell you what to do, so everything would be wasted in doing it wrong. There would be no books to tell you what to do. Reading would not exist or writing.
>
> Cheryl H.

Like Barry, Cheryl begins with an assessment of the issue 'No. It would not work because no-one would know anything' (C2.3). Unlike him, she is not concerned with spelling out the concrete implications of optional school attendance and choice of subjects in terms of her particular experience. The implications she draws are far broader. She is thinking, not of immediate consequences but long term consequences for society at large. She draws the same inference as does Barry about optional school attendance 'because they [children] didn't always come to school' (C2.2), and explains why in deductive sequence (C2.4) 'Because nobody learnt anything so there would be no exams for the teachers to qualify to be teachers because no-one was clever enough to make exams'. She then proceeds to hypothesize on the consequences of her initial premise 'There would be nothing to do. There would be no factories or shops', 'Science and exploration into space would stop', 'There would be no medical care' (C4.3s), and for each of the hypotheses she provides a causal explanation 'because nobody would be clever enough to make anything . . . because nobody would be clever enough to make factory foods', 'one one would be clever enough to man these things' (C2.1s). Cheryl paints for us a gloomy vision of a future without education. Her hypotheses are extreme, but they all add up to support for her opening contention. The reasons she advances for them may be a little repetitive, but what emerges is logical consistency for a point of view clearly articulated. We may want to question the truth of some of her suggestions, but granted her initial argument, what follows is consistent. Her response to the question is possibility-invoking, rather than tied to direct experience of the here and now. She sustains the giving of reasons for her assertions over the whole piece in a way Barry fails to do. Unlike him she has responded globally and emphatically to the suggestion of children's choice of school attendance, whilst ignoring the implications of the second part of the question — such dire consequences could hardly result from children's choice of school subjects alone. The reasons advanced for her view amount to an embedded generalization, that schools make people clever, and whilst her faith is touching, the truth of this premise is questionable. Her final hypothesis 'Reading would not exist or writing' is perhaps an inadequate one (C4.2); the notion of learning outside the context of school does not occur to her. Her piece is a good example of concrete-deductive rather than hypothetico-deductive reasoning; she does not envisage objections to her assertions and counter these as she argues her case.

The more developed pieces of writing from children of 10+ argued a negative response to one of the suggestions in the topic whilst ignoring the other. Those children who did perceive two distinct issues in the question, as did Barry, either confused the issues as they wrote their way into the topic or gave us two distinct responses, not synthesized into a whole. The task of weighing up the implications and consequences for and against the issues of optional school attendance and choice of school subjects proved difficult. Cognitively the task is testing in writing the childs' capacity to handle a 2 X 2 matrix — it is a classificatory task, which requires considerable thinking ahead. Those children who saw two parts to the question (five out of thirty-one), left the reader guessing as to what view they actually took on the matter. Those who could offer reasons for and against one of the issues in the topic had difficulty reconciling the two views. The ending of one child's piece read:

> Yes: I do think it might work but only if you got a method going. So that people/children would get some time to do work.
>
> No: I dont think it would work because people might stay home and not come at all.
>
> Penny D.

Here Penny is attempting to sort out for herself whether optional attendance would work or not. She can isolate a reason (C2.1) for and against the one issue, but is not able to combine these views into a coherent whole. That she attempts to sort out her ideas is a move in the direction of a classificatory approach to the question. This at least shows the beginnings of a capacity to foresee objections to one's own viewpoint and take account of them in arguing a case, at a fairly primitive level.

The ten year olds in our sample could give us single concrete reasons for their beliefs, but found the business of acknowledging potential resistance from an imagined audience difficult.

The demand for logical justification for a point of view drew more response from children at 10+ than it did at 7+. Even within pieces which were basically narrative reports, children gave assessments of their position with some attempts at explanation before lapsing into narrative anecdote. Pre-logical 'reasons' noted in the seven year olds, such as 'because we wouldn't get so cold in the mornings' appeared only in the weaker scripts at 10+.

Generally the reasons offered at 10+ were circumstantial, based on the daily operation of the particular school known to the child, such as

> I think they sud let us go home at a better time Because we miss all the films
>
>   Alan M.

It must be pointed out that some reasons offered at this age were implicit generalizations 'children would take the easy subjects', 'parents would disagree', 'people would make fun of them', but such 'abstracting' (C3.1) emerged only at the sentence level. The children in our sample at 10+ did not argue from generalized assertions as in propositional logic; they argued from concrete details, occasionally offering generalizations at an unsustained level. No child at 10+ offered, for example, an overall evaluation of the topic at the outset taking into account a response to both parts of the question. Further in only three out of thirty-one scripts at this age were generalized conclusions (C3.4) to an argument noted; as follows: 'So most people do not agree that this would be a good idea', 'So I think this is going too far', 'So it is better to be in school than out of school'. Most children at 10+, having started with an assessment (C2.3) failed to make their final stance on the question explicit.

8.2.3 Argument – thirteen year olds

The trend towards support of the status quo continued into this age-group. What does emerge however, is a classificatory approach to argument in approaching a quarter of the scripts whilst nearly all the others contained deductive sequences. The writers' disagreement with the topic means that we did not find an example of an argument for both parts of the proposition articulated. Resistance to the idea of change is strong; most children at 13+

could not even entertain the idea that children might behave responsibly if given the choice of school attendance. The fact that we allowed group discussion or class discussion as the preparation for this writing task may well have influenced the attitudes to school expressed in writing both at this age and in the children at 10+. Despite the fact that we specified as 'audience' for the task the peer group rather than the teacher, class discussion may have led to a consolidation of attitudes in defence of the status quo. Despite this limitation in terms of content, there emerged overall evaluations at the opening in half a dozen scripts, whilst most of the others started with assessment of one or other of the issues suggested in the topic. Further, concluding generalizations (C3.4) emerged in two-thirds of scripts in comparison with the odd two or three at 10+. Children at 13+ make their conclusions explicit. Some examples may make this clear:

> These seven points show just how ludicrous that suggestion really was
>
> Colin C.

> The society would soon change into anarchy
>
> Ron G.

> On the whole I think that some points of this would work but most of it, I don't think there is anyway of it working
>
> Mark S.

> So altogether it would not work out
>
> Tessa M.

It must be pointed out that such concluding sequences did not always appear as the final sentence in the argument — those children who wrote in a classificatory fashion tended to produce such conclusions at the end of a paragraph dealing with one or other of the issues. A quarter of the pieces ended on a conclusion of this type.

An example of the less successful writing at 13+ is Eddie's attempt at argument:

> "Would it work if children came to school when they like and could do what the liked there?"
> Lots of people in school would say that this is great, but you know, it wouldn't be, because if you didn't do what the school is trying to teach you, and you didn't pass your exames, you wouldnt get a job, well what I mean is you wouldn't get a job that you enjoyed, the money might be low, you wouldn't be able to go out for a good night out because of the money being low and you wouldn't be able, to get good job prospects, all this because you couldn't be bothered to try hard enough at school, it leaves you with a lot to say about the good of schools in the country no matter what you thought at the time.
> If people went to work any old time and didn't do the work, just sat around

playing card they would become unemployed, but in school you don't get kicked out, you would get a letter sent home and your parents who would dile with you and so would the school so that you can get another try at school.

If you had a system like this and you just had two or three hard nuts in the school then it means trouble broken equipment and a lot of younger children going to tutors or house heads, whoever there may be crying and you call for the other children and you punish them (after you know that they did it), and then they would get the younger children because they thought that they had creapt and its one big ring.

One thing about it, so you couldn't go to school for the buses didn't come, the teachers wouldn't mind much. If you didn't like History (like I do) you don't have to go to that lesson and the teachers wouldn't mind much.

Eddie M.

Eddie opens with an attempt at generalizing (C3.1), 'Lots of people in school would say that this is great' then goes on to assess his stance on the issue 'but you know, it wouldn't be' (C2.3), which he then infers (C2.2) 'because if you didn't do what the school is trying to teach you . . . you wouldn't get a job'. He then, unlike the younger children attempts to qualify the generalization underpinning his reason — the simple equation of school with jobs, the belief in the puritan work ethic behind such inferences needs qualification: 'well, what I mean is you wouldn't get a job that you enjoyed' (C2.1). He then goes on to speculate on the consequences, raising adequate hypotheses, which he then supports with explanations. The problem with Eddie's opening is that it casts about, trying to spell out the implications of optional school attendance, but does so in a random rather than organized fashion. The reasons he advances are also highly concrete ones. He attempts a concluding remark, 'It leaves you with a lot to say about the good of schools in the country no matter what you thought at the time' (C3.4), but he has not made explicit how this statement relates to the speculations which precede it. In his second paragraph he attempts to draw a comparison between the world of work and the world of school, but the point of this comparison is not made explicit either. In this paragraph he appears to be focusing on the suggestion of optional school attendance, pointing out that the consequences of it are less marked than in the workforce 'but in school you don't get kicked out, you would get a letter sent home and your parents would dile with you and so would the school . . .' Here, he is simply recording (C1.4) for us what goes on in his own school over the issue of absenteeism. He has lapsed into describer thinking. In his next paragraph he goes on to speculate about the effects of such a system on the school from within. He raises a hypothesis (C4.3), 'If you had a system like this and you just had two or three hard nuts in the school then it means trouble'. He supports this hypothesis not with reasoned argument, but with a narrative anecdote of bullying and tale-telling 'broken equipment and a lot of younger children going to tutors or house heads . . . crying and you call for the other children and you punish them (*after* you know that they did it) and *then* they would get the younger children' based on a loose chronology (C1.5). Within this anecdote he offers one explanation of why older children would be violent with other children 'because they thought that they had creapt'. He is attempting to describe the 'trouble' mentioned in his initial hypothesis, rather than give reasons systematically. However the narrative anecdote *does* illustrate the hypothesis he raises at the opening of the paragraph in a way that Sandra's little story at 10+ did not.

Up to this point in his response each of Eddie's paragraphs is thematically consistent with the initial assessment he gave at the outset — he moves from his consideration of the general bad effects of a change in a school system towards particular negative effects within the school. His final paragraph, however, neither sums up the viewpoint he has attempted to argue for, namely that change is bad, nor gives another instance of the same view. It is a volte-face to a consideration of the positive implications of a change. He toys with the possibilities of greater freedom for children:

> One thing about it, so you couldn't go to school for the buses didn't come the teachers wouldn't mind much. If you didn't like History (like I do), you don't have to go to that lesson and the teachers wouldn't mind much.

If the system changed teachers 'wouldn't mind' about the same things *as* they normally do. This plea for self-indulgence at the ending does not follow logically from the rest of his writing. Tacked on as it is it looks like a self-contradiction. At least, though, it is an indication that Eddie is beginning to see two alternative views on the issue. However his final paragraph is particularly context-bound. As with the ten year olds many children at 13+ explored the implications for the bus service of a change in school routine — for children on outlying farms the service is important and if not supported by sufficient numbers would collapse. The issue appears to have been raised in class discussion. Eddie raises it, without elaborating the context or demonstrating that the issue is relevant to his line of argument. He makes his opinion and beliefs clear, but the structure of his discourse is loose — he cannot sustain logical argument. He makes an attempt to 'acknowledge potential resistance' to his viewpoint, both in his opening sentence and in his final paragraph, the beginnings of decentring, but like the better ten year olds winds up in self-contradiction.

The middle-range of children at 13+ argued coherently for a point of view, taking into account both parts of the topic — the question of optional school attendance and pupil choice of activities. An example is Colin, who writes:

> No, there would be so many difficulties inherent in this idea that it would be a non-starter. A few of the problems would be (1) A fluctuating demand for teachers (everyone might come one day and but a few another day). (2) Some children not realizing the importance of education would never come (3) How *literaly* is the above question taken (could children go to school at midnight if the late film isn't any good?) (4) Some children would attend school for 4 or 5 hours every day, they would be at a very different level of understanding in their subjects than the people who seldom came and it would therefore be impracticle to put them in the same class, and as only 20 people might want to do R.E. it would be impracticle to split the class into the nessesery 4 or 5 levels. (5) In a school of 1600 it would not be possible to let children do exactly what they want (only 4 or 5 people might be interested in falconry). (6) The planning of the curriculum would be a nightmare. (7) The school lunch system would be useless as the lunches might be left one week and over subscribed the next. These seven points show just how ludicrous that sugestion really was.
>
> Colin C.

Colin begins with what appears to be a simple assessment of his position, but granted the context and the fact that he argues against both parts of the proposition in the piece as a whole, it is in fact an overall evaluation (C3.3). His opening statement gives direction to the whole piece — the 'difficulties' mentioned in his overall evaluation are then elaborated in full. Nothing irrelevant intrudes. He lists the difficulties in a series of generalized assertions, drawing out the implications of both suggestions systematically — these assertions act as summaries, 'a fluctuating demand for teachers' (C3.2), 'The planning of the curriculum would be a nightmare', 'The school lunch system would be useless' (C3.2s). He gives reasons for his assertions, 'everyone might come one day and but a few another day', 'as the lunches might be left one week and over subscribed the next' (C2.1s). He explores by asking his own questions 'how *litteraly* is the above question taken (could children go to school at midnight if the late film isn't any good?)' (C4.4). His fourth point is in fact a deducing sequence (C2.4) in which a concluding generalization is made explicit, 'It would therefore be impracticle to put them in the same class' (C3.4). He goes on to give a concrete example of what he means, relying on his peer-group audience understanding the context by using an abbreviation for the name of a school subject 'as only 20 people might want to do R.E. it would be impracticle to split the class into the nessesery 4 or 5 levels' (C2.1). He ends his list of problems, which proceed from generalization to concrete example, with a conclusion which does, in fact, summarize all that precedes it, 'These 7 points show just how ludicrous that sugestion really was' (C3.4). The beginnings of a classificatory approach to argument are apparent in his listing of points; however his writing is not fully classificatory. The list is not organized systematically into two sections which correspond to the two issues in the topic. His fifth and sixth contentions take up the issue of children's choice of subjects, his seventh point returns to the consequences of optional school attendance with which he started — in fact he has less 'proof' of the inadequacy of children's choice than of optional school attendance and has disguised this rather cleverly. The two issues *are* responded to, however, without him lapsing into self-contradiction, as did Eric. There is internal logical consistency from the opening evaluation to his concluding sequence.

An example of a classificatory approach to argument came from Arthur:

This system would be dubious unless several regulations were introduced. In each lesson such as English the pupils would be at different levels, there might be any number of pupils attending the lesson. This would be very awkward for the teacher if he had a CSE and A level student in the same class. Individual attention would have to be given to each pupil which would mean a drastic increase in the number of teaching staff, many of whom might become redundant if few turned up to the lesson. Thus English, Maths and Environmental study, games, and art and a science would have to be controlled as is now usual.
Secondly not all interests could be catered for in one school. In one 'year' e.g. third year some might like to do falconry, one chess, yet another piano-making and a third reading Shakespeare. Even in a school as big as ours not all these interests can be catered. Pupils must therefore travel to schools that have classes specializing in their hobby. This is not possible.
A far better system would be to give secondary school pupils a basic three years schooling and then allow less academic pupils to take an apprenticeship for half their school time in the fourth and fifth year. The more academic pupils could take the 'O' and possibly 'A' level. Meanwhile the less academic would be able to take a small number of G.C.E.'s or C.S.E.'s that would be suitable for their job. This system would help young people find work more easily and would prepare them for a working life. It would be far more practical than technical courses and this work experience would be constructive. It would drastically cut down on school costs, while giving a superior education. If it was found that the children had less general education, then secondary school education should begin at ten or nine so that a fairly broad background education can be given and a greater number of qualifications obtained.

Arthur M.

Arthur begins, not with an emphatic statement of opinion on one of the issues but with a tentative overall evaluation (C3.3) which contains a qualification, 'This system would be dubious unless several regulations were introduced'. His opening signals that he is evaluating both parts of the question as his use of the word 'system' implies. The qualification 'unless several regulations were introduced' is an indication that not only can Arthur express an opinion tentatively, but that he is decentred enough to realize that his opinion could encounter potential opposition; the qualification he adds strategically suggests that the issues in the topic are not simply ridiculous because he does not agree with them, that something positive could be said in their defence even if in the final analysis he happens to disagree. His opening generalization is in fact possibility-invoking. He follows this with an explanation (C2.1) which illustrates the problems of optional school attendance, 'In each lesson such as English the pupils would be at different levels', follows this with an assessment (C2.3), 'This would be very awkward for the teacher . . .' from which a result is inferred (C2.2), 'which would mean a drastic increase in the number of teaching staff'. A concluding statement (C3.4) ends his opening paragraph 'Thus English . . . would have to be controlled as is now usual'. Throughout the first paragraph Arthur is deducing (C2.4), giving causal links between his interpretations of the effects of optional school attendance on the school as a whole. Unlike the young children he has sorted his paragraphs out logically into considerations of each of the two issues contained in the topic, taking one at a time rather than jumbling both as did Barry at 10+. The opening of his second paragraph indicates that he is thinking in a classificatory fashion (C3.6) 'Secondly not all . . .' which implies that the first paragraph dealt with the first issue, the second will deal with the second. He goes on to generalize in a reflective fashion (C3.5), 'Not all interests could be catered for in one school' and again demonstrates the truth of his assertion by recourse to concrete explanation (C2.1), 'some might like to do falconry, one chess, yet another piano-making'. Again, he draws a conclusion (C3.4), 'Pupils must therefore travel to schools that have classes specializing in their hobby'. He then assesses the conclusion to which his reasoning has led 'This is not possible' (C2.3). To this point Arthur has operated in a classificatory fashion. He gives an opening paragraph reasoning out the implications of optional school attendance and a second paragraph on student choice of subjects, dismissing both possibilities not simply by assertion but by tightly argued reasoning sequences.

In his third and fourth paragraphs Arthur goes beyond the information given suggesting alternative changes to the school system of his own. A series of linked hypotheses are sustained when he projects (C4.5):

> A far better system would be to give secondary school pupils a basic three years schooling and then allow less academic pupils to take an apprenticeship for half their school time in the fourth and fifth year. The more academic pupils could

take 'O' and possibly 'A' level. Meanwhile the less academic would be able to
take a small number of G.C.E.'s or C.S.E.'s that would be suitable for their job.

Arthur's proposals at highest reach, like this, the level of adequate sustained
hypotheses, and he has some idea of possible objections to them, as his
alternative suggestions to curriculum for the 'academic' and 'less academic'
indicate. The system he suggests as a hypothetical alternative he then
attempts to evaluate in a series of assertions which are overall evaluations
(C3.3s) 'This system would help young people find work more easily', 'It
would be more practical than technical courses and this work experience
would be more constructive', 'It would drastically cut down on school
costs'. All his evaluating moves add up to positive support for his own projecting. He is not simply tied to the issues raised in class discussion, but goes
beyond them. Whereas it was felt that such projecting falls short of full
theorizing, because thematic rather than logical links are stressed within it
and the writer cannot subject all his hypotheses to critical examination, this
is the thinking from which full theorizing, the peak of adult intellectual
endeavour, springs. Arthur may not be able to envisage the effects on children
of enforcing of secondary school curriculum on nine or ten year olds for he
has as yet no theory of intellectual development in children against which to
weigh up such a proposal. He does, though, envisage that an objection to his
alternative system would be claims that education would not be general
enough as a result, and tries to counter this, albeit inadequately from an
adult's viewpoint. This is the beginnings of hypothetico-deductive thought,
as against concrete reasoning, and must be valued highly. Arthur's response
to the question goes beyond that of Colin in two respects: he can argue a
case in a classificatory fashion (C3.6), and he can project an alternative view
of his own (C4.5) which is original. Further, he is not resistant to the notion
of change *per se*; his whole piece ends with a consideration of potential
changes to the system of schooling he knows intimately, with some attempt
to evaluate them critically. Unlike other children at 13+ who suggested
changes to the school system, his suggestions for change are at a greater level
of generality and are more decentred. A comparison may make this clear.
Evan, one of the few children at this age to respond positively to the
suggestions for change contained in the topic, wrote:

> We also schould have a break in the afternoon, and have coffee in the breaks and
> dinner hour. We should learn about first aid and saving lives. I wouldn't have
> assemblies but would have something like tutor group . . . We all schould watch
> more television at school . . .

Evan M.

Whilst Evan is also capable of speculating about potential changes to schooling, his suggestions are far more concrete than are Arthur's. He sees change, not in terms of *systems*, but in terms of concrete events in the school. Arthur's capacity to propose an alternative system and to evaluate it goes far beyond this. He is arguing from propositions rather than from concrete events; his thinking is formal operational.

8.2.4 Summary — Argument

What, then, can be said of the pattern of development in the argumentative task? The trend here confirms that discerned on the explanatory task, namely that powers of interpreting, generalizing and speculating improve over this age range. At 7+ less than a third of children in the sample were capable of assessing their position on an issue and offering one or two restricted 'reasons' to justify the assessment. Most children at 7+ began their responses with statements such as 'I wish we could come to school when we liked', then went on to describe what they would do. Partial information dominated the accounts at 7+; few children wrote more than two sentences. At 10+, over three-quarters of scripts started with assessments of one or other of the issues in the topic and followed them with circumstantial reasons based on knowledge of a particular school. Within many of these children gave deducing sequences. At 13+ over three quarters began with assessments and the rest gave overall evaluations of their attitude to both parts of the topic and attempted to make explicit their own logic, unlike the seven year olds who found this very difficult. Generally, too, younger children found it difficult to draw an explicit conclusion from their deducing sequences. Explicit conclusions at a generalized level occurred in very few, in a quarter, in nearly two-thirds of scripts at each age respectively though not always at the end of the piece of writing, where adult logic would predict them. Usually such concluding generalizations appeared at the end of a chain of deductions, rather than at the end of the total discourse. It is not simply, either, that such interpreting and generalizing moves appear in more scripts at 13+ than in other age groups. From 10+ children draw more inferences, make more generalizations, offer more hypotheses than children at 7+, although they have difficulty organizing them coherently. At 13+ this development continues, with increasing powers of organization becoming apparent — the logical connections between ideas are made more explicit and the problems of self-contradiction noted at 10+ disappear from all but the weaker scripts. The same pattern emerges with our fourth category 'speculating'. At 7+, very few scripts offered hypotheses at the sentence level, at 10+ and 13+ about three-quarters, with several more at this last age projecting a set of related hypotheses in a coherent fashion. Previous research, such as Harpin (1973) would indicate that our results at 10+ are rather unusual. Syntactic markers of the hypothetical mode — clauses of condition, modal verbs, expressions of tentativeness in 'perhaps' and 'what if' statements made little appearance in Harpin's analysis of the syntax of nine—eleven year olds, yet they emerged consistently from 10+ in our sample. Our results indicate that when children are presented with a writing task designed to elicit hypotheses as the 'would it work if . . .' formulation of the topic encouraged, they do use hypothetical syntactic construction earlier than previous research would lead us to expect. The important point is that the cognitive and linguistic strategies for speculating appear when we ask children to speculate — the linguistic task is all important. We found little evidence of speculation even at the sentence level on the explanatory task, and it is not surprising that Harpin found little evidence of clauses of condition appearing with greater frequency the older the child was. His writing tasks, factual and creative, did not encourage speculation from children. Perhaps the reason why children at 10+ are said not to produce hypotheses in writing is that teachers and researchers do not ask them to do so, not that they are incapable. This speculation, however, does need qualification for as Barnes (1976) maintains:

> What is not so clear is whether tentative forms of words are always vehicles for hypothetical cognitive strategies: and this must at present remain an hypothesis. (p. 70)

What our results indicate is that when asked to perform a task, one which elicits hypothetical cognitive strategies, children at 10+ produce, at the sentence level at least, the 'tentative forms of words' not seen on other tasks such as explanation or narrative.

The pattern of results at the sentence level, mentioned above, is confirmed when the writing is classified in terms of its means of cohering. The results were as follows:

	Partial Information C1.3	Reporting C1.5	Deducing C2.4	Classifying C3.6	Theorizing C4.6
7+ (N = 31)	65	29	6	0	0
10+ (N = 31)	3	35	61	0	0
13+ (N = 27)	0	4	74	22	0

Figures to nearest percentage.

The trend here confirms that noted on the explanatory task, namely that children leave behind reporting/narrating as the means of organizing the writing as they mature. Deducing capacities, the ability to give a chain of reasons for an opinion, improve with age. Classificatory thinking does not emerge before 13+, and then only in a small percentage of the sample. We found no pieces which could be classified as full theorizing, an indication that the fullest form of formal operational writing, in which the writer submits his own speculative thinking to critical examination and anticipates objections to his line of argument as he proceeds, is beyond the cognitive capacities of children in this age-group. Whereas we found no evidence of fully decentred theoretical writing in our sample, we did find that capacities for decentring improved with age. Children at 7+ characteristically argue for coming to school when they like, citing egocentric reasons: 'I can stay home and watch television and eat sweets' — that is, if they give reasons at all. At 10+ the reasons offered for an opinion are more decentred: children explored the effects the system portrayed in the topic would have on other children, on parents, on teachers. At 13+ this trend continued, with children not only exploring the effects of the proposed system from a 'within the school' perspective, but from a 'society at large' perspective as well. As one boy aptly reflects 'The society would change to anarchy'. The reasons offered tend to confirm the results of Peel (1971), that prelogical explanation gives way to circumstantial and restricted reasoning chains which in turn give way to 'imaginative' or 'possibility-invoking' generalizations across the age-range 7—13 years.

8.3 Some Conclusions — Explanation and Argument

In applying the cognitive model to the two discursive tasks given to children at 7+, 10+ and 13+ on a total of 174 scripts we are in a position to make some tentative generalizations about development, bearing in mind the limitations of our sample. We did not apply the cognitive model to the autobiographical and fictional narrative writing of the students, largely because these tasks called for full describer thinking and would give us little evidence for cognitive development beyond the 'reporting' level in our hierarchy. Carlin's (1978) research into secondary school writing, suggests that our more developed model should be applied principally to writing tasks which stress the cognitive aspects, rather than the affective aspects of student's thinking. As Carlin (1978, p. 89) discovered:

> The cognitive measure of writing development proved useful in isolating certain features of the writing of each student, although it was generally less productive with narrative writing than it may have been with more transactional writing.

With our application of the developed cognitive model to discursive writing tasks we are in a position to demonstrate its full working, rather than to indicate its partial use.

The application of the cognitive model to the writing of low achieving and high achieving students in each age group across two tasks demonstrates that cognitive abilities within age-groups differ markedly. Nevertheless, some generalizations can be made which indicate development from 7–13 years. The younger children in our sample find it difficult to decentre when writing for an audience which is more remote, more abstract than the real audiences they encounter in speech situations. They are unsure of what information to give which will make sense to an outsider. The twofold nature of writing, the selection of information relevant to the topic, and to the needs of a particular audience, they find difficult. The result is that partial information character-izes the writing in this age group on both tasks, as do problems of labelling versus naming. There is less general coherence in their writing than in older children's; those that move past partial informing move to reporting as their main form of coherence. Even when reporting, as about a third of the sample did on the explanatory task, children of 7+ found it difficult to give both spatial and temporal sequences – they opted for one or the other. A similar pattern emerges on the argumentative task – partial information again dominated the accounts. Powers of interpreting, generalizing and speculating are only beginning to emerge at 7+, and then only at the sentence level. It is the rare child at 7+ who can give a chain of reasons for an assessment of an issue or can raise a relevant hypothesis. At 10+ children decentre more, elaborate the context more fully for a reader, offer chains of reasons for their opinions, even in cases where such deducing chains are still based on concrete phenomena rather than upon generalized propositions. They have difficulties with ordering information, but this is partly because they have more to say than do the seven year olds. They do, however, raise hypotheses and make generalizations which arise out of reporting sequences of events with greater consistency than do the seven year olds. They are more aware of the needs of their audience, though still have difficulty selecting what is relevant to the demands of a task and remaining logically consistent. The older children, at 13+, abstract more easily, summarize, give overall evaluations and conclud-ing generalizations more easily and have a greater grasp of the notion of relevance. Classificatory thinking emerges at this level, whereas we found no evidence for it in younger children. Furthermore, by 13+ children elaborate context more fully – partial accounts all but disappear at this age, and logical connections between ideas are made explicit. Whereas at 10+ children give generalized assertions on the argumentative task which they characteristically fail to elaborate on or to explain, children at 13+ show more capacity to support their generalizations with concrete evidence. The result is that problems of self-contradiction decline. Further, at 13+, some children manage to 'go beyond the information given', projecting a series of thematically related hypotheses, which none of the younger children in the sample manage to do. Our results bear out the developmental shifts postulated by Moffett (1968) which he sees in relationship to Bernstein's distinction between restricted and elaborated codes:

> The code differences run along the same lines as the developmental shifts we have discussed: ethnocentric to individualistic, increasing choice, increasing consciousness of abstracting . . . increasing elaboration. (p. 58)

We have found that older children decentre more, elaborate context more, select more, and generalize and hypothesize more than do younger children. Further, they are not bound by reporting or narrative as their chief means of cohering and have greater control over logical sequencing than do younger children. They are beginning to move towards what Bruner (1975) terms 'analytic competence' with language.

Chapter Nine

Affect in Children's Writing

In Chapter Four we discussed affective development. In Chapter Five we described a model of affective development, and we shall now examine samples of children's writing by means of this.

9.1 Affect in Writing

Let us compare the spoken English of an eight year old boy, Struan, with his written English on the same topic. The following was spoken to a group of his peers, with an adult present, in response to an invitation to talk about his holiday:

> well when we went to scotland em/we went to bendherloch and er/we out out em/to trulee bay/you see my grannie lives there and er/she lives very near the beach/and/so er/you see there was this speed boat on the beach/and this man who owned them let us go out in them/so we went out to this little island/and mm/we took a picnic lunch and it was fantastic we stayed in this little castle/oh boy we went down to see the dungeons/we/went up and saw a few swords and armour/oh it was fantastic that was/ooh/and then we went we came back/we went out to another one/and it was terribly it was exactly the same/but we went on the other side of the island you see because it was too far to walk/so we had to take the/speed boat and then then we came back/and then we went home

Subsequently he was asked to write about this holiday:

> When we went to Bendherlock in Scotland. We went to Trulee beach and my Grandma's and we saw two speed boat's and the man that was beside them said that we could go on them and we went out to an Island and we had a picnic.

The differences between these two in the presentation of emotion are great. In the spoken passage, as can be inferred, the emotion is conveyed primarily through the paralinguistics. The pace, tone, rhythms, timing all serve to communicate the feeling of immediacy and excitement. Again certain 'hurrah' words (the example 'fantastic' here) are accepted in the spoken language rather to convey a vague feeling of approbation than to convey a cognitive idea. Struan even goes so far as to use a non-word, 'ooh', to convey the shiver down the spine which he is generating in his audience. Another means of communicating excitement is by the use of emotionally charged words — 'dungeons', 'swords', 'armour' for example.

In Struan's written version all this has disappeared. Certainly there can be nothing carried by the voice. Anxieties about formal correctness appear, and the interesting details of the spoken version are omitted. This is presumably because Struan believes that he ought to start at the beginning and he runs out of steam before he reaches the dungeons (the picnic at the end of the writing is in the middle of the spoken version), but he may also believe that the written language need not be interesting. The expectations that children discern in their teachers, correctly or not, seem to influence their writing very considerably.

There is however a major problem independent of this. What is communicated without effort in the spoken language in the voice, stimulated so often by face to face contact, has to be carried in the written by stylistic devices — by the connotations of nouns and verbs and the enrichment by adjectives and adverbs, by a whole range of metaphorical language, by rhythm, and so on. The conveying of affect in the written language is much harder than in the spoken, and particularly for young children learning to write it is very difficult indeed; not least as it is essentially associated with other difficulties.

Some of these difficulties have been recently focused upon. Bartlett (1979) speaks of the way in which the writing process involves integration of skills and knowledge from several intellectual domains — the textual (aspects of language), the referential (objects, actions, events), the communicative (judgements about the audience, adequacy of the message, etc.). Scardamalia writes:

> Even a casual analysis makes it clear that the number of things that must be dealt with simultaneously in writing is stupendous: handwriting, spelling, punctuation, word choice, syntax, textual connections, purpose, organisation, clarity, rhythms, euphony, the possible reactions of various possible readers, and so on. To pay conscious attention to all of these would overload the information processing capacity of the most towering intellects.

Bereiter (1979), who quotes Scardamalia, observes that those matters do not seem to be dealt with sequentially but as far as possible simultaneously, and for this to happen two conditions must obtain: 'automatization of many parts of the writing process so that they can be carried on with infrequent or slight conscious attention' and 'highly skilled time sharing so that attention can range over a number of ongoing tasks without serious lapses or inter-ference'. He also comments that such performance would also seem to 'require attainment of adult levels of working memory capacity — if indeed this capacity grows with age'. The last condition is a saving one, otherwise it would seem to be theoretically impossible for anyone but 'adults' to write consecutive prose. Even so it is by no means easy, the more so when we bring into consideration also the matter of affect which the cognitive psychologists quoted do not specifically mention.

In Chapter Three we looked at the tendency of children's early written sentences to appear to be literal and factual. This is not an inevitable condition of such sentences, but it is a likely one because of the cognitive load which children are carrying in coming to write, and we posited a developmental process (3.3.5 above):

Sentence as literal/factual becomes metaphorical/affective

This is one element we look at in what follows. It is not always an easy process to discern. Overt statement of emotion, obvious metaphors, are often less effective and less skilled than implied feeling, indirect symbolism. Nevertheless the attempt seems worthwhile.

Our model of affect, it will be recalled, has as its dimensions Self (unawareness to self awareness); Others (growing awareness of other people, of needs of readers); Reality (relationship with environment, processing of universal and accidental constraints).

9.2 Autobiography

9.2.1 **Autobiography -- seven year olds**
The simplest piece of writing in our sample was by Peter G. 'The saddest was when my dog got knocked down'. Peter demonstrates the literal statement as an early type of writing. The absence of 'day' indicates the difficulty he has in holding the overall sentence. Clearly there is no self analysis (A1.0), sense of its effect on others (A2.0), no setting is given (A4.0), no explanations are offered to the reader (A3.1), there is no contextualization or distancing of the experience (A5.2). Another boy, Philip S. writes rather more

> One day we were walking by the country side And i wanted to look in a field and my dad walked on and chased him and i fell over on my face

He calls this his saddest day but the reason is not apparent (A1.1). The potential for emotional expression is present ('my dad walked on') but is not realized (A2.1). He assumes much about the environment giving the reader only a vague idea of time, place, and social relations. The piece seems on the surface to be a recall of a specific experience (A5.2).

In contrast to these two pieces is that of Jean G.:

> The saddest day was when my Grandad died and his wife was very upset because she had lived for 60 years with him and me and my sister were very very very upset to. We all had to go up to my Grandads house to comfort my Grandmother and stop her crying — and we stoped for two days i went with Granmar with my sister
>
> The End of my Story

Jean evaluates her emotions in terms provided by the title (A1.2) and goes on to explain the events that have brought the sadness, showing an awareness of what causes such strong emotion in herself (A1.4). She quite remarkably expresses an awareness of and an empathy with the feelings of her Grandmother: 'his wife was very upset', 'we all had to go up to my Grandads house to comfort my Grandmother and stop her crying' (A2.3). She includes an unusually detailed description of the social relationships within the family — the feeling of the grandmother for the grandfather, and the relationship between the two sisters and their grandmother (A3.3). The writer is very much aware of a real life event and describes it literally (A5.2).

We may sum up some of the general characteristics of the writing.

Over half the writers evaluated the experience of the saddest or happiest day (A1.2), not surprisingly since this was the task, but most did not state their feelings beyond this. Two writers showed an awareness of self-image (A1.3) — 'I was so sad that I was sent to bed without any tea'. Generally speaking the seven year olds did not express their own feelings explicitly no matter what wonderful or horrendous things were happening to them.

Over half the writers mentioned others as separate identities, but gave no indication of their attitude towards them. Some did not mention others at all: five gave the direct speech of others (A2.2). Only two showed an awareness of the emotions of others, one of whom was Jean G. (9.2.1 above). Mothers, or to a less extent fathers, appeared in half the pieces.

The writing of this age group varies from that in which there is no reader orientation to that in which sufficient information and interpretation is supplied to enable the reader to understand and reconstruct the situation, though not necessarily in detail. Thus Peter G. (in section 7.2.1.) gives us no setting or context whereas in other pieces, such as Jean G's, explanations for motivation are offered not ostentatiously but arising naturally: 'because she had lived for 60 years with him', 'to comfort my Grandmother'.

Some of the writers gave no indication of the setting (A3.1). Most pieces contained a literal account of a person or persons, place, time, objects, experience. The nature of the assignment prompted this. However in four pieces exaggerated behaviour indicated a less certain hold on reality. Thus in Donna H's piece (section 10.2.1) two boys are excessively punished for an unintentional offence. In Don H's piece, 'Craig' hit the writer with a stone and had to stay in for three weeks.

On this task seven year olds do not explicitly state their feelings or self-awareness; most show an awareness of others as separate identities, especially their mothers; they describe the environment adequately for the reader to understand why an experience is sad or happy. The nature of the assignment results in a literal treatment in most cases.

9.2.2 Autobiography — ten year olds
At this age we find that there is a tendency to make explicit the feelings of the writer in about half the scripts; the others implied their feelings by describing their experiences. Beth writes:

> The happiest day of my life was when I was on my friends pony both of us were cantering through the woods and having a lovely time. We sat down ate our picnic we had sponge cake, sandwiches, lemon Juice, doughnuts, etc. It was very nice we lied down on the grass and slept for a while.
>
> Beth B.

The feelings of the writer ('having a lovely time', 'it was very nice') are clearly stated. Nothing is said about the friend — it would be irrelevant to the purpose — but there is a sense of environment — the pony, the woods, the grass (A3.2). There is considerable attention given to the addressee or reader in the amount of gastronomic information given him to imaginatively join in the picnic (A4.2). The incident has the air of slight fantasy, but is presented in self-consistent terms (A5.2).

The difficulty many ten year olds have in expressing direct emotions is seen in Jessica's piece. The situation is presumably fraught with strong feelings, but the potential here is unrealized in her written expression:

> One day my brother went to dartmoor and a rock fell on his leg and he broke it and he had to take him to plymouth hospital to have plaster on his leg and Mrs. Sneddon was with him and Mr. Woodford took christopher home and Mrs. Seddon and christopher was home a gen and Mr. Woodford carrying christopher in door and Mrs. Seddon took his stuf in door and mum said to me and carol go to bed to sleep good light mum.
>
> Jessica H.

Jessica tells of the incident as consecutive events and no emotion emerges. Others are mentioned in terms of their actions but do not begin to appear as people (A2.1) and even the words quoted seem rather a conventional ending than presenting a facet of personality. The details are minimal — there is no attempt at scene setting (A3.1): the problems of organization involved are so great that the writer is preoccupied with them to the exclusion of the reader (A4.1). The incident is presumably a real one, but there is no attempt at interpretation (A5.2), or pointing a non-literal significance.

Although Jessica does not realize her characters many ten year olds are quite capable of doing so. Sharon H's grandma ('She is allways making a fuss over me and I dont like it') comes to life through her spervision of Sharon and her peremptory bedtime orders.

> One day I was pick up a pot of Jam and my Graman siad oh Sharon it is to havey
> for you but I was still happy Sharon it is time for bed
> good night Sharon good night

The writing of Francesca seems to contain a higher level of emotional awareness than many, chiefly expressed by implication, and through the environmental items selected.

> The happiest day of my life was on a Sunday when we had to go out. I don't
> know were the place was I don't know what it was called. It was by a little
> stream, and there were trees growing we could climb up to trees some were very
> high. There were rocks too with grasses growing on top. And a hill which had a
> path leading a long side the stream. You could climb up and down the hill it
> was a rocky hill. But it had lot of trees to catch hold of to pull yourself up. It was
> a long walk along the stream we walked about a quater of the way and quater of
> the way was about two miles. We got tired so we thought we should turn back
> there was a small water fall in the river. Because of some stones stuck in the
> middle of the stream. There were bushes you could hide under. They were very
> big not many people walked on the path. There was another path on the other
> side of the stream. There were trees coving the path, but alot of light still came in.
> Then we got back we had to go because the day was over.

Details of the landscape are given to create atmosphere. Exact information ('rocks with grasses growing on top') helps here. But the landscape is not merely a backdrop — the children's actions and emotions arise in inter-relationship with it — they climb up and down the rocky hill, pull themselves up with trees, get tired because of the two miles they have walked, hide under bushes (A3.3). Fiona is also able to report on her thoughts of that day, 'We got tired so we thought we should turn back' (A1.2, A2.1, A3.3, A4.3, A5.2).

In the writing of ten year olds as against seven year olds there was a tendency to state feeling at the 'I felt sad' level in about half the thirty-one scripts; in the others, as with the seven year olds, the feelings had to be inferred from the experiences. There is a slight development in the statement

of self-awareness. Thus Harriet C. is aware of the problem of accounting for
her own feelings, 'one day I woke feling very happy, I do not know why but
I did'; but this awareness is shown only by four writers.

Many writers still refer to other people in their autobiographies in the
barest terms (rather over half as against rather less than half of the seven year
olds) though about half of them now begin to realize other characters
through what they say, feel, or do (whereas only about one in five seven year
olds give words to others, and very few ascribe to them specific feelings).

As one would expect, partly because they are more in control of the
medium, the ten year olds far more than the seven year olds provided information necessary for the understanding of their themes. Only perhaps two of
the ten year olds produced context-bound writings (A4.1); most seemed to
be in effect approaching a general audience (A4.3), even reassuring them that
they will be taken along gently:

> The happiest day of my life happened on my holiday in july we went shopping
> and we made a trip to the beach this is what happened.

Perhaps the most notable development is in the use of environmental
items — physical objects, spatial and temporal descriptions, social relationships. About a third of the seven year olds assumed an environment: none of
the ten year olds did: and just under half of the latter responded in a way
that showed that the environment had been specially significant to them,
compared with about a fifth of the younger children. The sheer amount of
detail often creates an atmosphere, though the danger of insufficient selection
is present.

There is as one would expect an awareness of the real and imaginative
worlds; one writer placed at the top of her piece 'half true, half fauls'. But all
the writers give or purport to give a factual treatment. Nobody at this level
invests incidents with a symbolic significance. The language is on the whole
extremely literal, though there is an occasional (original) metaphor, as with
Clare Wroth: 'So I slept on the floor. I woke up with the cat lying on me like
I was a poofa'.

9.2.3 Autobiography — thirteen year olds

The verbal formulation of the task was varied for the pupils in this group. It
became 'The best or worst experience I have ever had'.

From a variety of points of view the most notable script is that by Nina P.
Like that of Jean G. at seven it concerns a death in the family:

> It was just like any other Tuesday. Normal breakfast, normal lessons, little
> did I know that this was going to be one of the saddest days of my life.

I got off the bus as normal, walked up the hill, opened the gate, walked down the steps, pressed on the latch. Then, it was different.

My Mum opened the door, her eyes were red her cheeks puffed out, she'd obviously been crying.
Bewildered, I asked "What's happened?"
Thoughts flashed through my mind, who's hurt, Dad, Nana, Papa?

I was led into the sitting room, Mum held me and said,

"Theres no other way I can break this to you, Papa died this morning".

The words were like a bombshell. I cried.

"Come and see Nana" Mum said "Shes been very brave".

I walked to the other room and flung my arms arond my Grandmother. Tears fell like raindrops, until all my emotions were drained.

"How?" I asked.

"He was just sitting on the bed, getting his breath when he collapsed, he was probably dead before he fell".

Dead, dead, dead, dead, the word ran through my mind, Papa is dead.

Memories flashed back, when he used to push me in my small pram when I was young.

His teasing, his twinkling eyes when he laughed.

I cant cry anymore, all I can do is remember, it hurts though.

The words, 'Papa died this morning', kept on in my head for days. I couldn't stop them, it was like a disease, my whole body longed for him to be back. I hoped it was just a nightmare.

I couldn't accept the fact that he was gone. I expect I will have to soon though.

I long for the day when I can think about him without it hurting too much.

I'll just put on a brave face, its all I can do.

Nina's grandfather dies, and she feels his loss very deeply. She draws a contrast between the events of a normal day and those after she gets the news of her grandfather's death. She tells of her grief not only through direct expression but also by reporting her words and actions: she is bewildered, afraid, exhausts herself with grief ('until all my emotions were drained'); she is compassionate with her grandmother, and recognizes they must live for a time with despair, waiting for the hurt to lessen. It would appear that she has a well-developed understanding of the progress of grief. She shows skill in her selection of actions and dialogue to heighten the reader's awareness of the feelings involved. She also shows an understanding of the effect of emotional shock: 'Dead, dead, dead, dead, the word ran through my mind, Papa is dead'; 'memories flashed back'. Here she appears to be going back over the cause of the shock, trying to sort it out, to come to terms with it. Nicola compares her experience to a nightmare, even wishing it were so that she could wake up and know that it did not happen in reality. In all she expresses a highly developed sense of the nature of the emotion within herself, an awareness of that of others, and a general disposition to be compassionate, an awareness of the way emotion works in such a situation – the recall of past incidents for example. Particularly interesting is the attempt to find metaphorical equivalents for the emotion in order to cope with it ('like a bombshell', 'like raindrops', 'like a disease', 'just a nightmare') as well as the realistic acceptance in the later sentences – 'I'll just put on a brave face, its all I can do'. The language may seem conventional, even trite, but we must beware of thinking that therefore the emotion is not genuine. Unique expression for unique emotion is a hard won achievement. With writers of this age it is a virtue that they are trying on language, even if it is other people's. (Summary: A1.4, A2.4, A2.6, A3.4, A4.3, A5.2).

Amongst the thirteen year olds about a third show an awareness of how they appear to others in a way that scarcely any of the younger children do. Andrew B. looks back on himself at seven when he was given a hospital bed and comments, 'This bed was a cot which I was very put out by because I thought I had grown out of cots' (A1.3). Gordon B. gets lost in his new school and 'looked like a fool standing there asking where Room 1 was' (A1.3). In Nina's piece quoted above there is a deeper understanding of her own feelings (A1.4). As would be expected this age group is rather more conscious of other people in its writing. The task of course does prompt introspection, but over a third ascribe emotions to others or describe their actions which imply emotions, as against a quarter of the tens and scarcely any of the sevens. The realization of them in terms of their own words or thoughts occurs in a few scripts.

Many pieces at this level are context-free. They sometimes contain asides for the general reader, contain information necessary for understanding or interpreting, have a careful selection of image and detail. (There is a tendency beyond A4.1 and A4.2 to A4.3.)

One of the more significant features of the thirteen year olds' writing is their use of environment. Arthur M. uses skilfully selected details in order to convey a moving experience. These details are physical – the assembly, the fists, the swimming trunks; and social – the gang, the indifferent (or terrified) 'female teacher', the boy as outcast. This writer has gone past feeling the need to use language merely for scene painting (A3.4):

> . . . The first thing we did was to have assembly, when I was the only (one)
> able to answer the Headmaster's question. I was nicknamed 'Magnus' — a bad
> start. I knew everything in the lessons, I could answer every question by means
> of a lecture, though I had not mastered the art of friendliness. As one or two
> fists told me.
>
> My popularity in the class was abismal. I was rated as an outcaste by everyone.
> I was bullied perpetually and brutally by gangs. Whenever the teacher turned
> her back they attacked. Often when she was looking. She took little action.
>
> I hated the school. I learned absolutely nothing. I was in a backward class with
> an intelligence better than most of the top class. Just because of my age. The
> 'supervision' was about as effective as a catapult used in war between Russia and
> America. Or worse.
>
> The worst part of the day was changing back from swimming. The entire class of
> boys threw their wet trunks at me. At short range. Hard. Being a femal teacher
> no supervision could be given. This happened nearly every day . . .

A development in the expression of awareness of the environment as significant in stimulating emotions has already been noted in the ten year olds. About two-thirds of thirteen year olds, compared with less than half of the ten year olds showed an ability to respond to the environment in such a way as to indicate that it had been especially significant and stimulating (A3.3). One might expect this, given the nature of the task ('my worst/best experience') but there were several examples of writing such as Arthur's that reached the A3.4 stage and illustrate the higher quality of the responses from the thirteen year olds.

In the pupils of this age we see a tendency not to describe but to interpret. Once again Arthur M's work will serve as an example. Here he obviously had a very hard experience to cope with. In retrospect he can deal with it by objectifying — by seeing himself as 'Magnus' who gave 'lectures' and as someone who 'had not mastered the art of friendliness'. He deliberately uses exaggerated imagery (the 'catapult') but the overall distancing and interpreting device is irony. It is most explicit in his apostrophizing 'supervision' but it is implicit throughout, particularly in relation to the teacher, and is supported by his sense of style, particularly the laconic grammatically incomplete comments. The category would be A5.5.

9.3 Narrative

9.3.1 **Narrative – seven year olds**

Elementary narrative illustrates many of the features we have already observed in the autobiographies. Dan, presumably responding to the picture of the
two boys, entitles his piece 'The Last Day of the War'.

> It was 10 days from the end of the war. the bombing had stoped. A girl went
> into a building them a bomb fell through the ceiling just then the two boys came
> down the street they came in they saw the girl.
>
> Dan P.

The statements are literal and non-emotive; the characters are treated in a
single dimension. The environment is not described, though the potential for
fantasy is obvious. There is little audience orientation (A2.1, A3.1, A4.1,
A5.2).

Nevertheless in the more advanced narratives it is likely that by the nature
of the form there will be less personal feeling expressed directly, and more
attention paid to the actors in the story, and to their thoughts and feelings.
This proves to be the case. Kate writes:

> *The Lost Two*
>
> One day Mark and Jon and there mum went for a walk in the woods when Jon
> said to Mark let's pick some flowers for mum and Mark said all right then, so
> they told their mum and off they went. Then they came to a fence Mark went up
> to the fence and touched it and then he said to Jon I think were lost then Jon
> said were not I now the way back all right then dont be a thick head and show me
> the way all rihgt all rihgt and he led him back to there mum.
>
> Kate B.

The boys are aware of the need to put their mother in the picture. A convincing dialogue in delightfully appropriate register is offered with the irritation clearly emerging. Given that the children were asked to illustrate a
picture and the one chosen here was that of the two boys behind a fence the
context is sufficiently established, though there is no attempt to provide a
setting. The story form is established by elementary markers ('one day . . .
back to here mum') but is a literal statement of events (A2.2, A3.2, A4.2,
A5.2).

Development can be seen in for example 'The Electric Fence' by Vicky:

> One day two boys were walking with their mummy in the market. They had not
> been there before and they thought they would have a look round and they did.
> Soon they came out of the market and found themselves in a field and they
> walked a little way father until they came to a whole, There was a piece of rope
> hanging down they decided to go down the rope to explore. When they got down

they saw footprints leading into the darkness. They decided to follow them. And they did. They walked on untill they came to a fence. It was pad locked they tried and they tried But it was no use. Suddenly they heard a clinking it went CLINCK CLACK they thought it came from Behind so they turned round and to their great surprise they saw another fence coming down. Chris said we are trapped And John said Dont be such a baby. And Chris said I'm not. So they decided to dig a tunnel under the fence. And they did. After that they back through the passage out through the hole and back to the market. And by this time their mum had gone home again. They walked a little further and they saw a policeman and they asked him their name and their address and the policeman took them home. The end.

Vicky H.

This story shows significant differences from those of most of the group. Chris and John are seen as separate people with John definitely the leader — their speech indicates this. Their words indicate their feelings as well as their actions — 'turned round and to their great surprise they saw another fence coming down'. The details are carefully chosen for their emotional effect (even the noise of the fence is verbalized): the children get lost, it is a fearful place, the fence is padlocked, there is a hole with a piece of rope hanging down, footprints, and so on. Great care is taken to provide the reader with appropriate information. The piece operates on a level of fantasy presented literally in conventional story form the nearest approach to metaphorical language being the 'CLINCK' of the fence. In the control of the emotion and the mounting suspense the story operates beyond most others from children of this age (A2.2, A2.3s, A3.4, A4.3, A5.2).

9.3.2 Narrative — ten year olds

In the writings of the seven year olds the ability to indicate the personalities of characters in narrative was restricted. Similarly about a third of ten year olds have characters at the single dimensional level, barely distinguishable as separate entities. Thus Matthew gives an account of a kidnapping and murder in which the characters are only differentiated as 'two men', 'little boy', 'another boy' and there is no specification of what would be the immense emotions involved (A2.1).

The two men had a van near by a little boy came along one man grabbed hold of the boy and put him in the van the man gaged the boy and tied him up they wated on the corner another boy came and the men did the same to him they drove to a shack near a river the next morning the snow was very deep the children saw some people and they shouted the men took some shots at the people they strangeled the two children ded and drove of at the other end of the road were some men from the army. The police put them to prisson.

Matthew W.

In contrast Cheryl has an ability to create character through a variety of means. Here is her piece in full:

The light house keeper sadly put the phone down. He thought of the sad deed he now had to do. The lighthouse keepers young companion had recently gone missing. The last anyone saw of him was when he set out to fetch some more oil for the lamp from the mainland. The sea had been rough and the gale was force 7, obviously too much for the little motor boat. The man had either been sunk or dashed to pieces on the rocks. An hour later the light was nearly out and there was a ship approaching. The motor boat of the lighthouse keeper drifted up with no lighthouse keeper in it. But, there were 2 containers of oil in it. The light had almost gone out when the new oil came in and saved the ship from wrecking on the cruel rocks.

The young man had seemingly got to the main land, collected the oil and been washed over board as he tried to get back. It was a miracle that the boat had come to the lighthouse without sinking. The coast guards had been searching for the man's body but had had no success. Now the old lighthouse keeper had the job of telling the man's poor family what had happened to their father.

He turned and walked slowly down the steps. Soon he was in the boat. He turned the motor and went off towards the beach.

When he reached the house where the man's wife lived with her 7 children, he did not dare tell the truth. All he said was "Mr. Tops has gone missing". Mrs. Tops who had been expecting good news, looked very unhappy. "Where's daddy, where's daddy", her children clamoured. Mrs. Tops had no answer to give them.

The old light house keeper left sadly. He would never forget the unhappy look of the man's wife.

Mrs. Tops was very poor. She worked as hard as she could but her health got poorer and poorer. Finally she was not able to get up off the mattress that she slept on. Gradually her children left her to earn money. 6 of them died. Only one was left. As she lay in the ashes of the long dead fire, feeling afraid of death, she suddenly felt she was being watched. When she turned she saw her father, as he was before he died. With him was her mother, as she used to be when she was young. Also there were all her dead brothers and sisters. "Come with us little sister, come with us". Then the little girl felt a longing to be with them; "I will come", she said. Suddenly she felt young and happy again. She jumped up to go with her family.

The next day they found her body. She was starved and had lost her family yet she died with a smile upon her lips.

Cheryl H.

The lighthouse keeper's emotions are indicated by the way he acts — 'sadly put the phone down', 'walked slowly down the steps', (A2.3) and by the way he speaks, 'Mr. Tops has gone missing' (A2.2). Cheryl is aware that intense emotion may not be expressed by words: when the children asked

where their father was 'Mrs. Tops had no answer to give them'. The thoughts
of the young daughter are given in terms of the vision she has of her family
as well as recorded directly: 'felt a longing to be with them' (A2.4). The
piece has strong literary and media overtones: it is obviously not 'sincere'
in the sense of being the product of first-hand experience: nevertheless it is
an achievement for a child of ten in process of discovering a language for the
emotions.

Cheryl's use of the environment is discreet and economical, giving only
essential details — 'The sea had been rough and the gale was force 7', 'saved
the ship from wrecking on the cruel rocks' (A3.2). Some children in this
group use the physical environment for scene setting: others, more centrally
as a means of communicating particular emotions. In Carol's piece it is used
to contrast stillness ('no sound no life') with disturbance (A3.4); it begins:

> A derlicked house in a bombed battered street no sound no life just a
> scurring of mice around the rubble. A building which once was a Hotel just lies
> in a smuther of dust, accross the street from the Hotel is a house well a ruined
> house it was Number 14 but their is not much left of it now, crawling around the
> ruins are a dog and two people scrating around for their lost posetions The street
> seems to be coming alive now. Then a lowd ringing was heard down to the
> airraid shelters quickly!
>
>   Carol W.

An overview of the A3 category shows only two writers assuming the
environment (A3.1), the majority describing or explaining it adequately
(usually the physical setting) (A3.3), and two, Carol and Catherine M, showing a higher degree of selectivity and evaluation of the environment in their
choosing of items to achieve an effect (A3.4).

When we look at the writers' ability to cater for the reader we find some
development in the ten year olds. Like the seven year olds, most pupils seem
to be writing for the teacher or for peers, and therefore their pieces have to
be seen in the light of the picture-stimulus for the reader to get the full
meaning; thirteen out of the thirty-three pieces could be considered context-
free and as catering for the general reader. In most cases the writer seemed to
be able to imagine what it was the reader needed to know to understand the
piece, and supplied it.

In narrative the relationship with objective reality is complex. Very young
children often see no dividing line between fantasy and reality, but normally
become aware of this before they reach school. Stories of what really
happened and what is 'made up' become distinct for them. An invitation to
write narrative tends to encourage them to write the latter. A piece which is
'made up' but which tends to describe rather than interpret we have classified

as fantasy (A5.3); a piece which is interpretative as well as descriptive we have classified as 'imaginative' (A5.5) (the distinction here is something of the order of that Coleridge makes between 'fantasy' and 'imagination').

Thus in Lynn's script we have an example of fantasy, even fantasy run rampant. She is telling in the first person, the story of destruction on the home front caused by war.

> . . . I went over to the two little boys and said Hello. they did not reply and looked even sader. I tryed again. Where is your mother tear began running down their little white cheecks "o I'm sorry" I said and they stopped crying. I climbed over the gate and took them by their hand a led them into the house and in the kitchen was their mother lying over the kitchen range. I quickly pulled her of and her face was burning as I pushed her onto the floor and poured water over her. The children stood by the door very still.
>
> Lynn T.

In some ways the piece by Roy is similar. It contains the grab-bag of bombs, scares, mysterious comings and goings common in the ten year olds' scripts; nevertheless it has some of the graces of art:

> ### The Black Street of Death
> A quiet Autumn's morning in the Street of Death. Theres a no entry sign because cars explode if they go down the streat of Death. Many lives have been killed and many cars have exploded and thats why they put the no entry sign there. But people still walk down the Street of Death and there are two people by the no entry sign. They look suspicious it seems as thoe they are looking for somewhere to plant a bomb because there Face'es are covered up with a hat and its not raining nor is it cold its fairly hot. I can't see there faces. They they look at a watch they see its time to do to something they start to go down the street of Death. Then they go in to a room and plant a bomb then they do the same when they get to the end of the road I saw they had some one and they got to the end of the Road and then people went in the houses and in the streat of Death. Then all the Bombs whet off and called the fire engines and they put the fire out and 50 people were killed then I told the police the number plate which was N534 12T and I described the van and the people then 3 days later Iheard that they found the van and 10 more dead people then they found the men and they were sent to Jail and thats the end of the Street of Death.
>
> Roy S.

Some beginnings of interpretation are provided by the hint of symbolism in the 'Street of Death'; journalistic and very imperfectly realized as it is. On the whole however the narratives of the ten year olds remain at the level of fantasy. They tend to treat their writing task as an exploration of violence. The pictures chosen to respond to are not particularly suggestive of violence, but that is what they suggest to the children. The troubles in Northern Ireland, the bombing, destruction, concentration camps of the Second World War, kidnapping, looting, are all grist to the mill, both with boys and girls.

9.3.3 Narrative — thirteen year olds

In this group are fifty-eight scripts by writers from 12½ to 14 years. Only six pupils from the original sample wrote straight narratives, the remainder varying the task by using news reporting, reviewing one of the photographs, or writing a play for example. The scripts were therefore supplemented by work from another school in a similar area.

The most noticeable aspect of the work of this group in contrast to that of the younger children is in the manifestation of emotion.

Don't Die Mummy

I ran downstairs quickly, I hoped mummy was alright, the doctor had come last night and daddy sent David and I up to bed. I rushed through the door and immediately stopped, to see my father in his armchair, crying. "Daddy" I wispered. "Why are you crying". My father lifted his head and murmured "You're to young to understand son, you're to young". I suddenly thought of mummy, "Where is she, daddy, where is she". Daddy quietly got up and stumbled towards the door "Follow me, son". I cautiously followed him and realised it must be serious, I wanted to cry, but held it back, as I stepped into the room I immediately saw the doctor kneeling by my mother, with his arm around David. "Come here" he said quitly, he put his strong arm around me and mummy opened her eyes and managed to whisper "David, David", I thoucher her hand and my throat started to burn as I gripped her hand. I looked at her and she smiled, her head dropped and her hand slipped from mine, my father ran from the room and I knew that mummy was dead. I sat beside her and wept for a few minutes until the doctor had gone, I heard daddy have a drink and light a cigar.

Andrea L.

As far as sincerity is concerned (i.e. relationship to a real experience) there are obvious false notes: the whole is staged like a death-bed scene in Richardson. The 'cigar' introduces an unintended comic note, whereas 'cigarette' would not, and the attempt subsequently to express the grief of bereavement — the father drinks, cuts off the mother's hair and strips her, and shoots himself in front of the children — is similarly unsuccessful. Nevertheless Andrea has developed the techniques for expressing emotion — the selection of significant words spoken by the participants, the use of more meaningful terms than 'said': 'whispered', 'murmured', 'said quietly', the observation of non-verbal behaviour, and so on (A2.2/3/4).

The development in the ability to ascribe emotions to others by direct comment, and by describing actions of others that imply emotion (A2.3) is marked in the scripts of the thirteen year olds in comparison with the scripts of the sevens and tens. We find this method used in about one third of our scripts from the seven year olds, in about one half of our scripts from the ten year olds, and in about two thirds of our scripts from the thirteen year olds. Vida gives a vivid enough example to make the point!

After they have supper and get sent to bed. A horrid, sexy, filthy man comes round and he and the woman who is Peter and Paul's stepmother go to bed with each other. The man gets drunk often and then starts hitting them.

Vida A.

Kay builds up the description of actions to the point where the gesture becomes poignant:

Slowly and silently they worked their way through the city remembering how the places used to look and how they looked now, hardly recognizable. Often they saw dead bodies or just limbs of bodies that had been blown off by all the blasts. Blood was splattered everywhere, shattered glass covered everything. All of a sudden Peter picked up a dolls head, he recognized it as his younger sister's (Jane). He showed it to Simon, who shouted her name over and over again.

from 'Abandon', Kay P.

However, it is when we look at the number of scripts submitted by the thirteen year olds that show the awareness of emotion in others through a description of their thoughts that we notice a really significant development (A2.4). Only one pupil out of the thirty-one seven year olds and only two out of the thirty-three ten year olds used it. Here are a few examples from those writers in the thirteen-year-old range.

I dragged myself from my mum and went to my room. Why should this happen to me, I thought, Mummy had said that God did things that were right, but he hadn't this time, why me, why does my mummy have to die.

Andrea L.

Nothing was said, it was an unfriendly silence, entering from an ugly main road, rebounding from the dead end wall hitting two men, setting thier silly little brains to work on a fools plot.

Sophie B.

Sonia would seem to have carried this method furthest. She uses a stream of consciousness technique. This is a quotation from her piece:

The Caged Animals

No parents. Killed by animals, and us just caged in this small confined place, and all alone with no-one to care for us, but them horrible drunken soldiers that guard this shabby inclosure, that we have to be imprisoned in.

No mother, to care for our small frozen hands or our tiny little faces. No mother to wash these small affectionate faces or to clean our muddy nails. But what is worst of all, is that there is no mother to love, and kiss.

No father either, to play games with us or to have long exciting walks with us. No father to read us playtime stories from the nursery rhyme books. But also the thing that is worst of all is that there is no father to love . . .

Five of the scripts of the thirteen year olds showed writers approaching very closely the realizing of a character fully by assuming and controlling a persona (A2.5), whereas only one of the ten year olds could be said to have shown this skill, and none of the seven year olds. Andrea L., quoted above, would be one example as she tells her tale through the first person, showing a control of the tale through the character of the 'I'. Another example would be 'The Refugee Camp' by Sasha wherein the 'I' is quite fully realized as a thoughtful and compassionate news reporter, moved to adopt a Vietnam refugee while on assignment: 'I closed the door behind him and flopped down on the bed. My mind kept going back to those two little boys. I went over to my bag, got out my pad and pen and started writing. I was so involved that when I looked up at the clock it said ten to seven'.

The outstanding characteristic of the development in the ability of the thirteen year olds to express an awareness of the significance of the environment in relation to emotions, lies not so much in their description of physical settings, though there certainly is a development here, but in their description and comprehension of the social environment — in for instance, the roles that their characters assume, and in particular the emotional relationships between family members (A3.3). For example, a characteristic of the seven year olds was their inclusion in many of their stories of a 'Mummy' from whom their characters get lost or who acts as security for them. About one third of the ten year olds referred to Mummy in an only slightly more psychologically distanced way. But in the scripts of the thirteen year olds, 'Mummy' becomes a significant 'other' who has her own emotions the same as any character, and plays a social role in the family.

If we look back at the part of Andrea L.'s script quoted above we find a young boy exploring the loss of his mother and its effect on his own emotions and on those of the father. Various writers explore family roles — mother, father, husband, wife, children, brother, sister. Sensitivity to these and other roles can be seen in the use of appropriate registers. A sense of register pervasive in the narrative is seen in Cara M.'s piece, where she refers to the social services agency who first cared for the children before Rowena got them as 'the welfare lot' — 'The welfare lot weren't really bothered so they let them go'. Charles G. has his father and son speak in appropriate register for a father and son down on their luck:

> Did you manage to get the woodbines and the fishfingers son?
> Yeah, but im not going there again.
> Why is that?
> They have got tonnes of security staff in there, there is mirrors on the walls and some screens.

Oh well, come on home, we'll have the fish fingers later on.
Dad . . .
Yeah? . . .

Examples abound of pupils choosing items in the physical environment to create an emotional effect or mood. Details are now often chosen for relevance and with accuracy. Tom R. in 'Two Lost Boys' shows an awareness of time by giving the exact time the lost boys went to the police station: 'It was 12 o'clock when they reached the station', and again, to show a time lapse: 'After another 20 minutes the boys were getting more worried and more frightened'. A single sentence sets the scene for mad destruction in Jos H.'s 'The War': 'The humming from the German planes could be heard almost hovering above waiting for a defenceless person to run across the street and be pinned to the floor by the bullets'. Corah in 'Changes' manages to ascribe a motive to the builder who created the atmosphere that very effectively sets the stage for her narrative:

> . . . The most obvious thing was that the house was gone. It had been demolished, probably by some uncaring man who had to earn his pay-packet by knocking down parts of peoples lives — big important parts that contained hundreds of memories. Now all that was left was rubble and a big empty-looking space. Next door, the Canterbury Inn was still standing, though it was never used. It looked shabby next to the cheap, ugly-looking big stones of the newly-opened bingo hall . . .

> Corah H.

On the other hand some writers go overboard in the use of descriptive details, not all of which contribute to the mood of the piece.

As far as use of environment is concerned then, about one-fifth of the thirteen year olds' pieces were judged to have reached the A3.4, the highest stage in this category; that is, they showed with a high degree of selectivity and evaluation an ability to choose environmental items to achieve an effect, compared with two scripts from the ten year olds and one from the seven year olds. Again at least half the thirteen year olds' scripts were judged to be written at the A3.3 level, compared with one-quarter of the scripts of the ten year olds, and one-tenth of the scripts of the seven year olds.

In catering for the needs of the general reader in their pieces this age group were very similar to the ten year olds — that is, rather less than half did so, the judgement centring on whether the piece was context-bound or context-free — whether it was considerably more meaningful to have the picture at hand or not.

The stance of the thirteen year olds to reality shows differences from that of the younger age groups. Many of the narratives are fast moving but operate

at a surface level, without much interpretation or engagement; thus the story
of an escape will have no symbolic overtones. The more advanced ones however demonstrate the shaping effects of art. In for instance 'The Loved Ones
Lost' by Adam R., there is an attempt to cope with the facts of death and
find consolation.

It shows the affective beautifully controlled through careful selection of
images, the presentation of character, and narrative comment. The writer
seems not only to be coming to terms in a poetic art-form with the emotional
meaning of the loss of a mother and father, and the feelings of a devoted
husband over the loss of a wife, but inserts the symbolic in the form of a
father-figure who brings a calm supportiveness to the boy at the same time
that he brings word of the father's death. Even the father's death can be
seen as symbolic in its appropriateness. This is one of the very few pieces in
the corpus designated A5.5.

The Loved Ones Lost

"It's happened son your mothers gone". "She was called early this morning".
My mother was not old but she was very ill. She had a bad heart and was always
seeing the doctor. We all knew that she would soon go and now the time had
come. My father stood looking up at the dull early morning sky. "She's up in the
heavens now though" he said. Taking his sea weathered hat from his tilted head,
he looked at me his only son. I looked at him and thought. What would happen
to him now, where would he live. He'll never go out to sea again he told her that
before she went. He's way past it now he only fishes for his food he never was a
success, the younger men with there new equipment jeered at the old boy when
he rowed out of the harbour with his hand full of line. Now what would they
say? They couldn't care less they never did. I looked at my father again and
quietly said, "Will you ever go out to sea again?". "No son never" he replied. He
turned and walked slowly away head down and bent over like an old mule driven
into the grown by its master. He disappeared down the cobbled path and over the
harbour wall.

He didn't see me for the next few days I didn't hear of him or see him either.

He wants to be left alone I thought, he dosent want no full. She depended on him
and he lived for her. Now she's gone and he dosent have anything to live for,
What's going to happen to him I thought, he mustn't die, he cant leave me I'm old
(only?) seventeen. Oh God please dont take him, Im his only son, Im to young to
live without him, please dont take him. Please.

"Calm down son" a Voice said. I quickly looked up. A tall man with sea boots
and a macintosh on looked down at me and said "Come inside son", "lets sit
down".

We got inside and he started to talk to me in a slow unusuall way.

"You know me son", "I was your fathers friend". The word 'was', hit me right in
the eye. "Was I said".

"Im sorry son" he said "Your father jumped over the harbour wall yesterday".
"His body was washed up by his own boat this morning on the early tide".

I rushed out and down the cobled path to the harbour wall, I climbed the steps
and leaned over the edge the wicked sea swirled below and I thought I heard my
father call. If thats the way he wanted to go, I thought then why should I stop
him. He loved her and I could now see that he wanted to be with her in the grey
sky. He's happy now I thought. He's happy now.

9.4 Argument

The argumentative and explanatory tasks were designed to elicit cognitive
rather than affective language. Affect scarcely emerged in the explanations;
there was however a certain amount in the argumentative pieces, and we shall
discuss this briefly.

9.4.1 Argument – all age groups

Seven year olds take an egocentric view – 'what I like' is the motive for
choice. Like John G. some of them think school could be improved considerably:

I think that school should be five days and the weekend should be five days
and you could go to school whenever you liked.

Steve T. expresses the opinion that 'Work is not nice to do', whereas
Kate B. thinks 'School is very good'. Vicki H. on the other hand, would do
away with school so she could stay home and eat sweets; Philip S., though,
likes school: 'It is quieter', and Jimmy W. says that Monday, Wednesday,
Thursday, Friday are 'my very very best days in school'.

The teacher who gave the assignment to the children found that they had
strong feelings and expressed them vehemently in the oral discussion that
preceded the writing. However, they did not make their feelings any more
explicit in writing than indicated above.

In the work of the ten year olds there is a move from the egocentrism of
the seven year olds to the decentred 'you' or 'others'. There is also a tendency
to include the feelings or attitudes of others in the argument. An excerpt
from Andrew P.'s piece will give an illustration of this tendency:

. . . And I think that teachers should have more pashents with children. And
some teachers have their favorite and thay seem to be in every thing. And they
school should pick the Good Wons not the favorities. I could Name a throw
(few?) of them But I wo'nt do that. I've herd that some teachers in other
schools havent got no pashents with children.

A characteristic in some of the children's writing is to describe an imagined world, though the imagined world is treated literally, as in this piece of Cheryl's (A5.2):

*Would it work if children came to school when they liked and
could do what they liked there?*

No. It would not work because no-one would know anything, because they did not always come to school. There would be no teachers because nobody learnt anything so there would be no exams for the teachers to qualify to be teachers because no-one was clever enough to make exams. There would be nothing to do because nobody would be clever enough to make anything. There would be no factories or shops because nobody could be clever enough to make factory foods. Science and exploration into space would stop, for no-one would be clever enough to man these things. There would be no medical care because nobody would make qualifications in medical care. As for doing the things you liked, well there would be no teachers to tell you what to do, so everything would be wasted in doing it wrong. There would be no books to tell you what to do. Reading would not exist or writing.

A continuation of the expression of an awareness of others in relation to making choices about school is noticeable in the writing of the thirteen year olds: whereas seventeen of the thirty-one writers at ten years of age wrote about their opinions about what would happen to others, over thirty of the forty thirteen year olds worked their arguments out in relation to others, and most of the remaining writers introduced the effects of such freedom on themselves in addition. With this decentring comes an accompanying objectivity, for fewer writers appeal to feelings in their reasoning, preferring to stick to facts and opinions. Even their imagined school-worlds are highly realistic. The arguments are, on the whole, designed to cater to a more general audience than were those of the ten year olds. There is a tendency for many writers to think that other children would become unruly vandals if they were given freedom of choice about whether to attend school, 'School would be in chaos'. Some of the writers are thinking of how a free environment would affect the behaviour and feelings of others, though most are less concerned with this, and more with presenting factual reasoning.

9.5 Summary

At the earliest stage literal statement is made with no affective elements. Generally speaking seven year olds do not express feeling explicitly, no matter what wonderful or horrendous things are happening to them. On the whole they do not realize others as separate identities, and find it difficult to fill out their characters by giving them words. (None of the apparent empathy with fictional characters was as powerful as that released in a real life situation of bereavement.) Reader awareness is not high — the reader is not given sufficient clues to reconstruct the situation and emotion. The world implied is on the whole a matter-of-fact world surrounding the writer, peopled by cut-out figures.

The ten year olds make an advance in terms of their ability to give the readers clues to enable them to understand the theme. There is greater explicitness about personal emotion, but in general terms ('I felt sad') and with little introspection. Other people begin here and there to become three dimensional, being given words and thoughts — it seems they are actualized more in an incident drawn from life than in a fiction. Perhaps the most notable development is in the use of environmental items; a background is usually there; sometimes it is specially significant in creating a mood, reinforcing an attitude. In narrative this group tends to prefer fantasy, often the fantasy of violence and crime, prompted by the media.

More realistic themes with greater psychological authenticity tend to be preferred by the thirteen year olds. There is an increased introspection, but also an ability to objectify self. Emotion is not necessarily expressed explicitly, but obliquely in the details of what people say and how they behave. Environment can be used selectively, not just as background, but in interaction with emotion. Interpretive and imaginative treatment is more consistently possible.

Chapter Ten

Moral Aspects of Children's Writing

10.1 Introduction

In this chapter the model set out in Chapter Five whose rationale was given in Chapter Four will be used to analyse aspects of the written work in the sample.

In applying a sequential model for moral development to children's writing we are extending the work of psychologists to the classroom. Piaget and Kolberg elicited the responses of children to stories containing a specific moral dilemma, by direct questioning in interviews with adults. We have found no studies in which the writing of children has been analysed for levels of moral thinking. The composition subjects we set were not on the whole intended to elicit explicit moral judgements. We did, however, expect that the topic 'The best/worst experience I have ever had', or its equivalent, would lead some writers to make implicit moral statements. The narratives written to a picture stimulus we also expected to produce 'moral tales', particularly that of two children standing beside a 'No Entry' sign. The argumentative task, 'Would it work if children came to school when they liked and did what they liked there?' we also anticipated would produce judgements which could be termed moral. The only composition where no evidence of moral thinking occurred was the 'How to play' one — though one child gave a digression on the evils of cheating which left her no time for the rules of the game.

10.2 Autobiography and Argument

10.2.1 Autobiography and Argument — seven year olds
Generally speaking the seven year olds in the autobiographical narratives judged the best or worst events in their lives in terms of damage to physical objects they possessed or in terms of pleasure or pain to themselves. Only one child judged as bad damage to others. A few children wrote stories in which a

punishment/reward orientation is discernible. On the argumentative task also this egocentrism is borne out — over half of the writers gave judgements of school as being good or bad in terms of personal pain or pleasure. A typical example of moral thinking (which we classify at M1) comes from John:

> The saddest day of my life was when we were at dartmoor I were feed a pony and another kicked me in the air and it hurt and I fell on the ground.
>
> John G.

Most children at this age judged their worst experience as damage to self or to objects belonging to the self — broken cups, paintstained jumpers, toes being damaged, fingers caught in doors. Happiest days were equated with birthdays or Christmas, most accounts featuring lists of presents. The same pattern appeared in the argumentative task — school was judged good or bad in terms of self-interest. For example:

> I think that there should be no school at all then I could stay home and watch television and eat sweets.
>
> Kathleen M.

Kathleen cannot decentre enough to realize that changes to the school system will affect others. She assesses her position in terms of what is pleasureable to the self (M1). Occasionally the principle of self-gratification is articulated precisely:

> *School Time*
> I think School Sould be changing and let children do what they want and have what they want. So remember you sould be allow to have What you Want.
>
> Tania T.

One of the most interesting accounts at 7+ demonstrates the upper limits of the young child's moral thinking, the shift from judgement in terms of physical consequences to a punishment orientation:

> *The Happiest Day of my Life*
> One day I was playing outside when I saw some boys and then they saw me and came up to me and called me names. So I whet in doors and when I whet out again. They were Playing with a tyre and this man had a new garig down the road and one of the boys roed the tyre down to the other boy but he mercd it and it whet right into the garig and the man told them off and then they whet home and when they whet to Sunday School when they got home a Pilceman was ther and he told them off.
>
> Donna H.

Donna entitles this piece her *happiest* experience, happiness being equated with seeing others punished! The boys in the story have done wrong and are punished by a telling off; both by the garage owner and by the policeman. What Donna does not yet realize is the distinction between intentionally damaging property and unintentionally doing so. The tyre rolls into the garage by accident — in the light of this the punishment seems unnecessarily severe. One suspects that Donna is more upset by the boys 'calling me names' than anything else. This is close to the Piagetan notion of 'immanent justice' — punishment catches up with the boys in the end, even if not related directly to the specific offence in Donna's eyes. There is an insistence on punishment: further, it is out of proportion to the accidental offence. Taken together, these two factors put the story at M2.

10.2.2 Autobiography and Argument — ten year olds

At 10+ on the autobiographical narratives we found a decline in the number of stories based on pain/pleasure to the self, an increase in the number of stories with motifs of heteronomy and the emergence of some stories in which empathy and reciprocity, judgements of others in terms of the status quo, appeared. An example of the punishment orientation comes from Tina who judges the 'saddest' day as one in which the whole world is conspiring to punish her: 'something in the hedge' frightens her, she breaks an umbrella 'it was not mine it was my mothes'. She disobeys her father after a petulant argument with him:

'I am going for a walk, no you are not yes I am and I ran out',

and parental punishment for her behaviour caps the bad day (M.2) 'You better get home to bed. you bad girl'.

The shift to judgement in terms of the status quo appears in Douglas' adventure story. Whilst an autobiographical narrative, one suspects that it is partly a fiction. It tells how he and his friend visit a Steam Rally, and continues:

> We were looking at a Fowler Engine when the driver asked us if we would like a ride are quick reply was yes we both climbed up and watched as the driver took the brake off and we slowly moved around the feild. Suddenly the driver sliped of the plate that he was standing on and knocked himself out as the hit the ground. I made a grab for the wheel but slipped and went sprawling on the foot plate. The was a sudden crash and then as I got up to steer another crash knocked me off my feet but lickily then the engine stopped and I ended up in a duck pund. We had destroyed a gate and ripped up a hedge. People came running from all directions and a newspaper reporter was soon on the scene. While we walked home I asked Snub why he hadnt tried to steer, Snub replied, "I couldnt because my feet had got tangled in some rope and I couldn't move". The next day I saw a paper with our photographs in and our story.
>
> Douglas M.

Whilst the bulk of Douglas' narrative is not concerned with notions of right and wrong, but with describing accidental damage to property, the ending of the story, where the two boy heroes have their photograph published in the newspaper, is an indication that fame or respect from the local community is seen by Douglas as good. Being judged as brave in the eyes of others for preventing further damage to property or injury to people — no one in the story is actually seriously hurt — is seen as good. Hence M3., 'Social approval in terms of whether behaviour pleases others', is the final orientation of the story.

On the argumentative tasks at 10+ judgement in terms of the status quo was the rule rather than the exception. Carol argues:

> I don't think it would work in my opinion its not a very good idea to come to school when you liked and to do what you like because everyone would never come to school hardly because they wouldnt want to learn, nobody would get any qualifications.

> Parents wouldn't agree either because they would not want you to be educated, anyway the country would become rough with school age people lounging about everywhere. At home mothers can teach you but you can't do half the things at home as you can at school. If you wern't educated you wouldn't be able to get a job. When your younger your mother and father would make you go to school because you wouldn't understand, there would be trouble when your old enough to make up your own mind weather to go to school or not.

> Personally I like school and I don't mind going. I would get fed up with doing what I liked. I think people would have a boaring life. Most people would just muck about. There are lots of oppertunitys at school and you do things you would not be allowed to do at home.

Carol W.

Carol's argument amounts to a defence of schooling remaining as it is. The reasons she offers range from attributing to other children pursuit of the pleasure principle (M1.) — 'everyone would never come to school hardly because they wouldn't want to learn', 'most people would just muck about' — to considering the effects on others in the social environment (M3) 'Parents wouldn't agree either because they would want you to be educated.' Carol realizes that a decision on such an issue is made by an implicit agreement between all parties — parents as well as children, and the ultimate effects of leaving the choice to children would be bad for society at large (M3) — 'anyway the country would become rough with school age people lounging about everywhere'. She sees the proper exercise of parental authority as being for the protection of the young; 'when your younger your mother and father would make you go to school because you wouldn't understand, there would be trouble when your old enough to make up your own mind'. Parents are right in terms of their conventional roles in protecting children for their own good. Carol judges the issue overall in terms of effects on others — reciprocity is extended in this argument to the immediate family circle; such a decision affects others, so others' views have to be taken into account. (Hence M3 overall). The basis on which she makes a judgement contrasts markedly with that of Kathleen and Tania at seven years. Carol can decentre enough to realize that other people's views must be taken into account.

Overall on the argumentative task at 10+, only a few pieces argued for changes to the school system in terms of 'the good is what I like and want'. Most children explored the effects of possible changes in schooling in terms of how they would affect others — parents, teachers, bus-drivers and other children. Most children argued in defence of the status quo, though elements of earlier forms of moral judgement were detected at the sentence level. The legalistic orientation of level M4 did not make much of an appearance; only one girl at 10+ ended her argument on the note 'But there is a law about going to school' in the context that such a law was a good one because it protected the rights of others. Generally, however, taking both the argumentative and autobiographical narratives into account, the trend at 10+ indicates that heteronomy gives way to socionomy at this age. The form of socionomy is, however, internal to the child's limited understanding of the social system; concepts of rights or fairness and justice do not really emerge at this age with any consistency.

10.2.3 Autobiography and Argument — thirteen year olds

At 13+ there is emerging the capacity to make moral judgements either in terms of conventional norms and rules or in terms of intention regardless of social status. Parents and teachers can now do wrong in the eyes of children; the Piagetan notion of the young child's unilateral respect for adults gives way to a notion of what is fair. On the argumentative task, most children at 13+ argue in terms of the status quo or of conventional norms/rules, looking at the implications for change in the school system in the light of how it might affect not only others within the school system, but society at large. Most children at 10+ claimed that children who didn't have to come to school would become bored; by 13+ most pupils drew the inference that such a decision would lead to an increase in crime — the legalistic orientation. The final paragraphs of Madge's argument that the school system should stay as it is begins with an exploration of the effects of optional school attendance.

She writes:

> The children that didn't go to school would be out roaming the streets. They'd become bored after a while, so they might committ some petty crime, like vandalism or small shop theft. These people wouldn't get any qualifications if they stayed away from school. So they proberly wouldn't get a job with good pay so they might steal extra money.
>
> The system wouldn't be fair on the people who wanted to do well in school, because in the classes they would go to would be people who just wanted to muck around.
>
> Madge H.

Madge's concern here is with the welfare of the social system, that the property laws be maintained. She pinpoints a concern for law and order in her statement that children would turn to crime and vandalism if given nothing constructive to do. Further, her claim 'The system wouldn't be fair on the people who wanted to do well in school' indicates that Madge believes that justice must be based on strict equality — the principle of equity M4. What worries her about the implications of optional school attendance is fairness to all children in the system. The same concern for fairness arose in Evan's piece, which argued overall for some concrete changes to the school system. His ending reads:

> As well as all this we should have more rights for example . . . I was blamed for doing something I didn't do and they didn't even ask any other of the class, I did and they said I was right.
>
> Evan M.

Despite the confusion as to whom the pronouns 'they' refer to, it is obvious from the content that 'they didn't even ask any other of the class' refers to Evan's teachers. Adult authority if not accepted here as being right all the time and Evan's experience of being punished for 'something I didn't do' leads him to questioning adult authority. Justice to Evan is based upon fairness — if adults can behave unfairly, then children 'should have more rights'. Again the orientation is M4.

In the autobiographical narratives at 13+ judgement of others in terms of intention rather than in terms of social status emerged. An example of an autobiographical anecdote which depicts this shift comes from Sally, who writes:

> My worst experience was seeing a little boy knocked down by a car.
>
> This little boy was standing with his mother by the main road. His mother was busy talking to another lady to see what her son was doing. The little boy saw something on the other side of the road. A car was coming, it hit the boy. The

boy rolled up over the bonnet then back onto the road. The little boy was
badly injured. Someone rang for an ambulance quickly. The car wasn't
travelling fast, but the boy just didn't look. The driver and his wife were very
shook up. This wouldn't have happened if the mother paid a little more
attention to her son, instead of to herself and a friend.

Sally M.

Obviously, underpinning Sally's direct judgement of the mother's behaviour
in the incident she depicts is a conception of the mother's proper social role
as being for the protection of the young (M3). The incident is judged as bad
because it hurts others, not only the child, 'The little boy was badly injured',
but others as well, 'The driver and his wife were very shook up'. However,
blame is not attributed to the driver of the vehicle, 'The car wasn't travelling
fast', but to the mother for her lack of care and concern for her child. The
mother's intentions are judged as self-interested (M5) — 'This wouldn't have
happened if the mother paid a little more attention to her son, instead of
to herself and a friend'. Sally has a clear idea of where to apportion blame
for the accident; it comes back to notions of parental responsibility, which
she takes seriously. She looks beyond the obvious cause of the accident, the
driver's failure to stop, to the mother's sin of omission, judging the mother
in terms of her intentions. Another example of the capacity to judge others,
not in terms of physical consequences of action, but in terms of intention
came from Colin who wrote a paradigmatic 'moral tale' as follows:

In 1971 I went for a holiday to Italy with the rest of my family. We went to
Rimini (on the Adriatic coastline) and stayed at a small hotel called the Seisle
my birthday is in June and that year we had our holiday early. (last week of
May 1st week of June) I was then 5 (nearly 6) and was passing through the phase
in which I "Hated the Jerries" I often critised them calling them "Stupid Idiots".
I say I was passing through this stage in fact I had only been attacking the
Germans for 6 months or so, this phase would generally have lasted several
years. At the age of 5 I couldn't swim a stroke (I learnt to swim at 9 or 10)
however Mum and Dad had no qualm's about me going of because the beech
(a lovely golden sand) was a gently shelving one. At the time I had a small (one
place) Inflatable boat and padle, this was my cheif joy, I would paddle around
with it for an hour. The boat was a fairly stable one. About two days after I had
been given the boat I was gently paddling it out toward the sea. the water
looked shallow so I put my leg over the side of the Inflatable and felt for the
bottom. The Inflatable capsized and slowly floated away from me. My head
bobbed up and down and I saw the boat 3 ft. away but I just couldn't swim
even that far. I lifted my head above the water and tried to shout for help,
however it sounded more like "hel" as my head sank below the waves then my
head was clear again and I shouted "He" (the rest was stopped as I swallowed
a mouthful of water) then my foot touched the bottom, the water was less than
4.5 ft. deep! This time I didn't rise to the surface on my own (I would have

drowned there and then) A large broad shouldered man picked me out of the
water with one hand and pulled in the inflatable with the other, after querring
wether it was mine (by pointing to it and me and lifting an eyebrow). he then
found my mother at some length in a foreign language. The language he spoke
was German. from that day I have never attacked "the Jerries".

Colin C.

Colin is exploring his own attitude change to a group of people 'The Jerries'
which by convention, upbringing and the world of television war movies one
would expect to be stereotypic. He speaks of his attitude at age five which
was to stereotype those not in his family or national circle as bad: 'I hated
"the Jerries". I often critised them calling them "Stupid Idiots" '. Here he is
recalling being at an earlier level of moral thinking whereby he judged
Germans as stereotypes (M3), attributing unfavourable attitudes to a whole
race. He is able to distance that earlier attitude, firstly by reflecting for us,
'I say I was passing through this stage in fact I had only been attacking the
Germans for 6 months or so, this phase would generally have lasted several
years', and secondly by placing the stereotypic label 'the Jerries' in inverted
commas. He is consciously aware of the limitations of such an attitude. The
near-drowning incident where he is saved by a 'large broad-shouldered man',
who speaks to his mother in German, triggers his change of attitude, 'From
that day I have never attacked "the Jerries" '. He sees through the stereotypic blinkers to the good intentions and motives of the man who saved
his life. He respects him regardless of race and conventional attitudes (M5).

Generally, then, our application of the moral model to the autobiographical and argumentative writing of children from 7–13 years illustrates
that it is a useful tool for analysing the content of children's writing. We
found general confirmation of Kolberg's finding that pre-conventional moral
judgement, anomy and heteronomy, decreases with age, and that his types
3 and 4, the 'good-boy' morality of maintaining good relations, approval of
others and authority maintaining morality, increase with age to thirteen
years. The pleasure principle, or definition of good as 'what I want and like',
dominates over half of the sample at seven years, declining to account for
only a few moral judgements at 13+. We found that heteronomy developed
to ten years, then declined at 13+. We found no evidence of 'judgement in
terms of abstract principles' in children of 7–13 years. We did find, though,
that whereas no children at 7+ judged adults' actions in terms of intention, by
13+ they were capable of doing so. As Kolberg (1964, p. 402) maintains:

> Large groups of moral concepts and attitudes acquire meaning only in late
> childhood and adolescence, and require the extensive background of cognitive
> growth and experience associated with the age factor.

10.3 Narrative

The responses to the fictional narrative task from ages 7–13 years did not give us the range of moral judgements demonstrated in earlier tasks. The 'moral' stories came mainly in response to the picture depicting two young people facing down a dark alleyway labelled with a 'No Entry' sign. Most children at all ages made the assumption that the young people in the photograph were up to no good and wrote us conventional crime and punishment tales. Hence in response to this task the punishment orientation and the judgement by status quo orientation appeared at all age levels.

10.3.1 Narrative — seven year olds

An example of a seven year old's response to the task came from Jean who wrote:

No Entry

> One day two boys went out one was called Chris and the other one was called fred. they put on their coats and set out side. they went along the path until they came to a sign post it said No Entry. i will go this way so i will to the other was where it says no Entry. I am going to tell mummy of you. OK said chris go on. So fred went home and told his mummy. he went back and told Chris. I am going back home said Chris and fred went back home. the next day it was snowing. We are going for a walk i am going the same way as you today said fred all right said chris. So they went passed the sign Post. they came to a gate and they stoped. they looked over the gate then they went home then they stoped again and ther stood a Policeman, Hello Hello what's up here then said the Policeman. I am going to take you to court. Oh no we are not. Oh yes you are. Shall we now yes so the Policeman took them by thir arm and took them in the Police car and they drove off to the Prison. The End.

> Jean G.

What is interesting about Jean's story is that wrong-doing amounts to disobeying a 'No Entry' sign clearly depicted in the picture as a traffic signal. The boy Chris disobeys the sign, whereas Fred has reservations 'I am going to tell mummy of you'. Adult authority is depicted as all-pervasive in the story, the sign 'No Entry' is taken by both boys to apply to people as well as cars. The boy Chris disobeys because of the pleasure principle (M1) — no other reason is offered. The two children then both disobey the sign 'i am going the same way as you today said fred' and punishment of course catches up with them. The policeman in the story is a stereotype; his words 'Hello Hello what's up here then' have the ring of the Noddy books about them (M3). The punishment orientation at the end of the story is unnecessarily severe 'they drove off to the Prison' (M2). There is no question that to the writer the policeman is doing the right thing in imprisoning the boys, no sense that the punishment does not fit the crime.

10.3.2 Narrative — ten year olds

Whereas the punishment orientation continues in the ten year olds' stories, the offences attributed to the children are much more realistic, ranging from petty-theft to kidnapping. As Helen writes:

> There was once two boys. They lived a no. 6 Bruce street. They were 10 years old and they were twins. There names were paul and Andrew. It was morning and the boys were going to have their breakfast. It was raining out side and very cold. After breakfast the boys were getting dressed. they were going to go out side "Come on Slow coach", said paul "All right fuss pot" mound Andrew. Paul said "Shall we kiddnap a baby — or are you scared" "no Im not" said Andrew "Come on then", said Paul. They soon came to a baby witch was out side a shop. "No one is looking" said Paul "lets not kiddnap a baby" said Andrew. "Don't be such a baby" said Paul. "I'll lift out the baby" said Paul. They took the baby to there hide out. The baby was crying so the went back to there house and Andrew got some milk. Soon the baby was asleep. Three day later a police man came to the door. He said "A baby has been reported lost, have you by any chance seen it any one with a baby like this". the police man showed there mum a picture of a baby. The two boys ran up stairs to there bedroom. Andrew said "I told you we shouldn't have tacken the baby. "Oh Shut up", Said Paul. When the police man went by the boy secret hideout he herd a baby crying. He found a door a went inside the hut. He found the baby. He went back to the boys house a told their mother. The boys were put in barestall for one year.
>
> Harriet C.

The villains of the piece, Paul and Andrew, do wrong on a whim (M1). ' "Shall we kiddnap a baby — or are you scared" '. Andrew agrees by giving in to peer-group pressure from Paul — the only reason he articulates for not doing the deed is fear of punishment (M2). Andrew continues to have reservations ' "lets not kiddnap a baby" ', but he is shamed into it by Paul — ' "Don't be such a baby" '. The deed committed, the boys actually look after the baby. Enter the policeman, representing the rule-based nature of society (M3). Andrew then articulates his reservations ' "I told you we shouldn't have taken the baby" ' — the deed is seen as bad, not in itself, but because the boys might get caught. Again (M2): fear of punishment is expressed. Finally, the boys' action is discovered and punishment catches up with them in the end 'The boys were put in barestall for one year'. Harriet makes it perfectly clear in this little narrative that the behaviour is anti-social and worthy of punishment. She depicts the clash between the amoral position of Paul and the beginnings of rule by fear of punishment in Andrew — the moral positions of the two boys are clearly distinguished, played off against each other. The implicit moral of the story is a conventional one — simply that crime does not pay. The goodies, the policeman and the baddies, the boys, are clearly distinguished and the forces of good triumph in the end (M3).

One of the few stories in which children were not depicted as being anti-social, but on the side of the forces of good came from Gordon B. From its title, 'Mystery! Can it be solved', to its conclusion, his narrative is a conventional one. The criminal in the story, 'Scarface Regon', is given a stereotypic name, the teenagers John and Joanne align themselves with the force of law and order, the police. 'Goodies' and 'baddies' are distinguished in terms of stereotypic roles (M3). Further, Gordon appears to have more knowledge of the operation of the police force than do either Jean at seven or Helen at ten — the roles of sergeant and constable are clearly distinguished in terms of conventional status. The sergeant is definitely in charge ' "Yes, constable over here" bellowed the sergeant', and the dialogue between the two pinpoints Gordon's awareness of the power hierarchy. The criminal is depicted as being on the run, ' "Its him all right, he bust prison a month ago" ' and as adding insult to injury by placing Joanne in a moral dilemma by his note ' "Little girl! don't get the police, If you do your boyfriend dies!" ' This indicates the motivation for Joanne's behaviour, in attempting to save John herself rather than reporting the ransom note to the police, is partly fear of the consequences the criminal will exact (M2) and partly care and concern for John, the close friend (M3). The story then moves into a tale of adventure and escape in which the children triumph in the end: 'They were both awarded medals for bravery against superior forces'. The criminal appears to have escaped at the end of the tale, but the ending indicates that concrete reward for good action is important to Gordon (M2). That the criminal isn't punished at the end is a real departure from most of the stories at this age-level. Gordon is the only child at ten to express reward orientation so directly.

10.3.3 Narrative — thirteen year olds

At thirteen the punishment orientation and judgement in terms of conventional social roles continues in children's stories. Awareness of types of crime seems largely influenced by television — terrorist activities, political assassinations, fratricide, kidnapping and theft all feature. The conventional judgement 'crime does not pay' is the clear orientation of stories in this age group.

A somewhat sophisticated narrative, reminiscent in plot of Forsyth's *Day of the Jackal* will serve as an example:

Sunday Express
The Assignment

A man strolled out of the "Banque de France" carrying an attache case. He had a long overcoat on over a typical French suit. The street was deserted as there was a steady drizzle falling, it was five thirty (English time). The man waved a taxi, which was coming up behind him, he climbed in and the taxi drove off up the street. At the top it turned right and disappeared from view. In the attache case was £7,000, inherited from his father.

Toledo Steele was British born, when he was a boy he went to live in Germany where his family lived. Aged thirty-eight he retired from his original job as a journalist, he is now unemployed, but for a special reason. As a journalist he went to France to report on an attack which was directed at General Charles de Gaulle. It was then that an idea formed in his mind, two years later he gave up his job. Just after he had left his job he heard the tragic news, or so it seemed at the time, that his parents had been killed in a car crash. In his father's will he had left Toledo £7,000. (his parents were quite old at the time) and everybody at that time felt sorry for Toledo. In Toledo's head the money was just what he wanted and, if he succeeded with his mission he wouldnt have to face his parents. On July the 2nd 1949 £7000 was placed in the 'Banque de France'. From July the 2nd untill August the 12th there was a lot of planning done, in the attic in Toledo Steele's house.

On August the 12th. an old man shuffled along the Beehive streets of Paris, he was carrying a shopping bag in his right hand and an umbrella in his left. Out of the shopping bag protruded a long French loaf. The old man had a couple of day's growth which was his beard, his face was cut from numerous shaves with a razor blade. On his head was a 'fishermans' cap, he wore a long overcoat which was unfastened at the front so that it flapped in the breeze untidily. He hurried on until he came to a side street, he continued along this road for about fifty yards then he stopped. He reached into his pocket, pulled out a packet of cigarettes lit one and looked around, he could hear the roar of the traffic in the square. Making sure no-one was around he slipped into an ally way, still carrying the bag and umbrella. Five minutes later a clean shaven man appeared from the ally-way, wearing a light coat over a dark jacket and trousers. Under his arm was a long French roll, reaching the main street he turned right and continued on his way until he came to a hotel called 'Croix de Malie' overlooking the square. He went in and booked a room for one, he was directed up to the second floor. At room 34 he stopped and went in locking the door behind. Toledo went over to the window and looked out down below the square. It was here that General De Gaulle would pass in his chauffer driven car.

At precisely 4 o'clock all the traffic was stopped, above all the confusion below, could be heard the unmistakable wail of the French police escorting General De Gaulle through Paris. At the window of the hotel Toledo looked out, on his knee was a powerful 'snipers' rifle. It had telescopic sights which were set to converge at 300 yards, attached to the muzzle was a silencer. As the convoy drew level with the row of houses on the far side, Toledo brought his rifle to bear. The cross section of the sights were exactly on General De Gaulle's temple. A shot rang out, Toledo Steele crumpled to the floor, his rifle clattering to his side. A round hole could be seen through the jacket, then blood began to ooze out. Cheif Inspector Collins looked down at Toledo Steele 'that was a bit too close' were his unspoken words.

Andrew B.

Andrew's tale of an attempted political assassination is very much an attempt to write in a conventional genre. The master criminal, the assassin Toledo Steele, is presented with details of family background, so that the reader focuses on him from the outset. The details of the planned killing are let out gradually, so that the reader is held in suspense. The master criminal is depicted as a man who knows he is doing wrong. 'In Toledo's head the money was just what he wanted and, if he succeeded with his mission he wouldn't have to face his parents'. Planning to kill is wrong, but the reason offered 'he wouldn't have to face his parents' is an indication that living up to the expectations of others (M3) is the basis for choosing to do wrong or not. Political motives are certainly not given by Andrew. We then follow Toledo Steele, the master of disguise, to the hotel room from which the assassination attempt will take place. Andrew elaborates the details to keep the reader in suspense. Then comes the reversal of expectations in the ending: 'A shot rang out, Toledo Steele crumpled to the floor, his rifle clattering to his side . . . Chief Inspector Collins looked down at Toledo Steele 'that was a bit too close' were his unspoken words'. Again, the police arrive on the scene in the nick of time. The policeman's action in killing the criminal is not questioned; the punishment is exactly suited to the attempted crime on the basis of 'an eye for an eye'. Again the punishment orientation (M2) is clear. We have a conventional crime-does-not-pay story. The criminal and policeman's roles are again stereotypes (M3).

10.3.4 Narrative — comment

Although the moral model can reveal levels of judgement the pattern of development may be obscured in this fictional narrative task. Children's moral judgements tend to centre on punishment and social stereotype regardless of age. Older children show more awareness of the springs of motivation of evil actions than do younger ones, and use stereotypic characters more frequently. Their punishments relate to the crimes their characters commit, unlike those of seven year olds where punishment is out of all proportion to the nature of the offence. This is, however, not unexpected when we consider the fiction children read, where they meet stereotypic good and evil characters associated with particular social roles. Conventional story forms are experimented with across the age-range of our sample; it is not surprising therefore that the child's moral thinking parallels that met in the actual models. The level of moral thinking in a *fiction* is not necessarily the most developed thinking the child is capable of — *imitation* may account for it. The fictional mode allows the child to employ moral attitudes, which he may not hold himself, or which he may have passed beyond. Our model allows us to rate only what is explicitly stated or directly implied in writing, not to assess the child. However, if it can be applied to children's writing, presumably it will reveal interesting results when applied to fictional writing in general. Such an application may give teachers of English confirmation of their intuitions about suitability of reading material for particular age-groups.

A further factor which may have influenced results on the fictional narrative task was the use of a visual stimulus for writing. We used pictures as a stimulus because this practice is a common one in the English classroom for fostering 'creative writing'. The practice is somewhat akin to the projective test measures psychologists use for research into attitudes and values generally. Certainly the most common test measure in research into moral development is the 'Projective method of story completion ' (Magowan and Lee, 1970), the story being given either orally by an adult interviewer or by reference to carefully selected pictures of children in moral dilemma situations. In Bull's (1969) research visuals depicting children in 'value of life', lying, cheating, and stealing situations were given to 360 subjects, in groups of sixty children matched for sex from ages 7–17 in two year intervals. For each of these tests given, girls appeared to give more socionomous responses than boys, particularly at ages 11–13 years. However, with Bull's projective test items children were given pictures on a 'same sex as respondent' basis – four sets of pictures for each of the moral themes tested were compiled where the age and sex of the child in the picture was varied on a 2 × 2 matrix; young, old; male, female. Children were asked to respond to the picture matched for age and sex with themselves. The main reason for doing this is, according to Magowan and Lee, that

> It is assumed that a child who completes a story projects his or her own judgements or emotion into the material by identifying with the central figure, who is usually depicted as the same age and sex to facilitate the process. (p. 537)

In our research we certainly did not ask children to respond to a 'same sex as respondent' picture – the identity of the children in it was masked by the fact that they were depicted with their backs to the viewer beneath a 'No Entry' sign, dressed in anoraks and jeans. There were no detectable sex differences in the responses to it; both boys and girls gave heteronomous responses at all ages in our sample. It appears that the type of picture used can influence the results – the intractable problem of all projective test measures. As Magowan and Lee succinctly put it:

> There may be a difference between the moral rules which are perceived to apply to self and those applying to others, particularly when 'others' includes children of different ages and sexes . . . If this possibility were real, different responses might be expected when the age, sex and social status of the figures in the stories are changed. (p. 537)

Further, in controlling for this variable in their six story completions given to children of 9—10 years and 11—12 years in sex-matched groups of fifty-six children each, these writers found that:

> more immanent justice responses were accorded to stories where the central
> figure was male, and this difference obtains for both boys and girls. (p. 540)

Our results tend to confirm Magowan and Lee's finding: children assumed that the people in our picture were male, so heteronomous responses or the punishment/reward orientation appeared at each age level. The conclusion we can draw is that the picture stimulus is not the best means for eliciting a range of moral judgements from children.

10.4 Conclusions

In analysing a normative sample of children's writing from 7—13 years, we found the sequential moral model a useful tool for analysis. We did not find any evidence of 'judgement' in terms of abstract universal principles, or individually developed systems. This, however, is not surprising granted the age-range of our sample and that we did not set out to elicit moral judgements directly. In Kolberg's (1964, p. 403) original sample, only four per cent of moral judgements at thirteen years were at his stage 6 or 'morality of individual principles of conscience'. In a follow-up study into the children in his initial sample Kolberg (1974, p. 446) reported that stage 6 did not emerge for one boy until the age of twenty-four years. Further studies such as those of Haan, Brewster Smith and Block (1968) on adolescents in freshman college year indicate that the bulk of late adolescents' judgements fall into Kolberg's stages 3 and 4 — judgements in terms of convention and the legalistic authority — maintaining morality. Out of 957 subjects in this study only 28 fell into Kolberg's stage 6 (p. 185). The development of principled levels of moral thinking appears from the research evidence to consolidate from late adolescence to adulthood, outside the age range of our sample. What then is needed is further research into the moral judgements of pupils as evidenced in the writing at ages 13—18, which may reveal evidence of the later stages of our model.

It is clear from our discussion that we need to know more about the levels of moral thinking children are exposed to, particularly in books and television programmes. We suspect that imitation of story models occurred in fictional narratives and accounts for the comparatively restricted nature of moral attitudes in this task. If so we need to ask certain questions. Do all young children's stories focus on a morality of heteronomy, namely that the good are rewarded, the wicked punished? How much literature goes beyond conventional norms and rules and gives us examples of the man of moral principle, prepared to question the status quo? When should we begin to expose children to more advanced forms of moral thinking? If, as we have demonstrated, a Kolbergian style model can be applied to children's writing, then surely it can be applied to writing for children, thus helping us answer the question of how the culture transmits its values and how these come to be internalized by the young. Other wider questions may be asked. Do we respond positively or negatively to adolescent thinking which questions our norms and rules? What morality do we as people expose to the children we teach in the way we apply school rules, for example? Teachers may, and probably will, object to being seen as responsible for the moral education of the young, yet the hidden curriculum of the school inevitably engages us in the area of morality. If we as teachers know more about the characteristics of children's moral thinking as they mature we will be less likely to condemn them for immaturity, and will have a more realistic notion of what constitutes true development.

It is important to emphasize that the cognitive-developmental view of morality which our model espouses has certain limitations. It is not a model which can be applied to children's behaviour — it focuses on the verbal judgements people make and not on whether these verbal judgements are put into practice. Again, it does not take into account the area of affect or emotion as it relates to the development of moral thought — it is perfectly possible that our responses to hypothetical moral dilemmas may appear to be more advanced than our responses to practical issues where our emotions are involved. But when all is said and done there is a moral dimension to much writing, and it is important to discern the nature of this in any discussion of the nature of personal growth with which teachers are so essentially concerned.

10.5 Summary

In two out of three pieces of writing previous research findings were confirmed; namely that young children tend to make judgements in terms of punishments/rewards and in terms of physical consequences of action; that by age ten children make judgements in terms of making good relations with others in the immediate social context, and that by age thirteen children are capable of judgement in terms both of fairness and intention, regardless of the social status of figures usually in authority over them. We found also that such a pattern of development was task dependent — fictional narratives led to a centring of attitudes at the heteronomy/socionomy axis.

Chapter Eleven

Style in Children's Writing

In Chapter Three we discussed the development of style. Young children's writing frequently consists of simple affirmative sentences; imperfectly organized; with insufficient awareness of the reader's needs. We have chosen to look at developments in these three areas. Thus the *syntax* of the sentence is transformed or otherwise changed; and the use of the various lexical items, *the verbal competence*, grows more exact. The overall *organization* becomes more coherent, partly aided by the use of *cohesive* devices. And the writer's *awareness of the reader* grows; together with his sense of the *appropriateness* of a particular register. These therefore, out of various possible features, are the ones we have chosen to use in our model. Additionally we shall look at the *effectiveness* of a particular piece which, for an individual reader, is a summation of all stylistic elements.

11.1 Narrative

11.1.1 Narrative — seven year olds

In her narrative Nancy writes:

> One day I was walkin down the street Then I saw a spaceship. Then he landed
> down then he said do you want to come up here Yes I do I want to go with you

This represents an early syntactic form (S1.1). The sentences are simple, the verbal competence restricted, with action verbs, absence of modifications, phrases like 'landed down' (S2.1). The organization is chronological (at a simple level narrative tends to structure material by requiring it in sequence) (S3.2); though the story is not complete as far as cohesion is concerned the main device is elementary — the use of 'then', and the pronoun 'he' has no noun antecedent (S4.1). The language is close to speech (S5.1) with however the common story opening 'one day'; the readers need (e.g. to know who speaks from the space craft) is not recognized (S6.1). In terms of effective-

ness this piece would for its limited contextualization and incompleteness
rate SN7.1.

The longest narrative produced in this group is by Jean G.

Title No Entry

One day two boys went out one was called Chris and the other was called fred.
they put on their coats and set out side, they went along the path until they came
to a sign post it said No Entry I will go this way so I will go the other way where
it says no Entry. I am going to tell mummy of you. OK said chris go on. So fred
went home and told his mummy. he went back and told Chris. I am going back
home said Chris and fred went back home. the next day it was snowing. We are
going for a walk i am going the same way as you today said fred all right said Chris.
So they went passed the sign Post. they came to a gate and they stoped. they
looked over the gate then they went back home then they stoped again and ther
stood a Policeman. Hello Hello what's up here then said the Policeman. I am going
to take you to court. Oh no we are not. Oh yes you are. Shall we now Yes so the
Policeman took them by thir arm and took them in the Police car and they drove
off to the Prison. The End.

The syntax here is a little more complicated. There are a few complex
sentences involving for instance an adverbial time clause (line 3), and an
adjectival clause (line 8), though the general pattern is still of simple
sentences (S1.2). The verbal competence is greater: the characters have
names, the exact words of the speakers are quoted, though the perambula-
tions of these characters are detailed rather than colourful (S2.2). The
organization is again chronological although the sheer physical action is
supplemented by conversation. Once again it is easier to organize a story
because actions take place in time. Eventually a conclusion emerges, but is
reached episodically (S3.2). Cohesive devices show an advance: the use of
pronouns once the noun has been given is understood — 'one . . . the other'
referring back to the 'two boys' in the first sentence, for example, though
elsewhere (the repetition of 'gate', line 13, for example) it is uncertain
(S4.2.). Sense of audience is increasing; 'I will go the other way where it
says no Entry' — is designed to inform the reader, even though it is presumably over explicit as far as Fred is concerned. The fact that the reader is
sometimes in doubt about who is speaking, however, shows an imperfect
awareness of his needs. Details such as the sentences about the gate are
arbitrarily included (S5.2). The register is moving towards the written style
particularly in the opening sentences (S6.2): there is some earlier dialogue,
though the policeman is a stereotype. This is in many ways a very good piece
for a seven year old. Overall effectiveness is limited by the amount of un-
selected information, and the lack of realization (S7.2).

11.1.2 Narrative — ten year olds

Ten year olds' narratives are on the whole much longer than those of seven year olds. The piece by Charles L. is in many ways typical both in its pre-occupation with crime and violence and in its stylistic features.

> We are fourteen year olds and our names are Bryan and Chris. A bank has just been robbed and we did it. We were not suspected at all. Three men are suspected theese are there faces

These are their fingerprints.

> They were caught in the bank and were recognized by the people in the bank (I don't know how). I said to Bryan "lets go out So we did I said they theres the bank" Suddenly Bryan Said "some body's following us" we hurried up his shadow was getting further back we turned a corner and heard footsteps coming closer and closer we hid but then someone screamed we were in a warehouse. Full of export good's (stolen). Then the Policeman appeared and arrested all of us. We were bound to be found out now. Bryan and I were trembling they asked why if we insisted that we never did anything. Bryan opened his mouth and let it all out. I was furious with him. They put us in jail Bryan said that we were guilty. I couldnt say anything else but say the truth. So we were put in prison and that is where I am now. "Come on out you come" that was the warden. I'm going for trile.

The syntax is not apparently much more complicated in general than that of the seven year olds — a high proportion of simple clauses. But it is a mistake to think of development here merely in terms of an overall increase in complexity. The point is that complex syntax can be called upon where it is required (e.g. 'they asked why if we insisted that we never did anything'). Although there is an over preponderance of short sentences, there are times when length of sentence is adjusted to meaning and effect; notice the differing functions of the first three sentences, for instance (S1.2—3). Verbal competence is represented by precise words ('trembling', 'recognized'), a knowledge of idiom ('closer and closer', 'bound to be found out') and a use of well-chosen detail in one place ('his shadow was getting further back'). The organization is interesting. The beginning takes us straight into the story. Indeed the variety of beginnings in this age group show that they are not imprisoned by the 'one day' or similar convention.

The year is 1944 and the war is still on

(Lynn T.)

A derlicked house in a bombed battered street no sound of life

(Carol W.)

'I am sorry', "I now please tell me the sad story"

(Jocasta P.)

A particular feature of Charles's narrative and others in this group is that he has ceased to be dominated by strict chronology. He begins in prison awaiting trial though we are not told this until the end when he is summoned by the warden. Meanwhile he has given us a retrospect on the crime. Control is not of course perfect — how he and his friend actually did commit the bank robbery is not mentioned (S3.3). Cohesion is good at the beginning. There are lexical links between the first three sentences except 'we' in the last two, but that is sufficient to relate them effectively, and the writer can obviously use elsewhere 'suddenly', 'so', 'then' and pronouns as noun substitutes. There is however a lack of cohesion in telling of the bank robbery since essential sentences seem not to have been written (S4.2). With this in mind reader awareness cannot be said to be high though there are indications from the asides from the reader ('I don't know how' and 'stolen') that in these places he is monitoring his own writing (S5.2). There is a dawning awareness of a writing model, the crime story (S6.2) though in this case, the attempt to use it is imperfectly successful. Effectiveness, judged by the two dimensional characters, the inexplications, the absence of individual or specific insights, is at about the SN7.2—3 level.

11.1.3 Narrative —thirteen year olds

This group, as one would expect, displays a greater variety of treatment. Thus, as with a narrative there are newspaper reports, reviews, interpretations of a picture, dialogues, some writers produce stories which have no apparent connection with a picture. Thus in some cases comparison with work in the earlier groups is not possible. Even so if the model we are using is to be of any general use it should be able to comment within limits on disparate material; and we find this to be the case. Here, for instance, is a piece by Nina P. written as a play:

Who Cares

"What do we do with the kids?"
"What do you mean, we do, thats your responsibility".
"Come off it, were both in this together".
"I suppose so, don't panic, we'll think of something".
"Well you'd better think fast we haven't got much time".
"I don't reckon its up to us anyroad".
"I know, we didn't ask for this job, did we".
"We could just leave 'em in the yard, someone'll see 'em".
"We couldn't do that!"
"Well I will if you wont".
"You can do it on your own then!"
"You're stupid you are. They're only a couple of kids".
"The job was to get rid of the mother, not them".
"What do you suggest we do then, go to the police and say
'heres a couple of kids, we've bumped off their mum so they're all on their own, you'll look after them, won't you'?"
"Dont be stupid".
"Your turn to suggest something now".
"We could put 'em on someones doorstep, they'd have to find somewhere for 'em then".
"And what if some old busybody sticks her nose through the net curtains and sees us, what then?"
"Alright, so that wont work".
"Our best bet is to leave 'em in the yard".
"Well I suppose I can't do much to stop you, anyway someones bound to find them".
"Come on then".

The men took the children out into the yard, left them staring through the wire mesh cage and drove away.

"What if anything happens to them".
"Who cares? I dont. They're only a couple of kids, just tough luck they got a rotten mother".

The car drove on into the night.

In Chapter Three (3.2) we referred to the general findings of 'linguistic' research that the more advanced the writer the more complex the syntax. A piece of work like Nina's shows up the limitations of this thesis. As for instance Harpin points out (1973), the factor most influential on the complexity of the syntax is the task set. As other pieces of her work demonstrate, Nina has access to a variety of subordinations when necessary. However, here she selects a series of simple structures of the S.V.O. (Subject, Verb, Object) type which are in keeping both with the idiom of the spoken language, and the tenseness of the situation being evoked. Competence in style in this particular is a matter of being able to select from a repertoire as appropriate. Thus the long last speech is in contrast to the laconic final sentence. We would rate this use of syntax as S1.5. The choice of individual words and phrases is careful. There is a good attempt at slang — 'kids', 'some old busy-body', 'come off it' — though this is a little old fashioned in terms of modern idioms. There is sensitivity to the way the words would be spoken 'What do you mean, we do' with the implied stress on 'we'. The title 'who cares' is picked up skilfully in the final words of one of the speakers (S2.3). This last is also a feature of organization. The obvious narrative line, the murder of the woman, is rejected, and instead we hear about it incidentally through the dialogue. Thus the chronology which we have noted in earlier pieces is interrupted by retrospections. 'We didn't ask for this job' is a reference back; the discussion is carried on about the children; then a further reference back — 'The job was to get rid of the mother, not them', which gives us crucial information. The bit of ironic imaginary conversation with the police introduces another dimension. The opening seizes the attention and focuses on the control issue. The conclusion — 'the car drove on into the night' symbolizes the indifference which the dialogue has argued out, and the title indicated (S2.4). Cohesive devices are confidently employed. In this conversation one statement is in some sense a comment on another. And in fact a device Nina uses is specific repetition with a different emphasis the second time e.g. 'we do'/'we do': 'think of something'/'you'd better think fast' (S4.4). The register is of a colloquial idiom with a slightly bookish flavour (how criminals are regarded as talking) (S6.3). The way of feeling through styles of others is common at this age.

The sensitivity to the reader is clear — explanations are inserted without distorting the convincingness of the conversations — 'we've bumped off their mum so they're all on their own' (S5.3). There is a high level of overall effectiveness, partly because of the way in which the actual information is inserted sparingly, thus sustaining the interest (SN7.5).

11.2 Autobiography

11.2.1 Autobiography — seven year olds

The structure which children use in their stories is sustaining: it provides a chronology which enables them to record events as they occur, even if there is no necessary connection between them. Thus many of the seven year olds write stories at some length. In contrast their pieces of autobiography are on the whole shorter, doubtless in part for this reason. They have to select and arrange events from their own experience, and this is a more difficult task. Some of the writers only manage a single sentence:

> The saddest day of my life was when Michael Healey fipt some glue on my head.
>
> Kenneth G.

> The saddest was when my dog got knocked down.
>
> Philip S.

Sandy B's piece is typical of several:

> On my holiday I went to the seaside and I went in the water and a crab and it Pinched and I went home and had my tae and then I went to bed

Where there is no clear narrative structure children often include in addition to the main incident the obvious punctuation marks of the day. These are particularly meals, getting up, going home, going to bed. The syntax is of simple sentences; cohesion devices are confined to 'and'; the register is very much of the spoken language; the piece is comprehensible but this is not of course the same as reader awareness. On all our categories the piece would be recorded as elementary.

Kate B.'s piece is longer and more detailed:

> My saddest day was when Richard and me came home and I had just come from a school Christmas party and when we came in the door and we were just going to take our hamster out but he was not there so then we went into the Front-room where mummy and Daddy were and we thought they had Hammy but they did not then they said we took him to the vet and he had to put him down then we ran to Mum and Dad and we cried and cried then Dad said he would buy us another one and he did. The End.

The structure is focused on the hamster, the organization being chrono-logical: the incident is not so much a 'story' as events recorded as they occur; the ending provides a satisfying conclusion (S3.2). There is a use of several cohesive devices, not just 'and', but 'when', 'but', 'so', 'where': pronominal reference is assured (S4.2) Syntax is more advanced than in the earlier pieces. She can use an adjectival clause (S1.6), a noun clause object (S1.7), but furnishes the constructions initiated by the time clause (S1.3) (S1.2). Verbal competence is in accordance with the general statement the piece makes (S2.1). Writing is close to speech (S6.1); the reference to 'Richard', as though the reader knew him, is an indication of the restricted audience awareness (S5.1).

11.2.2 Autobiography — ten year olds

Chronological organization is the predominant pattern we have seen with seven year olds. Both in narrative and autobiography they 'tell a story' in strict sequence. This is also true of many ten year olds, and we need not demonstrate the point further. It is useful though to look at how far a ten year old may vary this method of presentation.

This piece by Pauline represents, in a number of ways, development over the work of seven year olds.

> I had just moved into a new house. I had no friends my sister was only about 4 years old I looked for some friends but I couldn't find any. Then I heard a noise someone was bouncing on a matrue then I looked over the wall and there I found somebody I said who are you? what is your name? she said the same to me it was my old friend I knew in play school (she is in this school now) she is called nicola Thorn. We played skipping until it was time for me to go in. I had my tea and I watched television and I went to bed I said to myself I think that was the happiest day in my life. Nicola has been one of my Greasest friends right from that day. And she sometimes breaks but with me but she soon comes running to me when she is my friend again.
>
> Pauline G.

Pauline's introduction is immediately retrospective, marked by a highly economical but effective supplying of background. We come to the story 'Then I heard a noise' — which concludes with the conventional 'I went to bed', and the almost obligatory — 'the happiest day of my life'. But this is not in fact the end of the piece — there is a bringing of us to the present time, and a generalization about the friendship, which demonstrates that she sees it in context. (Organization S3.4.) Pauline's handling of cohesive details is satisfactory (e.g. 'I couldn't find any [friends]' — a substitution at the end of the second 'sentence') with an elementary use of 'then'. She is learning that sentences which stand alone are not necessarily unconnected. But the cohesive device whereby 'noise' becomes 'someone' becomes 'old friend' becomes 'Nicola Thorn' is of a different level (S4.3). Syntax is mainly of simple sentences but these are used effectively in the first part where they pace the story and heighten the interest (S1.2). Verbal competence is within expectation (S2.2). Register is oral, except for the early sentences which have the economy and organization of written language (S6.2). Notable is the sense of reader awareness. Not only are there asides ('she is in this school now') but all the necessary information is unobtrusively present. If we use the device of 'interrogating' the text, we find we receive answers. No friends — what of your sister? *She was only four.* Why did you not look for friends? — *I couldn't find any.* You heard a noise — what? *Someone bouncing on a mattress.* Who? — *Nicola Thorn.* Who's she? — *my old friend I knew at play school.* And so on (S5.4). Overall effectiveness would seem to be at the SA7.3 level.

11.2.3 Autobiography — thirteen year olds

The piece by Mary on her 'worst experience' demonstrates the command of aspects of style which we would normally expect in children of this group:

> This took place on the night of the 7th November. My mother and father had gone out to help my aunt who was moving house. So my brother and I were left. Suddenly we hard what we thought was a car we had a bet that it was mum and dad, so we both ran out and no one was there so I ran in and shut the door and my brother went to open the door and leaned on the glass, it was in the door. Then his arm went straight throw the glass. When I saw his arm he'd cut it very severely. I couldn't find my aunts telephone number. I then took him to the women down the road who I knew was a trained policewoman and would know what to do. She applyed pressure to the wound and took him down to the doctors by that time the bleeding had stopped. My mother and father arrived shortly afterwards and went down to the doctors by that time he had had 2 stiches and altogether he had 8. The cut was a V cut which is the worst cut you can get. I now have a brother who is proud of a scar and shows everyone.
>
> Mary M.

The organization of this piece is basically chronological, but Mary is able to interrupt the strict time sequence where appropriate. Thus the second sentence is retrospective to provide the necessary background — how mother and father had gone out. The opening sentence is exact and economical; the closing sentence, with its touch of humour, provides by implication the information that the wound healed satisfactorily. The events chosen all have their place — we do not get much unnecessary detail (S3.4). Cohesive devices vary in their sophistication: 'and' and 'so' are over used in the earlier part, though 'suddenly' and 'by that time' are also employed; pronominal subordination is insufficiently used, there being a tendency to repeat nouns; but elipsis is in the writer's repertoire — 'and went down to the doctors'. Semantic reference between one sentence and the next is clear even if not aided by grammatical means (e.g. first and second sentence) (S4.3). Use of syntax is variable; on the one hand there are phrases like 'we heard what we thought was a car' (line 5); on the other connections which should have employed an adjectival clause are made with a single sentence — 'the glass, it was in the door'. Use of tenses, and sequence of tenses is assured (as in the sentences concerned with the policewoman (S1.2—3). Verbal competence is good — there is a proper use of standard groups — 'cut it very severely', 'trained policewoman', 'applied pressure', 'arrived shortly afterwards' — as well as unexpected collocations — 'a brother who is proud of a scar' (S2.3). The register is conventional (this accounts for the lack of pronominal substitution in places) with a topping and tailing in written mode (S6.2). Very noticeable is the reader awareness —information and explanation is continuously though usually unobtrusively supplied. Thus we are told why the children were alone, why they went to the door, why they telephoned a policewoman (her medical knowledge) and so on. Mary is very keen on giving exact information — the date, the number of stiches, the nature of the cut (S5.4). The overall effectiveness of this piece is greater than appears on first reading — it is unspectacular, apparently matter of fact, but comes across by its precision (SA7.3—4).

11.3 Argument — all ages

Chronology gives strong support in organizing narrative and autobiography. Here in the task 'Would it work if children came to school when they wanted to and could do what they liked there?' the invitation is to balanced argument and hypothetical thinking for which the writers have no such obvious model. On the whole all groups write less on this task than on the other two.

On the whole the productions of the seven year olds are too short to make it useful to attempt to classify them by means of the model. Even so one point is worth noting — the attempt to think in the way demanded by the task elicits a certain type of grammar — the reason clause. Kenneth G.'s piece is typical:

> I wish I've never come to school. And no homework because I don't like the work.

This can only be described as heartfelt, and further comment would be tasteless.

11.4 Explanation — all ages

As we have seen in the previous two main sections the impulse to create narrative is strong and understandable. In the explanatory task in which writers explain how to play a game, we can see this impulse at work. One anonymous writer begins:

> When I used to live in the willage I used to play spot light a this is the rules of the game

In organizing their exposition in fact many of the seven year olds naturally give a sequential account which has only limited adequacy (S3.1.5). Curtis's is a fairly typical piece in that he states the number of players and the apparatus and then progresses through the game.

Battleship

> To play Battleship you need Two Players and one big board and two little boards and you have a lot of ships and you put the ships in lots of different Places and one Person says 5D and they could be RITE or they could be wrong, and if they our right you take away one ship if they our wrong you Don't take away a ship.

In most pieces it is the narrative which provides the main cohesion: otherwise formal cohesive devices (chiefly 'and' and the substitution 'they' for persons) are elementary. The last phrase ('you don't take away a ship') is a repetition whereas a substitution would be expected (S4.1). The interesting feature of the syntax is that the task prompts conditional clauses (S1.2). Verbal competence is restricted — there is a general imprecision (S2.1). The register is spoken, characterized by e.g. the use of 'you' (S6.1); there is only a very limited sense of what the reader needs to know to play the game (S5.1). Overall effectiveness is low (SE7.1).

The more complex the game the greater the difficulty in explaining it. Ten year olds tend to choose more complex games than the seven year olds, and thus sometimes meet greater problems.

On the whole in organizing the explanations this age group usually begin by setting out the dimensions of the game — number of players, type of apparatus needed — though there are still some tempted to go straight into narrative. Sarah S. seems as if she is going to short-circuit the task with her opening sentence:

> First you get all the things out and look at the instructions

Only one writer sets out to state the aims of the game at the beginning, but he distracts before he has given it:

> The object of the game is, you are given five crew cards . . .
>
> Barry T.

Usually, the object comes in the middle or at the end in such terms as 'the one with the most money wins'. There is a tendency in a fair proportion of the compositions to start well in organizational terms, and then to become uncertain as to the relative balance of some items as narrative, rules, description of items; even the place of personal comment, as in Sally M.'s piece on Stay Alive:

> . . . the person with some left is the winner. It is a very very good game. I sit
> and play and play with It is so good. The round things you put the Balls on
> are white or orange . . .

Cohesive devices are very much at the level we would expect from our study of narrative and autobiography at this age, but in addition there are those prompted by the nature of the game. 'The next player . . . the next player', 'After that'.

There is a particular problem presented in terms of word choice. On the whole the writers tend to know the technical vocabulary of the game — what they do not realize is that these are often specific to the game concerned, thus Margaret S. writes of the Wizard of Oz:

> The first few circles are red, on these you get a rub slippers card, and when you
> have got a ruby slippers card you can move on, but if you throw too many and
> go past the ruby slippers circle, you must go back to the beginning . . .

The syntax of many of the pieces is also typified in Margaret's piece, predominantly simple sentences but with time clauses, contrasts and prohibitions implied by 'but', and conditional clauses, in keeping with the alternatives in games.

Register is again frequently as in Margaret's writing. There is a tendency to use 'you' idiomatically as an instruction:

> You first of all get 8 or more players

This is nearly always drawn from the spoken language, but one of the writers is conscious that this is part of a particular register of games instruction.

> The things you will need
> Paper, Pencils, Felt tip pens, and imagination, a dictionary

This is Cheryl H., who is however also aware of the impersonal register for this purpose.

> This is a game for two players or more. Everyone must have a piece of paper.

A fair proportion of the writers are not aware of the kind of information the reader needs. In a task like this where exact instructions are crucial this is a particularly difficult task. There is goodwill towards the reader — an attempt to make him understand (the use of the word 'you' is significant here) but often the imaginative leap into the reader's mind is not possible over the whole piece, though it is frequently achieved in individual sentences. The thirteen–fourteen year olds show a big advance over the seven and ten year olds in their ability to organize their presentation of the game. This is a stylistic matter, but it is also related to the development of formal thinking. The account by Peter H. is fairly typical:

Monopoly

The idea of the game is to buy and rent or sell properties so profitable that player increase their wealth – the wealthiest becoming the eventual winner. Starting from "go", move the tokens around the board accordingly to throw of the dice. When a players token lands on a space not alreddy ownd, he may by it from the bank: otherwise it is auctioned off to the highest bidder. The object of owning property is to collect rents from opponents stopping there. rentals are greatly increased by the erection of houses, hotels, so it is wise to build them on some of your building sites. To raise more money, building sites may be mortgaged to the bank. Community chests and chance card gives instructions that must be followed sometimes player land in jail. the game is one of shared and amusing trading and excitement.

Peter organizes his writing by first stating the purpose of this game, and then explaining how it is played in a most economical way. The organization is not narrative; rather it is in terms of the principles involved at each stage: e.g. 'the object of owning property is to collect rents from opponents stopping there' (S3.4). Cohesion is competent – notice the use of 'otherwise' in line 9 (S4.3). Control of a varied syntax is good – the use of participal and infinitive phrases ('starting from go', 'to raise more money') to initiate sentences is a device we scarcely find in the other writers (S1.4). A high degree of verbal competence is to be found in the proper use of conventional language – 'the object of owning', 'greatly increased by', 'it is wise to' (S2.3). Use of register is slightly unsure – thus the instruction to the reader in the second sentence moves to a description of the player's behaviour in the third (S6.4). The needs of the reader are always taken into account – what he will want to know – so that explanations are inserted as appropriate – 'the wealthiest becoming the eventual winner', 'the object of owning property'. Reader awareness is further demonstrated by the personal touches – the bit of advice – 'it is wise to build on them' and the recommendation that the game is one of 'amusing trading and excitement'. The effectiveness is high – given the space available it is difficult to see what else the reader could expect to know (SE7.5).

11.5 Summary

There is a general movement from partial to complete organization of the writing. The narrative provides the earliest and most common structure, and it is often applied even where other systems are appropriate. It becomes more sophisticated in terms of time shifts. Other organizing systems begin to emerge with older children — logical, classificatory — related to growing cognitive powers. A notable feature becomes the variety of forms available, and a cognizance of the code necessary, but consistency may vary with the difficulty of the task — non-functional register switches occur; syntax and cohesion grow more controlled and can be used to produce specific effects, not merely to carry core content. Use of words and idioms, and a use of proper conventional language, grow more exact. There is sometimes a use of stock terms which need not be 'insincere', but an attempt to discover one's own language by trying on other people's.

Chapter Twelve

Jimmy, Catherine and John

In this chapter we shall look at the work of three writers, one from each age group.

12.1 Jimmy — aged seven

12.1.1 Jimmy — Narrative — 'the old old man'

> yes butt Ive got the real one
> you swin

So does the 'old old man' with 'grart glueme eyes', referring to a green crystal, taunt Jimmy; so does Jimmy reply with an oath in his story, 'The Meeting':

> I was walking around the East End of London when I met a old old man he looked at me with grart glueme eyes what are you doing here your to late rihgt. come with me he said and he led me into a dark mansion at 11 o'clock I shall leave you youve got to ours at finda green chrystal but if you dont find at 2 1 clock I shall kill you well ok I shall be in a different hiding places I shall be waching you all the time do you no weher it is what of course I don't thats why im asking you haaa OK man o no its 1 o clock I wondere if it is here not it half past 12 ah I found it Its 2 o clock so you found yes I have yes butt ive got the real one you swin I ran home he was never heard of a gan.

On this occasion we feel it permissible to normalize the conventions, even at the risk of distorting the meaning, to bring out some aspects of the piece.

> I was walking around the East End of London when
> I met an old old man.
> He looked at me with great/gloomy eyes 'What are
> you doing here? You're too late.'
> 'Right'
> 'Come with me,' he said, and he led me into a dark mansion. 'At 11 o'clock I shall
> leave you. You've got 2 hours to find a green crystal, but if you don't find it, at
> 2 o'clock I shall kill you.'
> 'Well O.K.'.

'I shall be in different hiding places. I shall be watching you all the time.'
'Do you know where it is?'
'What, of course I don't, that's why I'm asking *you*, heh!'
'O.K. man ...'
'O no, it's 1 o'clock! I wonder if it's here. No ...'
'It's half past 12. Ah, I found it ... It's 2 o'clock ...'
'So you found it'
'Yes I have'
'But I've got the real one!'
'You swine!' I ran home.
He was never heard of again.

Seven year olds conspicuously stick to a chronological organization, and
with it tend to record every detail, significant or not. Jimmy's story is certainly chronological, but he shows the ability to subordinate time to his own
purposes, by jumping from one time to another, until 2 o'clock, concern
about which he has already planted in us. The story is well begun, and
ended – with one of the traditional lines of finality. The jumps in time, the
doubts about which is speech and which is thought-track, and the doubts
about who is speaking (partly a failure of cohesion), indicate that he imperfectly conceives the reader's needs. He is, however, following a literary
mode, presumably a crime story, and is making a notable attempt at it. The
vocabulary has a melodramatic fitness – the 'old old man' with 'great gloomy
eyes' for instance (S1.1, S2.2, S3.4, S4.1, S5.2, S6.3, SN7.3).

Other features of Jimmy's story which mark it out from those of the
others in his group are the characterization and the emotion. Not only is the
old man described, but his words are given, revealing a particularly nasty
nature – he sets the boy under threat of death to find an object which presumably he already has. The sense of threat in the boy being taken to the
mansion late at night, and set an impossible task, with the old man watching
him from unknown vantage points ('I shall be in different hiding places. I
shall be waching you all the time'), is well conveyed. A seedy context (East
End, dark mansion) is provided (A1.1, A2.2, A3.1, A4.3, A5.3).

The story is a melodrama. As one would expect the characters are judged
by their physical attributes; that old men are bad is implicit in the description
of the protagonist (M1). Heteronomy emerges in the final sentences – the old
man 'was never heard of again' probably implies that he got his just deserts
for being a crook (M1.2).

Viewed for its cognitive elements Jimmy's story would come largely into
our 'describing' category, as of course would much narrative anyway. The
'old old man' is labelled rather than named (C1.1). Spatial and temporal
markers appear in the first sentence, so he begins in narrative reporting (C1.5).

From then on there is dialogue with a time sequence (C1.4) which is a little confused: strictly, 1 o'clock not 2 o'clock should be the crucial time. At the end the writer returns to narrative reporting (C1.5). There is however over and above the reporting a hint of evaluation (C3.3) — old men disappear if they threaten young boys.

In conversation Jimmy said that he got the idea from the photograph which he interpreted as an old man talking to a younger one. The main theme seems to have come from his reading at that time, Roald Dahl's *James and the Giant Peach*, and from the extended study of salt crystals which was the current science topic and which, according to the teacher, fascinated the children. Hence the mysterious use of the 'green chrystal' in the story. Jimmy said that he had the feeling that East London was a 'mucky' place, and that is why he set the adventure there.

12.1.2 Jimmy — Autobiography — 'the yougust rugb player'
Jimmy told us about the incident which forms the subject of his writing. A couple of years before, his brother woke him up in the middle of the night and told him his idea — to write to Roy Castle, who compered a TV talk show, to ask if Jimmy had been the youngest rugby player in Britain. Both boys were very excited at the idea, and when Jimmy was asked to write about his happiest day this incident 'came into his head'.

> The happeust day of my lif was whan my brother sent a lettre to roy castle to see if I was the yougust rugb player in england. I sarted at 2 and a half for under 8's for Oxford rugby club roy wroite back and said I dont no about yoar brother being the yougst rugby player in England.

It is very interesting to note Jimmy's obvious excitement at the incident expressed to us in conversation, remembered for over two years, in contrast to the matter of fact nature of the writing. As we have indicated children's resources to mediate feeling in the written mode are limited at this age. The only expression of feeling is the expected one in the first sentence picked up from the title. Nor are the similar feelings of Jimmy's brother included. Roy Castle's words are, however, quoted — in fact, judging by 'The Meeting', quotation is one of Jimmy's strengths. Adequate information is given the reader to understand the small incident (the explanation about his experience at Oxford). Beyond this, explanation is lacking — there is no attempt to interpret the event (A1.2, A2.1, A3.2, A4.1, A5.2). Cognitively the piece as a whole is at the reporting level (C1.5). There is no explicit moral dimension, though the worship of a hero figure is a hint of the heteronomy of childhood.

In a short composition (it is one of the shorter ones in the group) problems of organization are less likely to arise. Nevertheless what there is is well structured. The first sentence is a sort of abstract, the second elaborates, breaking the time sequence by retrospection, and the third gives the result without, as we have seen, evaluation. The piece is cohesive — thus 'wrote back' in the last sentence refers back to 'sent a letter' in the first, for instance. The syntax is surprisingly complex — a noun clause complement in the first sentence has a further noun clause subordinated by an infinitive. The register is moving towards the written mode: Jimmy is able to start sentences directly with the subject, rather than linking them with 'and'. The reader is given appropriate explanations — the reason for the letter, the explanation of the possibility of his being the youngest. The piece is short but coherent, with sufficient contextualization to be effective though it shows realization of the event as an experience rather than a report. (S1.2/3, S2.1, S3.2/3, S4.1, S5.2, S6.2, SA7.2).

12.1.3 Jimmy — Argument — 'wok onely in the morning!'

'I wolud like wok onely in the morning', writes Jimmy. In conversation he expressed some doubts about whether his teacher would approve of his scheme to have every school afternoon for games and sports — but he has decided to tell him anyway.

> *School*
>
> I think school is nice because thurday is my best day because we have drama and in the afetre noon we have p e. I wuode like to come in Monday Wednesday thursay firday are my very very best days in school I wolud like wok onely inthe morning.

This writing task imposes a heavy cognitive load. Naturally seven year olds like Jimmy can perform it only incompletely. He begins with an assessment (C2.3), 'I think school is nice', for which he offers an egocentric circumstantial reason (C2.1). The rest of the piece is taken up with simply naming the days of the week he enjoys coming to school (C1.2). Finally he states a preference without reasons (though we know he has them). The piece is characteristic of those of the seven year olds in that he can cite one egocentric reason for an opinion, but he cannot argue a case. He does not explore the issues in terms of the implications for others — parents, teachers, pupils. The overall coherence rates C1.3 as it gives partial information. Personal preference is asserted, and slightly evaluated ('My very very best days') (A1.2), but there is no sense of other people. The basis of judgement, what pleases self, is also elementary in moral terms.

Stylistically there is a 'chaining' organization — items follow without chronological or logical connection or order. There is no conclusion, reference back or summation. There is lexical cohesion by repetition, 'I', 'we', 'school', and one appropriate, one inappropriate use of 'because'. The absence of references back and of connectives between sentences indicates a reason for the disconnected structure. Syntax is apparently complex in the first sentence — main clause, noun clause object, with two further levels of subordination as reason clauses. But this is misleading. Syntax is complex but thought is confused. Verbal competence is restricted — 'onely' being perhaps the only word which helps to define meaning. The register is very much that of the spoken language. The reader may well not understand from Jimmy's last sentence that he does not wish to go home but to have sports and games. To begin to meet the terms of the question the task demands some kind of discursive style, some generalization, exemplification, sequence, balancing, rather than personal statement and assertion (S1.1/2, S2.1, S3.2, S4.1, S5.2, S6.1, SP7.1).

12.1.4 Jimmy — Explanation — '2 teams to kick'

Jimmy is very keen on sport. As we have seen he believes that every school afternoon should be devoted to it. Here is his response to the 'How to play . . .' task:

> *Subbetea Football*
> You need a pitch and goals and you need 2 teams to kick of have to players
> to flick and if they miss the ball the other one has his but if the players do it more
> than three times it is a free kick and if the player flicks and flicks another player
> over it is a free kick and if the first one up to ten wins.

Clearly this task is not in the moral or affective dimension but in the cognitive. Jimmy names (C1.2) appropriately: 'goals', 'teams', 'players'. He begins with a concrete list of ingredients for playing the game. He does specify some rules; for example, 'if the players do it [flick] more than 3 times it is a free kick'. 'if the player flicks and flicks another player over it is a free kick' (C2.1). He gives a rule summary for the ending: 'The first one up to ten wins. (C3.2). One wonders, however, what he means by 'one' — a person or the team? He begins by mentioning football as a team game, but by the end we are not sure. He gives explanations and the rule summary within an overall chronology. From the context he needs to specify that the scoring system relates to goal kicking. Here it appears to relate to 'flicking'. Nevertheless, the explanation of this rather complicated game is quite advanced for a seven year old, even though he forgets initially to mention the football, does not give spatial markers of the pitch, and fails to elaborate the context fully for the reader. He has some idea of the game as a system, but the piece reflects his as yet egocentric stance. His overall approach rates C1.3 in cognitive expression.

Stylistic organization is of course particularly related to cognitive organization in a piece of this kind. Jimmy does not try to make it into narrative as do some at this age, but states some of the *desiderata*, followed by some of the rules, and concludes with the way of winning, which is simple but incomplete, (there is no reference to scoring goals for instance). There are problems of cohesion. There is lexical cohesion by the repetition of 'flick' but this is confusing because earlier on 'kick' is used. The sequence 'to players', 'they', 'the other one', 'the players', etc. is similarly bewildering. And so on. A variety of syntax is presented in one long chaining sentence such as is common with children of this age: it includes three conditional clauses which, formally, are correctly used, but not completely clear for other reasons. Verbal competence is limited in this piece — although technical vocabulary is used ('free kick', 'flick', 'up to ten') the meaning is in doubt. Expressions like 'if they miss the ball the other one has his' are imprecise. The general looseness means together with the spoken idiom that the language is not very appropriate for this task. There is clearly an attempt to organize the material, but the imprecision, and lack of certain information make it only moderately effective, in no small measure due to the difficulty of the task (S1.1/2, S2.1, S3.2, S4.1, S5.2, S6.1, SE7.1).

12.1.5 Jimmy — Comment

Jimmy can write a story rather longer than many by children of his age. It's difficult to tell what's going on in places because spelling, punctuation and arrangement tend to be idiosyncratic, some links and explanations are left out, and in general his sense of what the reader needs to know is restricted. Even so the story is exciting, the main character, 'an old old man with grart glueme eyes' is sinister beyond belief and acts from an apparently motiveless malevolence. He is the simple character of melodrama where everyone is either very black or very white. It is usual at this age to write a story in strictly chronological fashion, including unimportant details. Jimmy can jump from one event to the next during the course of a day, leaving out intermediate details. He also, exceptionally, uses a good deal of dialogue which at once aids our realization of the writer's and old man's parts, and furthers the story. Of course dialogue is a way of modifying the strict chronology of 'what next?'. Again, many young children do not give much indication of setting or background: their stories take place in a kind of nowhere. Jimmy gives us some help here — a 'dark mansion' in 'the east end of London'. It is clear that his imagination has been fed by stories he has come across.

The story form is accessible to young children for several reasons, principally because life is a narrative — things happen, followed by other things
happening. As we saw in Chapter Four, the basic form of the sentence is
either narrative or description: 'The cat sits on the mat. The cat is grey.' Very
young children can tell stories in which the only sequence may be chronological — one event follows another without connections other than temporal — 'and then we did this', 'and then we did that' — but they are also aware
very early of the law of cause and effect: 'the dog eats the bone', for
example, is at once an event, and a reason for the bone's disappearance, even
though there is no explicit 'because . . .'. Causal relations often occur, but
between individual events rather than over the whole events of a story.
Jimmy for his age is remarkable in the overall coherence of his narrative.

In his autobiographical writing Jimmy writes rather less fluently than
in his narrative. He was delighted when his brother suggested they wrote to
Roy Castle to ask if he, Jimmy, had been the youngest boy to play rugby
football. But this excitement does not run over in the writing: there is no
attempt at even statements of the feeling by adjectives like 'pleased', 'excited'.
The full resources of the writer are in fact needed to make a factual statement. Whereas in his story the conventional form, and the fact that the story
is actually about fear help him along, in this piece Jimmy has to organize his
own forms, and the excitement is additional to the events. He uses the
chronological narrative, as so many writers of this age do, though he inter-
rupts it to insert an explanation, which is a flash-back, which indicates that
he started rugby at two and a half. For similar reasons presumably — tax on
the writer's resources — he makes no attempt at characterization except that
he quotes the actual words of Roy Castle's letter.

Neither task makes heavy cognitive demands in that what the writer is
doing in both pieces is to record events with little interpretation or evaluation. And in fact narrative, by whatever writer, must essentially operate a
good deal at this level. But when we came to the argumentative writing — as
in the topic set here ('Would it work if children came to school when they
wanted and could do what they liked there?') there is required an ability to
hypothesize and speculate. There are two issues — voluntary attendance,
voluntary choice of subjects. Most of our writers at this age do not notice
the two parts, give an immediate 'yes' or 'no', and then attempt to justify
their choice with reference to their particular school. Jimmy cannot cope at
the argumentative level — he merely lists the days of the week and the
subjects he likes.

Similar difficulties beset Jimmy in explaining how to play a game. Some
children take a narrative line and tell what happens from the beginning.
Jimmy does not do that — instead he takes several rules from the game — a

free kick, for example — selected on a rather arbitrary basis. The result is that we have items of perfectly correct information, but very incomplete inform-ation — aims, apparatus, rules, progress. Jimmy has no means of classifying and detailing these, though he doubtless knows them at a passive level. Partial information is a feature of much writing at this age — partly because of the difficulty of writing it down, partly because the writer doesn't realize it is missing, partly because he doesn't realize the reader will need to know it for comprehension.

12.2 Catherine — aged ten

12.2.1 Catherine — Narrative — 'It Fails'
In her story 'It Fails' Catherine has two boys planning to rob Lloyd's Bank. George objects that the bank is Welsh. David replies:

> So what I'm sure they have English money

This joke delighted Catherine: she discussed it with her teacher before writing. In fact she discussed with a friend her ideas for the story before-hand, as she says she usually does. According to her she got the idea from the bank she saw in the 'No Entry' picture, from thinking about her elder brother, and from her favourite reading, Enid Blyton's 'Famous Five' stories.

It Fails

"Come on brother aren't you hungry"
George ran down the stairs first dropping his hanky and then his
slipper fell off.
"Youre breakfast is in the oven Gorge"
shouted Mum going out of the back door to work.
"What shall we do today David." Ask's Gorge dropping is fork on the
floor. "Well I was thinking.
What about robbinga bank." Answers David.
"Youre joking" says Gorge. "No I am not"
"Well I don't know if we should realy David"
"Don't be an ass" shouts David going and picking up his shoes. "Mum wont know
or are you a coward."
"No I'm not I know we haven't much money but."
Says Gorge "But what. O do hurry up and eat that breakfast" O I'm so sorry."
David ran up stairs and washed. 1 hour later they were getting their coats on.
"Well David which bank are we going to rob if any." "Were going to rob Lloyds
bank" "But that Welsh" "So what I'm shore they have English money." They
caught the bus and went into town as they lived in London it was very busy.
They paid the driver and got of. "Now where do we go now?" asks Gorge "To the
back of the bank." "I dont really know if I should trust you." "O come on

squirt." Answears David walking of. "Wait for me im in this Loot with you."
Shouts Gorge running after him.
It took them 1 hour to get to the back of the bank. When they got there it was
11 o'clock in the morning. "I'm hungry". Conplains Gorge.
"Well you should have fineshed you breakfast."
"Oh be quiet". Mouth David" Says Gorge in a boasting manor. "Look hear's an
apple and be quiet." Do you want the London police after us!" "Look stop
talking to me as if I was a baby." "Well you are." "Oh come on David" "Or
write Gorge I'm coming." They quickly stopped when the saw a sighn.

Do you [NO ENTRY!] think we ought to go in David?" ascked
Gorge "Of course we can baby. You really are a baby
Gorge. I'm not shore if you won't tell anybody about what
were going to do." "Of course I won't I wouldent let you down now would I."
"Well I suppose you wouldent. Come on any way."
They went into the building and looked around. They saw a large door on the
right. They heard a few voices behind the doors "I'm scared David".
"I thought you would be Gorge."
"Hay whats that noise David."

"Your under arrest kids." "Its the police David." "I know Gorge I know."

Catherine is not bound by a strict sequence of events in the way many
younger children are, though there are still signs of the impulse to include
everything — incidents like paying the bus fare, for example, which are unnecessary. What is notable however is the way she can begin *in medias res*,
with a piece of dialogue. There are really two themes — the interaction
between the boys, and the robbing of a bank — both of which are neatly tied
up in the last exchange. The second theme is very much subservient to the
first; revelation of character being far more important than the narration of
unlikely events which are presented with no suspense or anticipation, and fall
a little flat (S3.4). Catherine is in control of suitable cohesive devices. In this
type of narrative, which moves through dialogue, conjunctions are scarce,
lexical cohesion and previous reference quite extensive. It is common with
this story convention that the first sentence should alert us, the second provide a context: 'brother' in the first becomes 'Gorge' in the second. Mum is
introduced by reference to George, and George introduces David. Mention of
'breakfast' allows a reference to 'fork' by lexical collocation: later George is
'hungry' not having finished breakfast. Continuatives — 'well', 'anyway' —
which throw the attention back to the previous statement: ellipsis, giving the
impression of natural dialogue — 'No I'm not', 'I suppose you wouldn't',
and synonyms — 'squirt', 'coward', 'baby' — all add up to a very skilled use of
cohesion (S4.4/5). Syntactically the story does not require complicated
structures, particularly as it is mainly in spoken idiom: it several times uses

the present participle to add action to words, e.g. 'answers David, walking off'
(S1.2/3). The diction and phrasing tend to be stock, largely from the Blyton
model — 'ass', 'squirt'. On one occasion where an exact word is required instead of 'boasting' — ' "Oh be quiet, mouth David" Says Gorge in a boasting
manner', her repertoire does not provide it (S2.2). The language is appropriate to the period Blyton model, taken with a pinch of salt (S6.3). The
reader is kept in touch, but is sometimes confused, about what happens in
the bank and why the boys should at one stage change roles — George becoming dominant and giving David an apple (S5.3). Effective in many ways,
partly from its lightness of touch, the story does not reconcile the two
themes and stops at the climax of the robbery (SN7.3).

Catherine does not express emotion directly in 'It Fails', but shows an
ability to understand it in the characters of the two boys (A2.3/4). They are
consistent (except for the one role change already mentioned), David being
the dominant entrepreneur, George the one with scruples and anxieties. There
is some well chosen detail: David's action in picking up his shoes reinforces
his disagreement with George:

> "Don't be an ass," shouts David going and picking up his shoes.

The writing is of course on the fantasy level (A5.3) written with tongue
nicely in cheek: the reader, as we have seen is carefully considered (A3.3).
The boys are deliberately presented as behaving at two different moral levels,
David from self-indulgence (M1) and George from scruples which David
ascribes to fear (M2). Amusingly David only offers two reasons to George
for not robbing the bank:

> "Mum wont know or are you a coward."

Cognitively the story operates, as so much narrative essentially must do, at
the level of reporting (C1.4/5).

12.2.2 Catherine — Autobiography — 'a small dog walket out'
A TRUE STORY

The Happiest Day of my Life

One morning I woke up to find mum shouting "Helen time to get up," "Okay".
I got dressed and went downstairs. I found mum cooking breakfast. I sat down,
and poured out the cornflakes. "Mum where's the milk." The milk man hasent
been yet. "Drats". I poured the cornflakes back into the packet. Buy the time I
had done that because they cep't on farling out. Mum had placet my breakfast
on the table. It was fried egg on toast the toast was a little burnt. It was
February and today we were going to Exeter, we were going to get my dog that
day. Dad came in with Honey woof went Honey. Then it was time to go. We

got into the car and then were on are way there. When we got there we went into
a room. There was a old lady on the floor scrubbing with a foaming brush. The
floor was covered with newspaper the old lady told us to stand on the newspaper
so we did. Then a man came in he looket at us. "Hellow,". He said he took us
along lots of cells with dogs jumping up at the doors. The rooms were about a
metre wide. Wewent along to a door and the man opened it. A small dog walket
out dad paid the man then we went home we named the dog Petra she was
beatiful.

Basically the organization of this piece of Catherine's resembles that of
her autobiography — a rather long breakfast episode, a journey, and the main
incident dealt with rather briefly. Detail is often unselective. The breakfast,
though interesting, has no necessary relation to the text, and does not anticipate it. In effect there are three parts — breakfast, charlady, dog — with only
consecutive connections: the conclusion, 'she was beautiful' only evaluates
the dog briefly, not the whole day (S3.3). The main cohesive device is 'I',
'We'. The chief limitation is the absence of substituting words: groups are
repeated in close proximity, e.g. 'we were going to Exeter. We were going
to get my dog that day' (S4.2). There is a preponderance of simple clauses
which produces rather a disjointed effect (S1.1), though she can join two
such clauses for emphasis: 'It was February and today we were going to
Exeter'.

Recording of detail, if over-meticulous, is accurate, with an occasional
notable phrase 'scrubbing with a foaming brush', but evaluation of the dog as
'beautiful' is conventional (S2.2). The broad characterization, the varying of
dialogue and narrative, the occasional humorous or whimsical observation at
breakfast, suggest a Blyton model, though 'Woof went Honey' perhaps owes
more to Ladybird (S6.2/3). The reader is taken into account, in fact is given
more information than is necessary (S5.2).

Catherine shows an ability to distance herself from the self at breakfast
time, and to see humour in her own irritation (A1.2/3). Other people in the
story exist as single dimensional, and act in effect as servicing agencies, to
provide breakfast, transport, a dog (A2.1). Circumstantial details fill in the
background — cornflakes, burnt toast, scrubbing lady, newpapers on the
floor (A4.3). The story seems to be an account of matter of fact; the writer
does not do very much in the way of interpretation (A5.2). As narrative the
story comes into the recording category (C1.5).

Particularly interesting in the light of our analysis is Catherine's own view
of the story. She says she 'spread out' the events so that the reader would
know how they had happened to the writer. In other words she does not have
a concept of the kind of coherence whereby the material is organized according to a postulated ideal development — relevant events leading to a climax,

for instance. Instead she wants the verisimilitude of matters of fact — the breakfast, the lady with the scrubbing brush, the dog, given more or less equal status. These she records with detachment.

12.2.3 Catherine — Argument — 'I think its a stupid idea'

Yes: I think it would work. But say the children must come least twice a week. At home most probely there Mums and Dads would give them a task to do each day like one day he or she would have to write a story another day they would have to do some maths and so on. Some of the children mite like going to school. So they mite want to help there Mums and Dads in the garden and house.

No: I don't think it would work the children would not get very good jobs. They would learn to talk in a bad way they wouldn't be able to read or write. I think its a stupid idea. They would say to there mums and Dads ("I going to school".) But realy they would go and play with there friends. If they went to school they would get a good job.

Perhaps Catherine really does think the proposal in the question a bad one. She expresses herself strongly enough, 'I think its a stupid idea' but at least she attempts to argue both sides of the question.

She begins with an assessment: 'Yes I think it would work' (C2.2), but does not explain why. Instead she qualifies her assessment — 'But say the children must come least twice a week'. She then moves on to making inferences about what children could do at home instead. 'At home most probely there Mums and Dads would give them a task to do each day . . .' (C2.2). The sentence beginning 'Some of the children mite like going to school' is a sort of summary inferring the subsequent sentence (C3.2). Catherine does not draw a conclusion from this; she is envisaging children learning at home as a possibility.

Her second attempt at argument begins in the same way with another assessment: 'No, I don't think it would work' (C2.2), 'The children would not get very good jobs . . .', 'They would talk in a bad way and they wouldn't be able to read or write'. She does not demonstrate, however, how these logically follow from the notion of 'coming to school when you like'. She then speculates (C4.2): 'If they went to school they would get a good job'; that is, she raises an inadequate hypothesis since clearly she does not think of the unemployment, or school leavers with or without qualifications.

Catherine proceeds by associations rather than deductions and does not come to an overall conclusion. However, the separating of arguments for and against the one issue represents the beginnings of the capacity to think in a classificatory fashion.

The moral thinking is interesting: the fabric of society represented by school is never seriously threatened. She envisages education as of great value and rather imagines the parents conducting school at home — though there are still some children who would go whether school was compulsory or not. After all school leads to the advantages which society gives — good jobs — the rewards for school attendance. The punishments for non-attendance are illiteracy, talking in a bad way, and presumably unemployment (M2).

The stylistic organization is again closely related to the cognitive. The overall debating style division is clear, but within each paragraph there is a cluster of ideas rather than a development (S3.2). In this type of writing it is helpful for the cohesive devices, such as initiators and conjunctions, to signal the argument. But here the cohesion, such as it is, is mainly provided by 'children' and pronoun equivalents throughout. Neither 'so' nor 'but' really affect the main tendency of the argument (S4.2). Syntax is comparable with the level of argument: at a theoretical level one would expect conditional, concessional, result clauses, antithetical constructions with an adversative like 'but'. Here in fact what children 'would do' or 'might want' forms the chief topic: structures containing these are in a sense conditionals, but all depend on one premise. They are not breaking new ground (S1.2). Language again is fairly restricted. The two words from the realm of mental operations — 'think' and 'idea' do not produce a reflective strain. Adjectives such as 'stupid' and adverbial expressions such as 'in a bad way' lack precision though others such as 'least', 'each day', and 'really' indicate an attempt at clearer definition. There are no sentence initiators and no generalizing statements, merely a few affirmations (S2.2). Clearly the general style is not very appropriate for this type of discourse (S6.1/2). The passage is perfectly comprehensible as it stands, but the information explanation load is not high (S5.2).

An initial discussion in class helped Catherine to organize her ideas and gave her confidence, but she did not really enjoy the writing. Unlike the narrative it was difficult to 'get going'.

12.2.4 Catherine — Explanation — 'How to play Speed'

How to play Speed

You are all dealt 7 cards each. Some of the cards have pictures of animals on them. Some have moter cars or planes other wise trains. The 1st person will put down say a card that has a train on it. Then you will put have to put down a card that has a train on. The first person who has no cards is the winner. Then the people add up the numbers that are on the card. On the animal cards they have 2 lots of numbers. You can get a card called lighting then you put in down when you like and change the subject.

Clearly this piece is not concerned with moral or emotional matters — it would presumably be regarded as a defect if it were. The reader wishes to receive a clear exposition, a cognitive task for the writer.

Cohesion starts with an explanation of the deal of the game: 'You are all dealt 7 cards each' (C2.1). She forgets to tell us how many people can play this game but it is implicit that she sees all games as competitive, 'all' suggesting more than one player. She then gives a description of the equipment required, the card pack: 'Some of the cards have pictures of animals on them, some have motor cars or planes otherwise trains'. She cannot talk about suits of cards but gives concrete names to the pictures (C1.2). Her overall coherence is chronologic (C1.5): 'The first person . . . *then* you will put down a card that has a train on . . .'.

She can summarize a rule for ending the game (C3.2): 'The first person who has no cards is the winner'. After this she continues with the chronological account: 'Then the people add up the numbers that are on the card', but doesn't explain why this is done. The final sentence is out of order. Catherine is attempting to explain the rule for changing suit but she adds it on as an afterthought: 'You can get a card called lighting *then* you can put it down *when* you like and change the subject' (C2.1). Catherine has problems ordering her information. The chronology of the opening leads her into omitting a rule explanation until the end. As far as this piece is concerned Catherine is an example of a 'middle range' ten year old. She can explain two rules but, working from chronological sequencing, she tends to leave out significant aspects of the game.

From the stylistic point of view organization of the piece reflects the cognitive problems mentioned. Catherine typically attempts a narrative organization, but this works only imperfectly because there are aspects of the game — apparatus, and rules particularly — which need to be explained descriptively. Thus the narrative first sentence is properly followed by two descriptive sentences: then however Catherine returns to the narrative and stays with it, so that it gets her to a conclusion before other necessary information has been given (S3.2). The somewhat imprecise character of the piece is reflected in the cohesion: 'all', 'you', '1st person', 'people' are insufficient to act as cohesive or differential referents. One cohesive device is used to rescue what is otherwise a general lack of cohesion — 'on the animal cards' referring back to the second sentence. On the other hand, 'otherwise' in the second sentence is unusually accurate (S4.2). Syntax consists of many simple active sentences with four in succession in the middle containing adjectival clauses (S1.2/3). Competence in expression is limited — the word 'card' constantly recurs; she does not use pronouns, or general terms like 'suit'.

(S2.1). Catherine explains in spoken style as though there is a listener present (S5.2), but there is much such a listener would need to know. Thus such a sentence as the last: 'You can get a card called lighting then you can put it down when you like and change the subject' – is confusing since no subject has been mentioned (S5.2). For reasons indicated the effectiveness of this piece is only moderate (SE7.3).

In writing this Catherine thought how her grandmother had taught her the game and tried to reconstruct the explanation. She found the exercise very difficult and became 'irritated' because she wrote so slowly. She likes her writing to flow.

12.2.5 Catherine – Comment

Catherine is ambitious in her story. She is aware of how such a story 'should' be written – on the Famous Five model – even to the detail of the appropriate slang. This model helps her considerably – she does not need to start with a conventional opening, but with a character speaking, 'Come on brother aren't you hungry?' which at once establishes the relationship of the two characters, and the breakfast scene. Thereafter she follows the events through to the bank robber, but interspersing the action line with conversation: she has some problems with which details to include – insignificant ones like paying the bus driver, for example. She has two themes – breakfast interaction, and the bank robber – and does not work out the relative importance of each. Children of Catherine's age are often capable of quite extended stories, though in our sample we found the longer stories tended not to have their material organized so coherently as some of the shorter ones. On the whole the children write chronologically, though experiments with time sequence, perhaps prompted by a literary model, begin to be possible.

It was the literary model that helped Jimmy to a certain detachment in his story. This is, however, more apparent than real. Basically the seven year olds have an egocentric viewpoint. Jimmy's autobiography, for instance, tells what happens to him, and is too short to offer insights into others, even if Jimmy were thinking that way. Catherine and her peers can be more distanced from people and events, and begin to be able to create character, though it is sometimes stereotyped. Even so the viewpoint is often egocentric: 'I' tends to be the main character in both story and autobiography.

Argumentative writing presents a more difficult task. Children have to deal with the cognitive problems as well as the stylistic organization. Like many in her age group Catherine does not realize the two part nature of the task – choice of attendance, and choice of subjects – and treats them as one, marshalling arguments for and against in distinct paragraphs, but the ideas are rather in heaps than in sequence. Other children tend to take up a single position and put down points to support it, again as separate items rather than a logical arrangement.

The explanation of how to play a game also presents cognitive problems. The writer has to state aim, rules, and procedures, and he has to bear in mind very much how what he writes will appear to a reader who has to play the game. He must thus monitor the effect of his words very carefully. Not surprisingly some children of this age find the task difficult, particularly if the game they have chosen to describe is at all complex. A straight narrative organization is not possible: at the very least it must be interspersed with rules and conditions — if a player does x, then y follows. Catherine chooses a narrative line, but this causes her to exclude much essential information. Whereas children have models for narrative they tend not to have for other tasks, such a argumentative and explanatory. Thus their difficulty with the more impersonal writing tasks, whilst it is partly cognitive, may also be due to a lack of experience of them.

12.3 John — aged thirteen

12.3.1 John — Narrative — 'At five o'clock today . . .'

John chose to write on the picture depicting two small boys peering through a mesh fence with some hovels in the background. His story reads:

As their fingers grasped the wire and their eyes followed the black smoke emitted by the straining train, their memories glided back to the evening three days ago.

Their father had arrived home from work, they had met him at the gate and walked beside him through the courtyard. He lifted them up onto his shoulders, they were laughing grabbing the lapels of his jacket to stay on. They entered the kitchen giggling uncontrollably. Slowly he lowered them onto the floor and kissed the woman who approached them. They put their hands to their mouths in a effort to cover their giggling as the man put his arms around her. He released his grip and wandered back into the hallway where he discarded his jacket. They had delved into their meal before he had returned and taking so much interest in their plates did not see him, but heard him come back into the room. The radio was a background to their parents conversation; but then, they fell silent, the whole room was suddenly cold, the radio was the only life, that moment; "At five o'clock today Britain and France declared war on Germany" the words swirled inide their heads "At five o'clock today Britain and France declared war on Germany."

Tears swelled in their eyes and trickled down their faces, blurred the image of the men in uniform, travelling in that blurred train.

There is remarkable quality of feeling in this piece. The writer's emotion is not stated explicitly; instead feelings of fear, threat, sadness are conveyed through what Eliot calls an 'objective correlative', an artistic form, in this case a story, through which they are mediated: a tragic incident in human history is interpreted imaginatively through the effects it has on a family and particularly through the two small boys (A1.5, A5.5). The children are delighted when their father arrives home from work and have one of the uncontrollable giggling fits of young children which is in ironic contrast to the political background. The emotions of the man and the children are skilfully conveyed by their actions — the gentleness of the man in 'lowering' the children and in embracing his wife, the children's attempt to stifle their giggling, their change of mood as they become preoccupied with eating (A2.3). There is a very skilled use of environmental detail, particularly the train: although 'grasped the wire' is unexplained and from one point of view needs reference to the picture, from another it does not — one may infer that it is a fence, but its very ambiguity helps to create atmosphere (A4.4).

There is a sense of style in the piece — a sense on the part of the writer that he is making an elegant whole. It is a very effective report (C1.5) with circular structure in which the end remembers the beginning; but with the addition of the telling detail of the troops. The flashback technique is employed in the body of the story, arranged chronologically with telling detail subordinate to the main design (S3.5). The main functional cohesive device is pronoun reference whereby 'he' and 'they' stand for the man and the boys throughout; but there is notable use of cohesion for artistic purpose, whereby 'blurred train' in the last sentence refers back to the 'blurred' image of the men; and also to 'straining train' in the first sentence (S4.5). Syntax is a matter of choice for the writer. The long opening sentence — two time clauses before the main clause — fills in the background. In contrast when there is the tension of the announcement of war there is a series of simple clauses: 'they fell silent, the whole room was suddenly cold, the radio was the only life, that moment' (S1.5). There is a good use of standard language — 'giggling uncontrollably', 'discarded his jacket' — but also an accuracy for specific effects — 'straining train', 'the words swirled'. It could be that in parts the emotion is a little over-written — 'tears swelled in their eyes and trickled down their faces' but elsewhere there is an impressive economy as in the complements used to lead up to the announcement — 'silent', 'cold', 'only life' (S2.3). There is clear awareness of the type of writing considered appropriate — concise, suspense-maintaining — as in for instance *The Silver Sword*, and John handles it confidently (S6.5), and — a confidence in dealing with the reader — the whole structure is an exploitation of the reader's need to have certain information if he is to decode the opening sentence (S5.5). All this adds up to a very effective piece (SN7.5), particularly in terms of the precious family group (M3) being threatened by war.

In discussion John confirmed the feeling that the story gives that it was consciously wrought. He said he had the beginning and ending of the story in mind before he wrote, but wasn't sure how he was going to develop the middle section. The repetition of the radio announcement was intentional; as John put it: 'The reader wouldn't know, it wouldn't make sense,' an indication that he realized that establishing the context of war was an important means of putting the children's behaviour in perspective. When asked *where* the children were in 'As their fingers grasped the wire and their eyes followed the black smoke . . .' John said he envisaged the picture as representing the backyard of the children's home overlooking a railway siding, but that he suppressed details of place because 'that would give away too much at the beginning'. John is aware of keeping an audience in suspense, of manipulating details for effect. When asked why he didn't give the children names, he said that he wanted them to be representative of any children disturbed by war. His writing here is very much modelled on literary examples, rather than on direct experience. He is exploring vicariously the world of separation and loss caused by war, focusing on action and feeling rather than characterization. An interesting comment from John's teacher — John, unlike most boys in his class, still enjoys writing stories, which is more characteristic of girls in the age group.

12.3.2 John — Autobiography — 'I can't have looked very pretty'
John's autobiographical narrative is based on a real experience. He entitles it 'The Worst Experience I have ever had':

> Being lost is an experience which one does not like to encounter frequently. Being lost when nobody finds you is worse. It was during our holidays in South Devon, when we were out for the day, when it started. I had decided to walk from the car, intending to be picked up later. Naturally, I took the turning from which we had come, the car however didn't. I began to feel a little uneasy as the time passed, and the tall hedges produced wild thoughts in my mind. Drizzle floated to the ground.

> I'm not sure how far I walked that evening, it seemed miles I had cut across fields and had become wet. On reaching a house, I knocked on the door, for by this time I was very worried. When it was answered I asked the way to the town at which we were staying. I was offered a lift and accepted it gratefully. (The next part I cannot remember).

> I do remember regaining consciousness and peering through a smashed windscreen at a crowd gathered outside. I kept perfectly still, least any bone should be

broken. I vaguely remember the journey in an ambulance and the kindness of
the ambulance men. My mother and father were at the hospital. Mother looked
relieved yet shocked at the same time. (I can't have looked very pretty).

My shoulder was very painful, but the cuts on my face were numb. After being
x-rayed I had my cuts stiched (very painful). I was in hospital for the rest of our
holiday.

John's autobiographical narrative is an example of highly competent
narrative reporting (C1.5, SN7.5). He gives both spatial and chronological
details of the experience he is describing, names (C1.2) the area in which the
accident happened, 'South Devon', gives spatial markers, 'Naturally I took the
turning from which we had come, the car, however, didn't'. He puts events
in a time order, in the process allowing for the passage of time, though this
is only implied in 'I'm not sure how far I walked that evening, it seemed
miles'. The chronology is in fact quite complex. He flashes forward, 'The next
part I cannot remember', after purposefully drawing out and elaborating
slowly the sequence of events which relates to being lost. Time is collapsed
in the penultimate paragraph — the journey to hospital, the appearance of
parents, and his being attended to for injuries are raced over in a series of
statements which suggest time passing rapidly. He is using the time sequence
to reflect the way the mind works when faced with an emergency. This is a
far cry from the simple chronological 'then . . . then . . . when' sequencing
of the younger children's narratives. He does not attempt to reconstruct what
he cannot remember, but leaves the gap for the reader to make the assumption that something drastic must have occurred. Within this sophisticated
reporting sequence, he offers explanations and interpretations of events: 'for
by this time I was very worried' (C2.1); and makes inferences for the reader
(C2.2): 'i can't have looked very pretty'. A term like 'naturally' (sentence
five) assumes a certain rapport with the reader — it implies that he is understanding of the situation: as does the use of 'you' (second sentence). The
most advanced feature of this piece of reporting is however its generalized
introduction. He begins with an overall evaluation (C3.3) of the meaning of
the experience 'Being lost is an experience which one does not like to encounter frequently. Being lost when nobody finds you is worse'. He does not
begin with concrete description and move to generalization; he begins with
generalization and moves back into concrete detail. The effect of this is that
the reported anecdote acts as an explanation of the generalization given at the
outset; the result is a tightly structured and organized narrative report, in
which nothing irrelevant intrudes, though the ending is abrupt (S3.5).

Other aspects of style contribute to the general effect. There is often an
ability to select syntax to support the meaning. This is apparent particularly

in the first two paragraphs: for instance, the crucial fact that the car turned in another direction, thus losing John, is recorded in a laconic simple sentence — 'the car however didn't'. Short sentences in paragraphs three, four and five however are less functional and could be due to pressure of some kind on the writer. The conclusion is a little sudden (S1.4). Cohesive devices are skilled — the repetition of 'Being lost' in the first two sentences to introduce a statement and a comment upon it, for example (S4.5). There is a good use of standard language forms — 'feel a little uneasy', 'accepted it gratefully' — together with less usual collocations — 'relieved yet shocked' (S6.5).

John's concern is to state his individual experience. The opening sentences, however, at once provide a context and an evaluation in that they indicate he recognizes the universality of feelings of loss (A1.2). He can look on himself as though from outside and plot the development of his feelings — he is first 'a little uneasy' and later becomes very worried (A1.4). He is conscious of how he must appear to others — 'I can't have looked very pretty' (A1.3). Other people's feelings are not the principal concern of the writing: even so he catches the complexity of his mother's emotions when she sees him in hospital: 'Mother looked relieved yet shocked at the same time' (A2.3). One feature of the writing is the way he interrelates landscape and emotions — the tall hedges and drizzle produce 'wild thoughts', the long walk across wet fields parallels his becoming 'very worried' (A4.3).

The moral attitudes in this piece are implied not stated. The writer explores the effects his accident has on those close to him in his environment. The ambulance men are judged as well intentioned in terms of their social role. John is concerned at worrying the family group, particularly his mother. He does not blame his parents for driving off in the wrong direction. Parents are judged as well-intentioned and concerned and judgements are thus conventional (M3).

John said he enjoyed writing the story. It was redrafted in part. The beginning came easily; he liked it and he did not feel the need to change it. But the section on the walk through the lanes was altered in writing a fair copy to make the event seem longer — he wanted the words to move as slowly as the experience had felt slow. The indications that the end of the piece is not on a par with the beginning find support in John's comments. He admits to being embarrassed about writing down his physical injuries and said he used parentheses in this section as an ironic relief from the other details, 'People don't want to hear how hurt you are'. The 'rest of our holiday' seems to mean a long time in hospital — the implication the reader tends to draw — but this was apparently only two days. When he was then asked whether he intended to give an impression of a severe result of his accident he said he just wanted to finish off the piece quickly.

The flash-forward from the statement 'The next part I cannot remember' he saw as being successfully managed by the inclusion of the aside to a reader. When asked whether he could have accomplished this by more explanation, he said he wanted the next section to come as a shock and was conscious of withholding full information so that the reader would guess something awful had happened. All his comments about the writing of this piece reveal a student confident in writing for an outside audience, aware of written conventions and beginning to exploit them for effect.

12.3.3 John – Argument – 'The present system . . . works well'
John's response to the topic 'Would it work if children came to school when they liked and did what they liked there?' reads as follows:

> I think the present system of schooling works well compared to what I think the one suggested would turn out like in practice. My main reason for thinking this is that I believe children who could have a choice of going to school or not, would not go, most of them if not all. The idea of learning, sitting and working whilst they could be doing practically anything they wanted seems stupid. There would be a few children who would realise the importance of going to school, and a few whose parents would insist upon it. The children may become interested if they could choose which subjects they wished to do, but the, surely, it would defeat the idea of going to school. The aim of the school must be to give its pupils an understanding of the things around him, a basis to a job and help to communicate with each other. If a pupil was to have a choice of subjects e.g. he may choose to learn about motor mechanics as he is interested in motors, then he would not (unless he wanted to) learn the basic subjects e.g. Maths, English, etc. With the present system he may not be able to learn about motor mechanics in school, but once he has learnt how to read he can find a book about it and teach himself (which would probably be more satisfaction giving). When he was eventually to leave school what chance would he have of getting a job? Thousands of boy had learnt about motor mechanics. Which children would learn about politics and economics, who were capable of running the country? The society would soon change to anarchy.

John tackled the explanatory task with confidence, as we shall see, but he had difficulty in organizing the argumentative task coherently. He begins with an overall evaluation (C3.3) of the two suggestions contained in the topic: 'I think the present system of schooling works well compared to what I think the one suggested would turn out like in practice' but this is not as well articulated as the generalizations he managed at the opening of his two previous pieces of writing. He is, however, responding to the full implications of the topic, as his use of the word 'system' implies. He goes on to explain why he thinks optional school attendance would not work (C2.1), 'My main reason for thinking this is that I believe children who could have a choice of going to school or not, would not go, most of them if not all.' He then goes on to qualify his reason, by drawing inferences about children's and parents' reactions (C2.2), 'There would be a few children who would realize the importance of school, and a few whose parents would insist upon it'. At this point, rather than drawing an explicit conclusion on the topic of optional school attendance he changes gear and moves on to a consideration of the second part of the question, student choice of school activities. He slides from one issue to the other without making explicit the logical connections between ideas or the conclusions he is drawing from them, though it is obvious from the context that he is arguing against optional school attendance. He leaves this implicit rather than stating it directly. His argument against choice of school subjects is argued more explicitly. He begins with an adequate hypothesis (C4.3), 'children may become interested if they could choose which subjects they wished', draws another qualifying inference (C2.2), 'but then, surely, this would defeat the idea of going to school'. He then gives an overall evaluation of the purpose of schools (C3.3), 'The aim of the school must be to give its pupils an understanding of the things around him' and uses a concrete example of a child selecting motor mechanics as his only subject to illustrate that the aims of schooling would not be met in this instance (C2.2) 'If a pupil was to have a choice of subjects e.g. he might learn about motor mechanics . . . then he would not learn the basic subjects e.g. Maths, English'. He then goes on to conclude (C3.4) on the logical alternative to this view, 'With the present system he may not be able to learn about motor mechanics, but once he has learnt how to read, he can find a book about it and teach himself'. Having raised the example he moves in his final paragraph to exploring the implications by raising hypothetical if not rhetorical questions (C4.4), 'When he was eventually to leave school what chance would he have of getting a job? . . . which children would learn about politics and economics, who were capable of running the country?' These speculative questions lead John to a reflection (C3.5), 'The society would soon change to anarchy,' a reflection perhaps rather extreme for the evidence he has marshalled, though a fitting concluding sentence with the weight of rhetoric behind it. Overall John's argumentative piece indicates that he can speculate, he can raise appropriate questions, he can generalize, he can explain and draw inferences from generalizations, but that he does so in a loosely organized fashion. His attempt at discussion of both parts of the question is the *beginnings* of classificatory thinking (C3.6) as his means of cohering;

however, his logic is not always as fully explicit as we would expect in tightly organized classificatory writing.

The concern John expresses for the smooth running of society in the final sentence of his argument, 'The society would soon change to anarchy' is the main example of explicit moral judgement in this piece. It reveals a conformist orientation in his thinking, a concern for law and order and social equilibrium which he thinks would be disturbed by changes to the school system. This is an example of M4 — a judgement of self—others in terms of conventional norms/rules. His concern is for the rule-based nature of society to continue. 'Anarchy' is bad by definition.

John's style in this writing is less assured than in other tasks. The syntax of the opening sentence is clumsy. The second: 'my main reason for thinking this is that I believe children who could have a choice of going to school or not, would not go, most of them if not all', with its cumbersome modifying phrase, seems to have been started before being properly thought out. The third sentence lacks a subject to which 'they', the pronoun in the subordinate time clause, could relate. John, however, has a clear grasp of complex sentence structures and uses adjectival clauses effectively. He demonstrates ability to rearrange the sentence for emphasis as in : 'with the present system he may not be able to learn . . .'. In his last paragraph he effectively juxtaposes statement with question (overall S1.4). The organization of the piece is fairly clear (S3.4) with its introduction, elaboration and its difficult conclusion. The paragraphing, however, does not follow the pattern of ideas. The second paragraph should begin with 'The children may become interested if they could choose . . .' for this is where John raises his second issue, of which 'The aim of education . . .' is the topic sentence. The final sentence in the paragraph is an effective summing up. John gives plenty of signals for the reader, 'My main reason . . .', 'The idea of . . .', 'but then surely . . .', and involves his reader by questioning in the final paragraph (S3.4) directly addressing him. The piece is couched in a largely impersonal register with emphasis on logical form, though occasionally the personal pronoun intrudes: 'I think . . .', 'I believe . . .' John makes appropriate use of nominal phrases to add weight to his argument, 'the present system', 'my main reason', 'the aim of the school' (S6.4). But there are such discrepancies as 'what I think the one suggested would turn out like in practice', 'most of them, if not all', 'seems stupid'. Such phrases are close to speech; one could argue that since the audience for the task was John's 'peer group', such informality is appropriate as a means of appealing to an audience. The imbalance between the formality of such abstract terms as 'system', 'reason', 'anarchy' and colloquial ones 'seems stupid', leads us to rate appropriateness at S6.3. Again John is able to employ a range of *cohesive* devices, but with more lapses than on previous tasks (S4.4). Pronoun reference is handled competently, except for one occasion in which concord is broken as in 'its pupils and understanding of the things around *him*'. John employs superordinate terms, 'reason' and 'idea', categorically. There is some effective parallelism in: 'the *aim* of the school must be to give its pupils an *understanding* . . . a *basis* for a job and help to communicate . . .' There are few problems with verbal competence. John's definition of the aim of school is a good attempt at nominalizing; he employs weighty abstract terms, such as 'society', 'anarchy', 'system'; and gives helpful conjunctive ties such as the adversative 'but then'. 'Stupid' seems inappropriate and imprecise in context just as the repetition of 'a few' in the sentence beginning 'There would be few children . . . a few whose parents would insist . . .' is unnecessary. Hence S2.4. In overall effectiveness we rated this argument at SP7.3.

The foregoing analysis of John's argumentative piece indicates that on the cognitive and stylistic dimensions John achieves less well than on the explanatory task. The point must be made, however, that argumentative writing is difficult — not only must the writer make the logical connections between his ideas explicit, but he must also decentre enough to counter objections to his point of view as a strategy for convincing his audience that he has the right to make his assertions. The complex interrelationship between writer, reader and topic under discussion creates problems. Our analysis indicated that this piece of writing was not as carefully constructed as the previous ones. John told us that he had indeed written it quickly, but that it took 'quite a bit of thought'. He was particularly pleased with his final sentence, and said that he had thought out the general direction of his argument as moving from the effects on the child to the effects on society at large. He wrote the argument in class, then took it home for his parents to disagree with his views, so that he could hear the positive case in order to counter it. Apparently his parents agreed that 'it wouldn't work', so he saw no reason to change what he had written. What we have is a 'fair copy' rather than an edited version: 'Mum helped with the spelling, but she wouldn't disagree with me'. He felt that the writing task was difficult because 'You have to get your facts right'. John understands the conventions of the discursive mode, and has some notion of rhetorical strategy. He raised questions in his final paragraph to encourage any reader to agree with him. His readership, despite the colloquialisms apparent in the piece, was a 'wider public'. He used his parents as a sounding board to confirm his sense of audience.

12.3.4 John – Explanation – 'First I will define'

John's response to the invitation to describe a game to a non-expert was again one of the better responses at 13+. He took the task seriously and wrote at considerable length. His account of the card game Canasta is very long and detailed, so we only quote the first third here:

Canasta

This card game to me is better than most and almost equals bridge. It differs from other games as two packs of cards are used. The game can be played with two, three or four players. The rules are slightly different for each.

First I will define some of the terms used.

The Pack

Canasta is played with two pack of 52 cards, with four jokers added. The jokers and eight two's are called wild, that is they can be used as cards of any denomination. The values of the cards are as follows:

Jokers	= 50 points each
2's	= 20 points each
Aces	= 20 points each
K, Q, J, 10, 9, 8	= 10 points each
7, 6, 5, 4, black 3's	= 5 points each

red threes count as one hundred, if all four three's are held by one partnership, the score is 800.

The Meld

A meld is three or more cards of the same number. A player melds by withdrawing three or more cards from his hand and laying them on the table. One wild card can be used in conjunction with two cards of the same number, e.g. 10, 10, 10 and 10, 10, 2 are valid melds but 10, 2, 2 is not. No meld can contain more than three wild cards. Partners may add to one another's melds.

Red three are never melded: but are put down on the on the table and another card is taken from the pack as a replacement. Black threes can only be melded at the end of a hand when a players is going out, and then no wild cards can be used. Wild cards cannot be melded with one another.

Making a Canasta

The main object of the game is to meld seven cards of a kind. This is called a canasta and carries a very high score. A canasta may be natural or mixed, red or black. A natural canasta contains no wild cards and has a value of 500 points. A mixed contains wild cards is worth 300 points. The be a valid canasta it must have a base of four natural cards. When a canasta has been made it is folded up and if mixed a black card is put on top. Any other cards of the same number (or wild cards) may be added.

John can organize his writing in a classificatory fashion, rather than remaining tied to chronology. He begins by giving the reader generalized information about the game, rather than starting 'First you pick the players . . .' as most of the children at ten do. His first sentence, 'This card game to me is better than most and almost equals bridge', is an overall evaluation (C3.3) to which he adds a further reflection, 'It differs from the other card games as two packs are used' (C3.5) and then offers an explanation (C2.1), 'The game can be played with two, three or four players'. He then summarizes (C3.2), 'The rules are slightly different for each'. His opening paragraph makes it clear that he sees games as systems, not as instances of spontaneous behaviour as do younger children. He then proceeds to classify (C3.6) information that the reader needs – his subtitles for paragraphs 'The Pack', 'The Meld', 'Making a Canasta', 'How the Game is Played', 'Making the First Meld' – indicate that he is classifying information in a logical rather than chronological order. Within this classification of information explanations of terms in the game are offered (C2.1), 'The jokers and eight two's are called wild, that is they can be used as cards of any denomination'. When he summarizes rules (C3.2), 'One wild card can be used in conjunction with two cards of the same number' he follows the rule summary with a concrete explanation (C2.1):

> e.g. 10, 10, 10 and 10, 10, 2 are valid melds but 10, 2, 2, is not.

He leaves the exceptions to the general rules for 'melding' until the end of this section in a series of rule summaries (C3.2's), 'Red threes are never melded . . .', 'Black threes can only be melded at the end of a hand', 'Wild cards cannot be melded with one another'. In the section entitled 'Making a Canasta' he gives an overall evaluation of the game's purpose (C3.3), 'The main object of the game is to meld seven cards of a kind', then goes on to elaborate on the distinction between *types* of Canastas after a summary (C3.2), 'A canasta may be natural or mixed, red or black'. His explanations (C2.1s) are succinct: 'A natural canasta contains no wild cards and has a value of 500 points. A mixed contains wild cards is worth 300 points'. He gives lists for values of cards and scores for hands in descending and ascending order of value – again a classificatory thinker at work. His way of proceeding is to generalize, then give concrete explanations. Again, a reflection on tactics (C3.5), 'The majority of players set themselves to capturing the pack in the early stages of the game', is followed by (C2.1), 'That is pick up the pile that contains the discarded cards'. Later on, beyond the section quoted here, we get examples of, for instance, hypothetical thinking (C4.3), 'suppose you drew a 9, you would discard one of your loose cards, probably a low card but not, for the moment, the three'.

In the section quoted there is no narrative. Later there are occasional brief sections resembling narrative; but effectively they are rather statements of principle:

> The pack is cut for partners: the people with the highest cards are partners: the first deal is made by the person in front of the one with the highest card.

As we see a variety of organizing principles is used — basically analysis in sections, within which John might, for example, define and then demonstrate, illustrate quality, as in the first paragraph of The Meld. Clearly this is to be rated highly (S3.6). There is strong lexical cohesion in the repetition of technical terms, 'game', 'card', 'joker', 'pack', 'face up', but the range of cohesive devices is also used with confidence: for instance in the first sentence ellipsis ('than most'), substitution ('this card game differs') and 'each' ('two three or four players') (S4.4).

John's *syntax* is highly developed (S1.5). He uses a wide variety of syntactic structures with confidence. Complex sentences are constructed lucidly and participles and infinitives are employed to maintain proper relations within sentences: 'If with hand X you R–O discarded a King or a 5, then having a natural pair to match the discard and the count for the meld you can pick up the pack and make your first meld'. He makes much use of the '–ing' participle preceded by a preposition, 'A player melds by withdrawing three or more cards from his hand and laying them on the table'. Both here and generally he uses modifying and elaborating phrases effectively: 'Before a side has made its first meld a player can pick up the pack when he has a natural pair matching the last card by his R–O, together with the count required to meld'. John rearranges sentence units to avoid monotony, 'With the hand we are considering, you could meld . . .', 'the rest of the pack you take in your hand . . .', 'the remainder he puts in a pile . . .'. Balance and antithesis are achieved as in 'once a side has melded it can take the pack *not only* with a natural pair *but also* with one matching card'. The syntax is controlled, sentences varying according to semantic needs.

An interesting feature of the writing is at once the awareness of an accurate technical vocabulary (S2.5), used appropriately (S6.5) together with an awareness of the reader's need to understand (S5.4) so that there is a constant movement between statement and explanation: a word once explained is assumed to become part of the reader's vocabulary and is used for further explanation.

John's account of Canasta is so assured that we naturally wondered whether it was simply a copy from the instruction manual — a legitimate possibility since we had not sought to disturb normal classroom conditions for writing. He explained that he chose to write about Canasta because he had difficulty explaining the game to his sister two evenings before the task was set in class. He was originally going to write on basketball, a game he enjoys, but chose Canasta because the rules were fresh in his mind, having had the experience of an oral attempt at the task which arose directly from personal experience. In prompting his sister to remember the rules, he clarified the rules for himself. The rule about making the first meld with a score of fifty he actually forgot in playing with his sister but remembered it as the actual game proceeded. This rule takes primacy of place in his written account of the game. His family did not possess a rule book for card games, but he had an idea of how they were laid out from having seen one belonging to a friend. When asked whether he wrote his account under sub-headings imitating rule book format his answer was surprising: 'No, I did it the way my friend taught me.' He put down some cards and said 'That's a meld. That's a canasta' and it worked. John appears to have worked from memory of the way he was taught to play and the problems he encountered when teaching his sister. When asked whether, in writing, he had his sister in mind as the reader he said, 'To myself and my sister I was explaining it more simply'. His chief concern with writing the account, was 'to get it right'. He was interested in the task and saw it as a challenge, writing for 'anyone who wants to learn it'. When asked whether he wrote in this fashion in any other of his subjects at school, using sub-headings and examples, he said that Geography was the subject which had taught him how to do that. John wrote the account himself over two hours, and he found it an intellectual challenge but 'it got tedious after a while'. He had models of discursive writing at the classificatory level from which to draw from his school and home environment, but he drew upon memory of these models and did not copy. John's account is a reminder that if students are asked to write on subjects close to their direct, first-hand experience and to assume the role of an expert in a *real* sense, they write well and with confidence. John took on the task and made it his own, finishing it, despite it taking so long, for his own satisfaction.

12.3.5 John — Comment
The main point to emerge from an analysis of John's writing at 13+ is that he is not tied to the personal or the narrative but he has a clear idea of form and function. He knows the conventions and content considered appropriate in various modes of writing; expressions of affect, for instance, do not occur in his impersonal writing. In the personal writings he does not merely record simple emotions. His emotion in the narrative is mediated and objective in terms of a story about the outbreak of war; the characters are realized in

outline, and perhaps John would have difficulty with detail, but that is not the object of this particular piece. In his autobiographic writing he shows an ability to look back on his past life and to comment on himself objectively. Many writers, particularly younger ones, find this difficult.

In the tasks requiring more advanced cognitive skills John can operate on a level beyond anything the ten year olds can attain to. He demonstrates that he can analyse material, can generalize, draw inferences and make hypotheses which are relevant. He can write in classificatory fashion and is not tied to narrative as his chief means of organizing experience into words. Within his narratives he handles more complex forms of organization than a simple chronology; he uses flashbacks and time disjunctions effectively. He also generalizes within narrative. His argumentative task indicates that he finds argument more difficult to write than either explanation or narrative. What he does not yet do is sustain a hypothetico-deductive argument in which conclusions are drawn from generalizations. This is not surprising granted the findings of Martin, Rosen and Britton (1966, p. 28) on the examination performance of 500 students at 'O' level. As they state:

> The articulate story writer can be a very poor writer of argument. We cannot therefore say of him that he is a good writer or a bad writer, but we can begin to say what he can write well and what he cannot yet write well. This is, of course, to put it optimistically, and to assume that some kind of writing calls for greater maturity and experience than others.

The point is not that John is a poor writer of argument in comparison with other children of the same age, but that he is a less confident writer of argument than of narrative or explanation. John generalizes, classifies the two issues under discussion, evaluates his stance, raises hypothetical questions, but does so in a loosely organized fashion and from a basis of his experience with schooling. His writing indicates that he is in transition between the empirico-inductive reasoning of the concrete operational thinker and the hypothetico-deductive reasoning of the mature adult thinker. His generalized conclusion is not supported by the evidence he offers, though he can speculate about the possible as well as draw inferences from what has happened in his experience. His lack of confidence with argument is also reflected in his stylistic ratings for this task.

In terms of moral development, there is nothing unusual about John's performance: he consistently, across three tasks, makes judgements in terms of convention or status quo, as did most children at thirteen. He adopts a person to society perspective in his thinking about right and wrong, rather than the concrete individual perspective of early childhood. He has an understanding of the rule-based nature of society as his comments about 'anarchy' at the end of his argumentative piece demonstrate.

In terms of stylistic development, John is an able writer at thirteen. His style alters to suit the conventions of a particular mode. We found more evidence of impersonal modes of address in the argumentative and explanatory than the narrative and autobiographical writing, more evidence of passive constructions, more evidence of the use of abstract terms. He can adjust his syntactic structures according to the requirements of the subject field and can use short simple sentences alongside clauses of concession and embedding in terms of his semantic needs. In terms of reader awareness, he rates highly. His impersonal pieces reveal a capacity for context-free elaboration, for making things explicit; his personal pieces indicate that he can use implicit means for keeping his reader informed. He employs a wide range of cohesive devices in his writing generally, and has a high degree of verbal competence, choosing the most appropriate word for the context. In terms of effectiveness his narrative and explanatory tasks were rated more highly than was his argumentative task as has been mentioned earlier: but in general he is a highly competent writer.

Chapter Thirteen

Summary Matters

13.1 Introduction

This is not the place to write the book again by way of summing up. Certainly lines of development were suggested in the early chapters and in the models. It need come as no surprise that an analysis of the children's writing in the sample bears out these lines of development since the models were developed in association with a study of the children's writing. But this fact does not invalidate a possible hypothesis that a similar description could apply to a larger sample or even to the written work of children in general. It is merely that we make no such claim here, not having the evidence to do so. The following comments are based quite explicitly on the writing we have been studying.

13.2 Writing Development

13.2.1 Seven Year Olds

Writing is difficult. The writer has to hold and give exact movements to a pen to make marks on paper — with young children particularly the muscular co-ordination required is not attained easily. He has to write in code — the noises he makes with the words of his mouth are silent, and he has to represent their sounds in a not very logical system of letters. He has to convey meanings many of which came through his tone of voice, his facial expression, his bodily movements and positions. In writing all these are denied him. He has to produce an extended and shaped construction — in speech this is less frequently required. Nor has he any listener to indicate to him how well he is communicating. We may write, as Virginia Woolf says, for the 'face beneath the page' — but that face is often shadowy, and sometimes it is not there at all.

Young writers — say our children of seven — will often write slowly, though some produce only a few words, others over a page. Spelling may vary from the completely original, which covers what might be a clear story with a thick crust of opacity, to the completely conformist. Punctuation even with the best writing will tend to be forgetful, with the worst it will be non-existent or splendidly random.

A basic problem is one of construction. Writing tasks are nearly all extended. In the spoken language this is much less so. Conversation, for instance, is a mutually supported interchange of fairly short items where the form of our words is suggested by what prompts the other gives us — we know whether we are required to question, to answer, to comment, and so on. In the written language one obvious form of organization offers itself — the narrative. Because life is chronological — events happen in time — then to relate what happens comes naturally. Quite young children can recount events in the order in which they happened. But what a 'story' requires is some sort of coherence, some logic of connection between the parts, some subordination or exclusion of less significant detail. And when the story is written the requirements become more rigorous.

With seven year old children the ability to 'report' is usually present (though we did find a few children unable to handle even the reporting of short sequences). The report may be of miscellaneous items because they happen in the time sequence. The sheer ponderous act of writing down slowly one thought at a time makes for disjointed discourse. There are however certain rituals: particularly noticeable is the obsession with getting up, breakfast and other meals, watching television and going to bed as punctuation marks to the day. But stories are also beginning to have some coherence as well as a time sequence, though this may not carry through the whole. Themes which help children to write coherently are those with which they are familiar from literature or television — one which recurred was that of virtue rewarded, vice punished, where the pay-off line is clear. This means that they should be given as many models as possible not just the stereotype.

Because they are secure in the narrative children use it also in writing for which it is inappropriate. Thus seven year olds cannot think analytically in the way required by the discussion of whether school should be voluntary and subjects a matter of choice. Instead some of them made a decision and developed it into a hypothetical story of the *first I would do this/then I would do that* variety. Clearly narrative has little use in this connection, and without it the writers found themselves in considerable difficulties of organization.

This task also requires the ability to objectify — to see the effects of the decision on others — parents, teachers, the school as a whole. Few children can do this — they tend to express their personal preferences. This egocentrism is in fact characteristic of much of their writing taken altogether. Of course when they are asked for 'the happiest/saddest day of their lives' then it is to be expected that the writer himself will be the centre of attention. In this case then it is particularly significant to see how far other people are involved, and the kind of interest shown in them. In the narratives we would expect the degree of egocentrism to be manifested in such devices as the first person narrator, and indirectly in the degree to which the characters are realized as individual identities. Realization takes place through the giving of significant dialogues, the mentioning of significant actions, the insertion of interpretative comment, and so on. Most seven year olds whilst showing an awareness of others are unable to manifest them as separate beings (though there are exceptions to this). Again, their own emotions are expressed, but not self-critically.

One feature of the writing of some children of this age is the partial information it contains — partial, that is, from the point of view of the reader. A person speaking can often assume a good deal — his words are 'context-bound': a person writing, unless it is a personal letter, must normally assume much less. His writing is expected to be context-free — to contain within it the clues for its decoding: thus we expect sheer fact, when and where something takes place, reasons and explanations, why it takes place. We do not expect these to be obvious, much less gratuitous, but woven into the texture of the writing. In the writing of young children much of the information is often missing. This is due no doubt partly to the need to concentrate on the sheer mechanics of writing; partly due to an unawareness of just what the reader needs to know, particularly in an extended piece. That quite young children of three or four can monitor their own language for its effects on others is demonstrable, but there they are operating orally and the signals of feedback, from the listeners, or the possibility of them, is always present. We have taken it as a mark of development when awareness of the reader's needs is apparent in writing. Seven year olds vary very much in this awareness.

Basically the written style of most seven year olds is a spoken style. There are the marks of the spoken language — simple active sentences linked by obvious conjunctions, particularly 'and', 'then', and 'so'. The spoken style is less likely to substitute pronouns for nouns and noun groups and is more likely to move from topic to topic without connection; and this is true of the children's written style. There is little sense of what is usually considered an appropriate register for the particular writing. Verbal competence is obviously restricted. There is much use of general verbs 'be', 'have', 'go', 'say', 'take', 'put', and though these are amongst the most common verbs in English, their use is even more common in proportion in the writings we examined. Nouns also are general — 'man', 'boy', 'lady', 'policeman', often without qualification. The use of qualifiers to focus the meaning of a noun or verb, or of a more specific verb for the meaning, is not common. Words tend to have a simple single connotation at this stage. For instance — 'man', 'lady' — and the flavours brought out in contexts like 'manly' and 'ladylike' would not be appreciated. Again concrete rather than abstract words are used. On the whole formulations in conventional language which form a large part of the stock of written idioms can be employed. But spoken idiom is of course used. As Jean's policeman says, 'Hello Hello whats up here then'.

13.2.2 Ten Year Olds

In the writings of ten year olds the narrative mode is used at greater length. Stories and autobiographies are predominantly chronological, but an ability to modify this emerges. Writers no longer need to get up, eat a series of meals, and go to bed. They can begin with a significant incident which plunges us *in medias res*, and end with a further significant incident. Retrospection is possible: on the one hand with a short reference, perhaps by way of explanation, to some prior event; on the other the major part of the writing may be a flashback from an event described at the beginning, which is led up to once again at the end. This last however is not very common amongst this group. It is more usual to find extended writing in chronological mode, sometimes with two or more incidents described in fair detail, without the writer being unsure about the relative priority he wishes to give to each, ambition and a growing facility having taken over.

We have previously characterized the sentence as being of two kinds — the narrative and the descriptive. We can apply this distinction to forms of personal writing. In many of them there is the narrative proper, and an element descriptive of the narrative — which explains it, or elaborates it for the benefit of the reader. Kernan (1977, p. 91) grandiosely calls these semantic and expressive elaboration. The former 'serve to provide information that is necessary to the desired semantic interpretations of the narrative'; the latter serve to make the narrative interesting to, and appreciated by, the audience. Or to put it simply, they explain and elaborate the narrative.

As we have seen the narrative line can be modified by adjusting the sequence of events. It can be held in suspension while a description is made, while an example is given, while an explanation is offered. Dialogue can be added which heightens the interest: it may be illustrative or it may itself further the narrative. There is an increase in these elaborating aspects of language as between the work of the seven and ten year olds. It goes along of course with an increased awareness of the needs of the reader — the writer is not just going along inside his own head.

Time then is an element which is present in the work of writers at all ages; space is not. It is only at 10+ that location begins to be established — it is part of the elaboration we have just mentioned. The events younger children write about often take place in a nowhere. Most members of this group however can indicate a context, even set a scene. Details of environment — landscape, for example — can be used to create atmosphere: in fact, sometimes there is over much detail rather than too little. The expression of emotion by other means, e.g. adjectival, adverbial, metaphorical, is not common, though if prompted by a title many writers will obviously say dutifully, 'I felt happy/ sad'. The outlining of sad or happy events however is of course perfectly possible.

The viewpoint in many cases is still egocentric, and scarcely anyone evaluates his own emotion. More attention is paid to other people, and in the stories characters are portrayed, though often not beyond the single dimensional level. This point having been made, it should be said that there is the occasional writer who explores character and emotion with considerable skill and depth.

As far as the argumentative and explanatory writings are concerned many writers of this group still attempt to apply the narrative model to tasks for which it is unsuitable. In an explanation of how to play a game a 'recording' level of thinking needs to be superceded by, or at least supplemented by, a classificatory one. Thus aims, method of winning, apparatus, lay-out, rules, progress of the game must all be present, and some form of superordinate thinking is important. No child of this age gives a full classificatory account of the game; but where a chronological account is given it may include ordered rather than random lists of information. However the advance that the ten year olds significantly make over the seven year olds is that their accounts are much more complete. They are very aware that there is a reader who has needs, whether or not they succeed in meeting them completely.

Some writers of this group are beginning to have an awareness of register. In narrative this may occur in dialogue, or in the general sense of knowing some of the conventions of a story — Enid Blyton was one of the models. This, however, is much less true in the argumentative and explanatory tasks. In 'How to play . . .' there is some sense of presentation derived from rule books, in some writers, but others offer friendly colloquial advice: 'you shake the dice . . .', and so on. In the 'voluntary school' task there is no ready model available anyway, and the analytical procedures which produce a rational and objective organization from scratch are not available to writers of this age.

There is a bigger repertoire of syntax than the seven year olds have. The question of using it appropriately is now more pressing than the question of possessing it. Few children can use it completely appropriately over a long stretch of writing, though there are areas of success. On the whole the use of vocabulary and idiom is more competent; a written register is more common. There is some ability to employ technical terms. Some children begin to experiment with 'fine writing' — phrases not their own for experiences they will later find their own words for. These are obviously not to be condemned as clichés but encouraged as signs of an exercise of growing powers.

13.2.3 Thirteen Year Olds

In the work of the thirteen year olds one of the immediately noticeable features is their ability to differentiate usage. Their sense of the 'appropriate' register and form for a particular type of discourse has developed considerably. This is partly due to growing cognitive powers — the ability to classify which is valuable in the explanatory task also suggests a way of presenting this task. Again, on the argumentative task their growing ability to hypothesise has in some cases suggested the outlines of the form. Thus Arthur generalizes and then goes into detail: 'This system would be dubious unless several regulations were introduced'. Of course the ability to use particular registers must also come from acquaintance with them, and there are obvious literary models behind much of the writing, particularly the narrative. The importance of acquaintance with literature in helping children develop their individual forms of writing is borne out by our study. The eighteenth century would have thought this obvious. Writers as diverse as Pope and Blake (how diverse can you get?) went through a self-imposed apprenticeship of 'imitation', and whilst we would not advocate this, it is clear to us that acquaintance with good models is necessary. Thus Enid Blyton's style proves helpful to children as far as the narrative line is concerned but also leads to stereotyping in character.

On the whole writers at thirteen are much more in control of the core narrative. Necessarily it will be chronological, but the time sequence can be adjusted with confidence with prospects and retrospects, and much gratuitous information has been excised. There are also the elaborations which put flesh on the basic structure. These are the devices which make the writing context-free by constantly giving the reader information and explanation. Sometimes the writers are unsure here (one piece is characterized by a staggering number of 'asides') but they are not in doubt of the need to cater for a reader. In a few cases the core narrative as such is missing, and the story is carried in dialogue or in a stream of consciousness. Another feature which distinguishes the work of the thirteen year olds from that of the younger groups is their concern with emotion. Younger children can certainly describe events which concern the emotions – death for instance – but the emotions are not expressed or interpreted. In the writings of some of the thirteen year olds however there are the beginnings of self-awareness and of awareness of others as psychological beings. In the sense that an awareness of self shows some ability to objectify self, this, as well as the growing understanding of others, carries on the general movement away from egocentricity which we have noticed in the developing child.

Often the writers' very eagerness to write well can produce an impression of 'insincerity' where the language seems second-hand and the emotions expressed exaggerated. Sometimes the reaching out for metaphorical language, even the 'objective correlative' of the story, seems to result in exaggerated or melodramatic emotion. Where there is a specific literary model this feeling of overwriting, and of second-hand emotion may be particularly strong. It behoves us to be careful however. Certainly emotion may be insincere in the sense that it is merely copied; but frequently we find it seems that writers have a unique experience but not, at this stage, a unique language. Stratta, Dixon and Wilkinson (1974, pp. 15–20) write of the process whereby a writer attains to a three fold uniqueness – of self, expression, form. The writer works through the stock language and stereotype perceptions associated with it to an individual perception expressed in individual terms. This is a hard won end – we can scarcely expect children to have gone through the process by the age of thirteen.

As far as language is concerned there is a much more confident choice of syntax in relation to meaning in all but the less successful writers. Normal cohesive devices such as reference and substitution are commonly used as a matter of course. The development comes in the way some writers use them as a deliberate device of style – repetition, parallelism, etc. Thus Sonia (9.3.3) begins each paragraph in a similar way: ('No parents . . . No mother . . . No father') and develops each as appropriate. Some writers can employ irony and disjunction. As already mentioned there is sometimes overwriting, and a search for metaphor which varies in its success. As against this the command of technical vocabulary in the description of certain games is impressive.

It is very important to emphasise that the comments we make in this book are comments not on the children themselves but on their writing. In everyday life people make assessments of others, whether conscious or not, in good measure on their behaviour. Writing may stand only in an oblique relationship to the individual who behaves, and is in any case only one aspect of him. Thus the moral attitudes we have discerned in the writing are within prediction. Young children judge in terms of punishments/rewards, and physical consequences of actions: ten year olds in terms of good relations and immediate social context: by thirteen they are capable of judgements in terms of notions of fairness and intention, regardless of the social status. But we have no means of knowing what these children's judgements or behaviour would be in 'real life'. Again the ways of coping with reality expressed in the writings are not necessarily an indication of the stance of the person behind the writing. As a generalization we might say that young children cope by means of fantasy, older ones by treating actual situations imaginatively. But this *is* a generalization, and is only an indication of how they do it in writing on a particular occasion.

But when all this has been said, language *is* behaviour, writing *is* behaviour. We argued in Chapter One that the 'growth' model of English teaching is important, but that a 'context model' is more comprehensive. Our view of the child is of a communicating being whose personal and social growth is developed in a context of relationships. Writing provides one important source of knowledge of the child's behaviour the teacher has available in furthering this process.

13.3 Conclusions

We have complained irritably that terms like 'maturity', 'development', 'growth' are tossed about in educational circles, and particularly by English teachers (who claim special rights on them) without any more than a hint of definition (and sometimes not that). We have therefore attempted, if not definition, at least description of the process of 'development' towards 'maturity'. We see this as a movement from dependence to autonomy; from convention to uniqueness; from unconsciousness to awareness; from subjectivity to objectivity; from ignorance to understanding; from self to neighbour as self. If it be objected by a wry observer that this is a personal, or at least a culture-bound definition, we shall answer with deafening agreement. We prefer it to, for instance, that of Nazi Germany where the desirable end product is an aggressive psychopath. In our description, however, there is no 'end product': maturity is not a state which is finally attained to: one does not arrive, one is continually arriving.

We have turned our attention specifically to the written language of children, and looked at the developmental descriptions of them available. On the one hand there are many 'linguistic' descriptions which count anything that can be counted. Their conclusions after years of painstaking work on both sides of the Atlantic is that on the whole children of (say) thirteen write longer stories than children of (say) seven, use longer sentences, know more words, etc. Dismayed by the prospect of not being able to better such world-shattering results, scholars have turned to other lines of inquiry, such as the description of function categories, and the most influential developmental model is of this type, that of the London Institute Writing Research Unit. This has proved valuable in heightening awareness of many features of language, particularly such matters as the relationship of language to the self. In our view however it has grave limitations which have become clear over the past decade. It is crude in that it gives a single procrustean description to each piece of writing; it is limited in that effectively this description is in cognitive terms only. It would be disingenuous to pretend that we do not see our work as dissenting in major ways from the approach of the London Unit.

In English teaching there are various basic assumptions; one or more of these influence the teaching whether the particular teacher can formulate it explicitly or not. We have preferred that which regards the child as a 'communicating being', emphasising both 'communicating' and 'being'. In an attempt to do justice to both the complexity of written work, and the complexity of the relationship between writer, writing, and reader, we have devised four 'models' — cognitive, affective, moral, stylistic, and demonstrated their application to pieces in the sample on which they were validated. With these schemes of analysis it is not necessary to make a single judgement on a single piece; one may make a variety of judgements, commenting on aspects of it at sentence or even word level. The items in the scheme are coded for convenience of analysis, but it is not intended that they should be added to produce a total score. If they were the result would be quite meaningless. The whole point is to draw attention to the many facets of a piece of writing — to describe, not to prescribe.

Thus the models are not meant for use as a day to day marking scheme. The teachers who cooperated with us on the project were firmly against any summary or simplification which might seem to imply this. They felt that one of the strengths of the models lay in their detail which paid due regard to the varieties of activity going on in the process of writing. In one sense they are assessment instruments, but only in the sense that assessment is an essential part of education — we constantly need to make assessments of children's development in order to help them develop further. In other words assessment is to be regarded rather as a teaching than a measuring device. Of course the wider range of criteria in our models is already employed by many experienced teachers. The most we can offer them is perhaps to make explicit some of the judgements they already make interesting. We have greatly profited by the advice of such teachers in the evaluation of our trial materials.

As far as extant marking schemes of the 'Grammar, Style, Content' variety are concerned we have expressed considerable misgivings. The definition of all three terms seems to be in doubt — 'style' as we have seen seems often to be considered in relation to a norm of the Augustan essayists; whatever 'content' means examiners never seem to be advised to consider it in terms of the nature of the thought, or the quality of the feeling. Of course with public examinations there is a big difficulty. The child cannot be regarded as a 'communicating being' (there is no way his totality can be viewed) but must be thought of essentially as a repository of skills. Under the circumstances an enlightened impression mark on more than one composition is the best that can be expected. But if it is to be enlightened the internalized criteria which are used for judgement must be wide and humane.

We have demonstrated that it is possible to discern with some objectivity features in children's writing which are likely to occur as they develop. Although we have taken the sample for our work from age groups (at seven, ten and thirteen) this is merely for convenience. The writing of some children at ten will be more advanced than some at thirteen for example. Our sample is small (about 150 children in all) and we do not claim that our findings would apply to all other children, or even to these children on other occasions or with different tasks. But here we must distinguish: the broad line of development may be correct; statements of the kind 'ten year olds generally exhibit features x, y and z' may not. Motivation, teaching, amount of reading, background, and so on will certainly influence the performance, so that these features may be found elsewhere with eight year olds. Even so these are good reasons for supposing that, for example, stylistic organization which requires systematic classification and subordination will not occur before early adolescence since it is a function of cognition. Similarly, rounded characterization will not occur until the writer is able to think other than egocentrically. And so on.

We are very conscious of the tentative nature of the models. As tools for the analysis of writing they are, as far as we know, the first of their kind. In the cognitive and moral fields there is indeed the work of Piaget and others; but in the affective and stylistic we have found scarcely anything to draw on, and this explains the very provisional nature of these two models. But we have felt it better to make them available for comment, use and modification rather than to sit on them coyly — Pope advocates nine years — in the vain hope of reforging them perfect. Certainly they need to be extended to cope with the work of older and younger pupils; and an extension of similar categories to the oral field is an interesting possibility.

The enquiry raises many fascinating questions which cannot be answered here. Thus writing is not just communicating; it is thinking and feeling, and learning to think and feel. What kinds of writing need to be done in order to maximize the learning? Is the apparent discrepancy between performance in personal and in discursive writing inevitable? What could be done to develop the discursive writing particularly of younger pupils? Do they have difficulty because of the task or because of its unfamiliarity? Children's narrative writing seems to benefit by exposure to models; how should this information be exploited? Should they be given more discursive models? As it is they often attempt to cope with discursive topics by narrative. And, to mention just one more — perhaps the most significant and the most delicate — what, in the communicating being, is the relationship between the communicating and the being?

We have emphasised to screaming point in this book that to assess the writing of children is not to assess the children. Even so the terms in which we have chosen to debate this matter draws attention to the nature of the relationship between the children and the writing. Our approach considers the question of how children develop as people — and thus the emotional, moral and cognitive education that is offered. In other words language is inseparable from living.

Appendix A

Models for the Analysis of Writing

Models for the Analysis of Writing

Cognitive Model

C1 *Describing*

C1.1 Labelling — the mere concept word e.g. 'There is *man* and . . .'

C1.2 Naming — the specific word e.g. 'Mr. and Mrs. *Jones* went to town'.

C1.3 Partial information — some concrete details given, but unorganized and unsustained, e.g. 'wene you get to near the red circle you would of de caught'.

C1.4 Recording — simple concrete statements about the here and now or there and then in a list; language close to speech, e.g. 'it hit my head I fell over and Antony said are you all right yes . . .' Past and present time confused.

C1.5 Reporting — some linking between statements in a chronological/ spatial sequence, e.g. 'I went to school. Then I found my books had gone, so I went to the house tutor . . .' or 'There was an old house on the moor behind our village . . .'

C2 *Interpreting*

C2.1 Explaining — saying why something is so or how something is done, e.g. 'I was happy because it was my birthday', 'the card sorry means you can send one of the other players back . . .'

C2.2 Inferring — e.g. 'I think he's more sad than happy because he's alone', 'This wouldn't work because children wouldn't bother coming to school'.

C2.3 Deducing — links between statements, causal links e.g. 'teachers will be in short supply because there will be much broader choice of things to do. That teacher won't be able to cover all the subjects, so choice of subjects wouldn't work'.

C3 *Generalizing*

C3.1 Abstracting — using abstract terms as well as concrete ones e.g. 'People

228 Assessing Language Development

say children should go to school', 'The *players* move alternately, white beginning . . .'

C3.2 Summarizing — e.g. 'So you see Topcat won', 'The object of owning property is to collect rents from opponents stopping there', 'The first person to do that is the winner'.

C3.3 Overall Evaluation — e.g. 'So Topcat won by being more clever', 'The main object of the game is to meld seven cards of a kind'.

C3.4 Concluding — e.g. 'So he decided never to enter the race again', 'These seven points show just how ludicrous that suggestion really was'.

C3.5 Reflecting — generalizing with reference to external rules or principles e.g. 'This phase would generally have lasted several years'.

C3.6 Classifying — links between generalizations sustained in a classificatory system.

C4 *Speculating*

C4.1 Irrelevant (even if beautiful) hypothesis e.g. 'If we didn't come to school we would get sick and die', 'The elephant's trunk was stretched by a crocodile'.

C4.2 Relevant but inadequate hypothesis e.g. 'His trunk is to breathe better', 'if we didn't come to school the buses wouldn't come'.

C4.3 Adequate hypothesis — 'His trunk is for feeding with'.

C4.4 Exploring — asking tentative but relevant questions 'What would happen if . . .' e.g. 'But what would we do if we didn't come to school?'

C4.5 Projecting — a set of organized hypotheses about a possible future, loosely linked e.g. 'A far better system would be to give secondary school pupils a basic three years schooling . . .' The writer goes beyond the information given, but cannot subject his thinking to critical scrutiny.

C4.6 Theorizing — sustained hypotheses in which links between one item and the next are hypothetico-deductive. Propositional logic rather than concrete reasoning as in C2.4.

Affective Model

A1 *Self*

The writer expresses his emotion and his awareness of the nature of his own feelings, or implies his emotion by describing action from which the reader can infer that the writer was in the grip of an emotion.

A1.1 The writer expresses or implies his own emotion, mechanically in some written work, explicitly in others, e.g. 'My feet were as wet as any-thing', 'I am afraid that day is a long, long, way away'.

A1.2 — not only expresses but evaluates emotion, e.g. 'The saddest day of my life', 'I did not like it indeed'.

A1.3 — shows awareness of self image, of how he appears or might appear, e.g. 'I looked like a fool'.

A1.4 — shows awareness of the springs and complexities of emotion, e.g. 'I got rather nervous about it and I couldn't find the way and went into another room and looked like a fool standing there asking where room one was'.

A1.5 — shows a general attitude or disposition, e.g. 'I long for the day when I can think about him without it hurting too much'.

A2   *Other people*
The writer shows an awareness of others both in relation to himself and as distinct identities.

A2.1 — records the mere existence of other people as having been present. This is the single dimension: others are present — acting, speaking — but no emotion is apparent by inference, e.g. 'The two boys went for a walk with their mother and they got lost and they came to a fence and that fence was electric and they was not lost . . .'

A2.2 — begins to indicate the separateness of others by, e.g. giving their actual words or significant actions. 'I woke up, had my breakfast' is probably not significant; 'the old man smild' may well be.

A2.3 — the thoughts and feelings of others by quotation of actual words, perhaps as a dialogue, or by description of them, or actions indicating them. More perception called for than in the previous category though it might be fairly conventional.

A2.4 Analytical, interpretative comments on aspects of character and be-haviour, or insightful quotation or dialogue.

A2.5 Consistently realized presentation of another person by a variety of means, perhaps by assuming persona.

A2.6 Ability to see a person and his interactions in extended context (e.g. a character in a novel).

A3   *Reader*
It is often argued that writing to an unknown or not well-envisaged reader will be poorer in quality since it lacks focus. Certainly the imaginative leap of the writer into the minds of others so as to grasp what terms have meaning for them must characterize effective com-munication.

A3.1 —- reader not catered for. Writing context-bound, incomplete information, links missing.

A3.2 — the reader is a person or type of person to the writer. He may not be conscious of this, but rather attempts to fulfil expectations within the situation. He may do so partially but imperfectly.

A3.3 — the writer caters specifically for the reader, e.g. by relevant information, explanation (sometimes asides), shows an empathy with him, telling him what he needs to know to be able to interpret what he is told.

A4 *Environment*
The writer shows an awareness of physical or social surroundings, a sense of time and place. On the one hand the environment may be a source of special stimulus. On the other hand a 'restricted code' may not offer the necessary context. Getting the register right is a sign of awareness of social environment.

A4.1 — assumes the environment.

A4.2 — describes or explains the environment, barely adequately giving background details, or gives enough details to clarify the background.

A4.3 — responds to the environment in a way that shows it has been especially significant and stimulating.

A4.4 — chooses environmental items to achieve an effect, thus showing a higher degree of selectivity and evaluation than that suggested by A4.3.

A5 *Reality*
This is concerned with how far a writer recognizes a distinction between the world of phenomena, and the world of imagination, between magical and logical thinking; with how far the writer's own preferences or beliefs can come to an accommodation with external reality; with how far the literal-metaphorical aspects of experience can be perceived in complexity.

A5.1 Confusion of the subjective and objective world. This seems to occur with young children who believe that stories are 'true'.

A5.2 — gives a literal account without evaluation.

A5.3 — interprets reality in terms of fantasy.

A5.4 — interprets reality literally but in terms of logical possibilities.

A5.5 — interprets reality imaginatively in terms of art, perhaps symbolically or metaphorically.

Moral Model

Attitudes/judgements about self/others and events.

M1   Judging self/others by physical characteristics or consequences, e.g. 'She was ugly, so she was bad', 'He broke fifteen cups — naughty'. Judging events by pain-pleasure to the self, e.g. 'It was a bad day. I hurt my hand'. 'It was a good birthday. I got lots of presents'. 'A bad accident — the fence was smashed up.' Principle of self-gratification — 'anomy'.

M2   Judging self/others and events in terms of punishments/rewards. 'I won't do that, Mummy will hit me'. 'I'll tell Daddy on you and he will beat you up'. 'If I do the dishes, Mummy will give me a new bat'. Events judged as rewards/punishments, e.g. 'I must have been naughty last night, the fridge hit me'. Heteronomy.

M3   Judging self/others according to the status quo. Mother, father, teacher, policeman good by right of status; the wicked witch, the evil step-father bad by right of convention, e.g. 'I hated the Jerries, I used to call them stupid idiots'. Reciprocity restricted to the child's immediate circle, e.g. 'I won't do that — it will upset mummy'. Social approval/disapproval internalized in terms of whether behaviour upsets others or not. Stereotypic thinking. Events judged in terms of effects on other *people*. 'It was a bad accident. All the passengers were badly hurt'. Socionomy (internal).

M4   Judging self/others in terms of conventional norms/rules, e.g. 'It's wrong to steal. It is against the law'. Conformist orientation. Rules are applied literally on the principle of equity or fairness. 'It's not fair. We all did it, so John should be punished the same as us. We all broke the rule'. Socionomy (external).

M5   Judging self/others in terms of intention or motive, regardless of status or power, e.g. 'She didn't mean to drop those plates, so she shouldn't be punished'. 'Teacher was wrong, because she punished all of us instead of finding out who did it'.

M6   Judging self/others in terms of abstract concepts such as a universal respect for the individual rather than in terms of conventional norms of right/wrong conducts. The morality of individual conscience. Rules seen as arbitrary and changeable. Autonomy.

M7   Judgement of self/others in terms of a personally developed value *system*.

Stylistic Model

S1   *Syntax*
      This category is concerned with the relationship between grammatical
      units within the sentence. There is development from the simple to the
      complex sentence and from the use of restricted and unvaried means
      to the selection, as appropriate, from a wider range of more varied
      structures.

S1.1 *Simple sentences with few modifiers or compound sentences without
      subordinates.* The most common conjuctions are 'and', 'so', 'but'
      (often used in an additive rather than contrastive sense). Where sub-
      ordinating conjunctions are used, there is not true subordination.

S1.2 *Short, complex sentences with some short modifying phrases.* Occa-
      sional use of adjectival clauses. Frequent use of adverbial clauses of
      time, place; clauses of cause and condition are used but not firmly
      established. Noun clause object very common.

S1.3 *Longer complex sentences employing adjectival clauses and most
      types of adverbial and noun clause.* Some re-arrangement of sentence
      units to stress meaning. More confident and elaborated use of modi-
      fiers. Some embedding.

S1.4 *Sentences become more varied and 'tighter' in structure.* Use of parti-
      cipal and infinitival expression embedded within the sentence. Clauses
      of concession and adversative constructions employed.

S1.5 *Greater control and facility with sentence structures.* Ability to adjust
      sentence structures according to the requirements of the subject field.

S2   *Verbal Competence*
      This category is concerned with the writer's capacity to express his
      meanings effectively, to define his terms adequately and communicate
      successfully an increasingly wide range of experience. There may be
      changes from the concrete to the abstract, and to a more diverse, dis-
      criminating and precise use of words; from the literal to the meta-
      phorical; from the stock to the individual statement.

S2.1 *Vocabulary limited.* Literal, not metaphorical, concrete, not abstract.
      A limited range of modifiers.

S2.2 *Increased range of vocabulary but still tied to the concrete and familiar.*
      Increased use of modifiers, temporal and causal initiators, adjectives.
      Circumlocution rather than precision in describing complex experiences.

S2.3 *Increase in number and range of words to express feeling and mental
      processes.* Many more modifiers related to the quality of experience:
      metaphor. Developing ability to use conventional language. More

effective and precise use of initiating words and phrases. Experimenting with new words.

S2.4 *Ability to use abstract terms and express an abstract idea.* Use of general terms and superordinates: more extended use of metaphor.

S2.5 *Greater discrimination in choice of words.* Clearer definitions, greater precision in use of words. Ability to select the most effective word for the context: in control of choice.

S3 *Organization*

This category is concerned with the relation between the separate sentences and the whole composition. There is development from a relatively uncontrolled and incoherent handling of material to a more controlled and coherent organization.

S3.1 *Little coherent structure.* Ideas are juxtaposed rather than related. There is little elaboration or integration.

S3.2 *Experience, ideas and observations are related to a single focus but without coherence between the parts.* In narrative structure takes the form of a cluster of events without focus. In discursive writing a 'primitive chain' structure is often adopted.

S3.3 *Sequence and structure are based on a simple linear or chronological pattern.* Elaborating detail where employed is not yet selected and organized with a clear aim. Introductory and concluding sentences are most common in narrative and least common in discursive writing. The connection between one fact and another is not always made clear.

S3.4 *More complex organization,* though the sum of the parts does not yet make a whole. Interruption of a straight-sequential pattern by, for instance, retrospection or anticipation. Other patterns such as a logical one emerge.

S3.5 *The relationship between the parts and the whole established.* Explanation and amplification handled more coherently. Appropriate subordination of material within the paragraph. Introduction and conclusion employed with confidence.

S3.6 *Capacity to control ideas and organize structure by a variety of means.* Complex experiences or ideas often presented by balance or contrast. Image, symbol, the use of a predominant tone and atmosphere become unifying factors.

S4 *Cohesion*

Cohesive devices are employed to maintain continuity between one part of the text and another. Just as grammar establishes the structural relationship within clause or sentence, so cohesion established the semantic relationship within the text. There is development from the relatively unrelated to the fully related parts in a text.

S4.1 *Few cohesive devices employed effectively.* Pronouns where used, sometimes have no specific referent or are used imprecisely. Ellipsis, when employed, often shows no clear understanding of the referent, e.g. 'If they miss [the goal?] the other player has his [turn?]!' Little lexical cohesion. Most common conjunctions: 'and', 'so', 'then'.

S4.2 *Marked increase in cohesive devices.* Sequential and concluding conjunctions, e.g. 'afterwards', 'finally', 'eventually'. Use of temporal conjunctions, e.g. 'when', 'first', 'first of all'. Use of causal conjunctions, e.g. 'so', 'because'. Use of 'but' in an adversative/contrastive way. Some use of demonstratives as adverbs of place, e.g. 'here', 'there'. Some substitution, e.g. 'one', 'other', 'some'. Nominal substitution, e.g. 'one', 'the same' and verbal substitution, e.g. 'do so', 'be so'. Appearance of low level general terms, e.g. 'people', 'things'.

S4.3 *Greater awareness of textual coherence to clarify and define meaning.* Emphatic cohesive conjunctions, e.g. 'too', 'even', 'also'. Use of comparatives, e.g. 'identical', 'similar', 'more', 'less', and superlatives, e.g. 'the weathiest'.

S4.4 *Development of logical coherence.* Use of superordinates. A wider range of adversatives employed, e.g. 'however', 'on the other hand', 'though'.

S4.5 *A wide range of cohesive devices employed.* e.g. reiteration, synonyms, antonyms, parallelism, contrast, assonance, alliteration, echoic words, etc.

S5   *Writer's awareness of the reader*
This category is concerned with the degree to which the writer can put himself in the place of the reader and see with his eyes. Initially a process of decentring, reader awareness includes such aspects as the writer's orientation to his reader, the degree of explanation and elaboration of detail to assist the reader and the relevance of that detail to the message communicated. At first there is an implicit assumption of the reader's omniscience. Later the reader is assisted towards understanding by explicit means. Later still, in more sophisticated expressive and poetic writing, various devices are employed deliberately to control the reader by implicit means.

S5.1 *Writer assumes the reader's awareness of the context.* Few modifying or elaborating details to assist the reader in understanding the context. Verbal syncretism.

S5.2 *More elaboration of detail but without focus or reference.* Explanation and elaboration still have no clear objective or function or are seen egocentrically. Selection of detail seems arbitrary.

S5.3 *Detail related clearly to a theme or focus.* Marked increase in elaboration and explanation; more use of modifying expressions and emphatic devices including asides and parentheses.

S5.4 *Writer assuming a more confident stance to reader.* Increasing use of initiatory, anecdotes and evaluative comments. More information provided in a more coherent way.

S5.5 *Writer communicates with reader by sophisticated means.* Irony, parody sometimes employed to relate to reader implicitly. Fable, allegory, the use of image or symbol etc. indicate a relationship with the reader in less overt and obvious ways.

S6 *Appropriateness*

Appropriateness is the writer's ability to adapt his style or register to the field of discourse and to recognize and respond to the conventions of particular kinds of writing.

Development from the inappropriate use of writing conventions to appropriate — recognition of the stylistic conventions of particular subject fields and kinds of writing — is significant within this age span.

S6.1 *Writing close to speech.* Little awareness of writing conventions. Little awareness of stylistic differences according to subject field though in narrative conventional opening and closing sentences are often used.

S6.2 *Dawning awareness of writing models.* Modifying and elaborating expressions more appropriate to writing conventions. There are still inconsistencies in register, however. Second-hand writing. More varied opening and closing sentences used in narrative. In discursive writing an undeveloped and unelaborated discursive style is perceptible.

S6.3 *Appearance of 'literary' English and employment of 'literary' effects.* Re-arrangement of particular units within the sentence, experimentation with short, simple/longer, complex sentences for particular effects, some sentence patterning. In discursive writing a less personal style emerges.

S6.4 *Greater awareness of written conventions.* More varied means allow the writer to experiment in a variety of ways, e.g. in use of figures of speech — suspense, bathos, humour, control of effects. Appropriate use of lexical emphasis, lexical cohesion, initiating expressions.

S6.5 *Appropriate adjustment of register to requirements of subject field.* Ability of writer to assume a variety of roles and discriminate between the different demands of subject, audience and context.

S7   *Effectiveness*

The effectiveness of a written composition depends upon the writer's ability to respond appropriately to the demands of his subject and his readers. Objective criteria will never wholly supply the place of the personal judgement and personal response in assessing a piece of writing. The realization of an experience in writing, the unity and coherence of a composition ultimately depend upon an interaction between writer and reader in which the reader creates for himself from what the writer has offered.

In the discursive modes, the task of assessment is easier than for writing in the personal modes. In one, the duty to one's reader to enlighten and to persuade is paramount and the means employed must be subordinated to that end. The writer is not his own master; he must employ recognized, conventional, public means of communication. Within the personal modes, the writer is less under the constraints of a particular subject field. His means of communication will be unique, he will organize his experiences in terms of his own vision and his own style.

The degree to which his reader understands him will depend partly upon a recognition of writing conventions but partly upon the writer's own unique handling of his material. Often the reader lags behind the writer's vision and has to become familiar with the writer's vision before he can truly appreciate it.

The following scheme represents a tentative attempt to plot development in the four writing tasks which the pupils carried out:

SA   *Autobiography*

SA7.1   A string or chain of events related without proper emphasis or adequate contextualization. The writing is not shaped to assist the reader in determining its significance. The experience is unrealized.

SA7.2   A coherent composition with some elaboration and contextualization but without imaginative or emotional unity.

SA7.3   A coherent, if sometimes brief, composition in which there is adequate contextualization, explanation and a simple expression of feeling without the writer's being aware of the springs and complexities of his feeling. The recollected experience has been shaped but not examined.

SA7.4   An elaborated composition in which various literary effects are employed to heighten the narrative but without proper integration of the parts into a satisfying and imaginative whole.

SA7.5   A fully contextualized and elaborated composition in which the writer shows self awareness and reflective ability but is unable to distance the experience or transform the recollection into a total imaginative unity.

SA7.6 A satisfying composition in which the experience is fully realized; the feelings are explored and examined. A variety of means are employed to achieve the immediacy of the experience for the reader.

SN   *Narrative*
SN7.1 Little coherent narrative pattern. Events are described in a chain or cluster without adequate sequence or contextualization.

SN7.2 Unelaborated narrative pattern without any exploration of the nature of the events or experience described.

SN7.3 A narrative in which there is some elaboration, and some heightening of effects but the sum of the parts does not make a satisfying whole. The writer's approach and handling of material is not consistent throughout.

SN7.4 A narrative which strives after particular effects rather than a unified vision. The writer experiments with a variety of literary devices and techniques, there is much 'second hand' writing and no sustained emotional or imaginative involvement.

SN7.5 A fully realized and imaginatively satisfying narrative.

SE   *Explanation*
SE7.1 There is an inability to plan or organize material into a coherent account. Information is neither contextualized nor related to an overall design.

SE7.2 A coherent account but without sufficient information provided for the reader's understanding.

SE7.3 A coherent account with certain features elaborated without an understanding of the underlying principles. No precision in defining terms.

SE7.4 An over-elaborated account with some awareness of the underlying principles and broad structure but without classification or abstraction. Detail obscures the main design.

SE7.5 A coherent, austere account which shows an awareness of underlying principles and broad structure but has insufficient information for the reader's understanding.

SE7.6 A clear, coherent and fully elaborated account. Material handled confidently with adequate explanation and exemplification. Terms adequately and precisely defined.

SP   *Argument*

SP7.1   Statement, narrative, description or assertion rather than discussion
        or analysis. Little explanation or elaboration. Little organization of
        material.

SP7.2   Discursive style attempted but ideas are not developed or arguments
        sustained. Explanations are egocentric and argument primitive.

SP7.3   More elaborated discursive style with appropriate introduction and
        conclusion. Argument seen as a sort of 'chain'. There is an attempt to
        handle abstract ideas but without definition or analysis.

SP7.4   Discursive style established. Material is appropriately organized in
        paragraphs with topic sentences. Argument is sustained and handled
        with confidence but there is some limitation in the writer's awareness
        of the implications of his subject so that argument is often glib and
        other considerations unexplored.

Appendix B

Photographs — Visual Stimuli for the Fictional Narrative Task

The children were asked to write a story for which one of the following pictures could serve as an illustration (See Chapter Six, section 3).

1

Permission to reproduce these photographs is gratefully acknowledged:

from Press Association Photos for *Sign of a Stricken City* (2); from Roman Vishniac for his photograph *Grandfather and Granddaughter* (3).

The publishers have made every effort to contact the copyright holder of *The Children Watch* from *Italia Mia* by Gina Lollobrigida (1) but without success, and apologise for any infringement of copyright.

◀2

3▼

Bibliography

Adolph, R. (1968), *The Rise of Modern English Prose Style,* Massachusetts Institute of Technology.

APU (Assessment of Performance Unit) (1978), *Language Performance,* DES, Room 1/27 Elizabeth House, York Road, London SE1 7PH.

Applebee, Arthur N. (1978), *The Child's Concept of Story,* University of Chicago Press.

Ashley, Jack (1973), *Silence Falls,* Bodley Head.

Aston, Alasdair (ed.) (1978), *Hey Mister Butterfly,* Inner London Education Authority.

Bannister, D. (ed.) (1970), *Perspectives in Personal Construct Theory,* Academic Press.

Barnes, Douglas, and Todd, Frankie (1977), *Communication and Learning in Small Groups,* Routledge and Kegan Paul.

Bartlett, Elsa (1979), 'Learning to Tell a Story'. Paper given at the CCTE Ottawa Conference, May 1979.

Becker, W.C. (1964), 'Consequences of Different Kinds of Parental Discipline' in Hoffman L. and Hoffman, L.W. (eds.), *Review of Child Development Research,* Russell Sage Foundation, New York.

Bell, Vicars (1953), *On Learning the English Tongue,* Faber.

Bereiter, Carl (1979), 'Development in Writing'. Paper given at the CCTE Ottawa Conference, May 1979, to be published in Gregg, Lee W. and Steinberg, Ervin R. (eds.) *Cognitive Processes in Writing,* Hillsdale, N. J. Erlbaum.

Berse (1974), 'Criteria for the Assessment of Pupils' Composition', *Educational Research,* 17.1.

Bloom, B.S. *et al.* (1956), *Taxonomy of Educational Objectives: 1 the Cognitive Domain,* Longman.

Britton, J.N. (1978), 'The Composing Processes and the Functions of Writing' in Cooper, C.R. and Odell, L. (eds) *Research on Composing: Points of Departure,* National Council of Teachers of English.

Britton, J.N., Rosen, H., and Martin, N. (1966), *Multiple Marking of English Composition*, Examinations Bulletin No. 12, HMSO.

Britton, J.N., Burgess, T., Martin, N., McLeod, A., Rosen, H. (1975), *The Development of Writing Abilities*, Macmillan Education.

Brown, Christy (1970), *Down All the Days*, Pan Books.

Bruner, J.S. (1964), 'The Course of Cognitive Growth', *American Psychologist, 19, 1–15*, Reprinted in Open University *Language in Education*, 1972.

(1975), 'Language as an Instrument of Thought', in Davies, A. (ed.) *Problems of Language and Learning*, Heinemann.

Carlin, Eric S. (1978), 'Theories and Measures of Writing Development'. Unpublished M.Ed. dissertation, University of Exeter.

Carroll, J.B. (1968). *Development of Native Language Skills beyond the Early Years*, Education Testing Service, Princeton, New Jersey.

Chomsky, Noam (1965), *Aspects of the Theory of Syntax*, Massachusetts Institute of Technology.

Cooper, C.R. and Odell, L. (eds.) (1978), *Research on Composing: Points of Departure*, National Council of Teachers of English.

Creber, J.W.P. (1964), *Sense and Sensitivity*, University of London Press.

Crystal, D. (1976) *Child Language, Learning and Linguistics*, Edward Arnold.

Crystal, D. and Davey, D. (1969), *Investigating English Style*, Longman.

Daniel, Evan (1898), *The Grammar, History and Derivation of the English Language*, London, National Society's Depository, Westminster.

Davitz, J.R. (1969), *The Language of Emotion*, Academic Press.

Dearden, R.F., Hirst, P.H. and Peters, R.S. (eds.) (1972), *Education and the Development of Reason*, Routledge and Kegan Paul.

Devereux, E.C. (1970), 'The Role of Peer Group Experience in Moral Development', in Hull, John P. (ed.), *Minnesota Symposia on Child Psychology*, University of Minnesota Press, Minneapolis.

Diederich, Paul B. (1974), *Measuring Growth in English*, National Council of Teachers of English.

Dixon, John (1975), *Growth Through English set in the perspective of the seventies*, Oxford University Press (3rd edition, 1975).

Donaldson, M. (1978), *Children's Minds*, Fontana/Collins.

Emig, J. (1971), *The Composing Processes of Twelfth Graders*, N.C.T.E. Research Report No. 13, National Council of Teachers of English.

Enkvist, N.E., Spencer, J., and Gregory, M.J. (1964), *Linguistics and Style*, Oxford University Press.

Halliday, M.A.K. (1973), 'Relevant Models of Language', in *Explorations in the Functions of Language*, Edward Arnold.

Halliday, M.A.K. and Hasan, R. (1976), *Cohesion in English*, Longman.

Harpin, W.S. (and associates) (1973), *Social and Educational Influences on Children's Acquisition of Grammar: A Study of Writing Development in the Junior School*, University of Nottingham School of Education.

Harpin, W.S. (1976), *The Second 'R': Writing Development in the Junior School*, George Allen and Unwin, Ltd.

Harrison, B.T. (1976), 'The Literate Response', unpublished Ph.D. thesis, University of Exeter.

Harrison, B.T. (1979), 'The Learner as Writer: Stages of Growth' in *Language for Learning*, Vol. 1, No. 2 Language in Education Centre, University of Exeter.

Hartog, Philip (1907), *The Writing of English*, Clarendon Press, Oxford.

Hartog, Philip (1944), *The Marking of English Essays*, Macmillan.

Hartog, Philip and Rhodes, E.C. (1935), *An Examination of Examinations*, Macmillan.

Hepburn, R.W. (1972), 'The Arts and the Education of Feeling and Emotion' in Dearden, R.F., Hirst, P.H. and Peters, R.S. (eds.) 1972, (see above).

HMSO, *Teaching of English in England* (1921).

Holbrook, D. (1961), *English for Maturity*, Cambridge University Press.

Hourd, M. (1949), *The Education of the Poetic Spirit*, Heinemann.

Hunt, K.W. (1963), *Grammatical Structures Written at Three Grade Levels*, N.C.T.E. Research Reports No. 3.

Jakobson, R., 'Concluding Statement: Linguistics and Poetics', in Sebeok, *Style in Language*, Massachusetts Institute of Technology.

Jones, R.M. (1968), *Fantasy and Feeling in Education*, University of London Press.

Kelly, G.A. (1970), 'A Brief Introduction to Personal Construct Theory' in Bannister, D. 1970, (see above).

Kernan, K.T. (1977), 'Semantic and Expressive Elaboration in Children's Narratives', in Ervin–Tripp, S. and Mitchel–Kernan, C. (eds.) *Child Discourse*, Academic Press.

Knight, Roger (1977), 'Examiners' English', in *English in Education*, 11.2 Summer, 22–32.

Kolberg, L. (1958), 'The Development of Modes of Moral Thinking and Choice in the years ten to sixteen,' unpublished Ph.D. thesis, University of Chicago.

Kolberg, L. (1963), 'The Development of Children's Orientation towards a Moral Order: I, Sequence in the Development of Moral Thought', *Vita Humana*, 6, 11–33.

Kolberg, L. (1964), 'The Development of Moral Character and Moral Ideology', in Hoffman, M.L. and Hoffman, L.W.: *Review of Child Development Research*, Vol. 1, N.Y. 383—431.

Kolberg, L. (1968), 'The Child as Moral Philosopher', in *Psychology Today*, 25—30.

Kolberg, L. (1969), 'Stage and Sequence: the Cognitive-Developmental Approach to Socialization', in Goslin, D.A. (ed.) *Handbook of Socialization Theory and Research*, Rand McNally, 347—480.

Kolberg, L. (1976), 'Moral Stages and Moralization', in Likona, T. (ed.): *Moral Development and Behaviour*, Holt, Rinehart and Winston, 1976, 31—53.

Kolberg, L. and Kramer, R. (1969), 'Continuities and Discontinuities in Childhood and Adult Moral Development', in *Human Development*, 12, 93—120.

Kolberg, L. and Turiel, E. (1971), 'Moral Development and Moral Education', in Lesser, G. (ed.): *Psychology and Educational Practice*, Scott Foreman, London, 1971.

Kolberg, L. and Colby, A., Gibbs, J., Speicher—Dubin, B., and Power, C. (1977): *Assessing Moral Stages : A Manual*, Harvard University Press.

Labov, W. (1972), *Language in the Inner City*, University of Pennsylvania Press.

Langer, S.K. (1957), *Philosophy in a New Key*, 3rd ed. Harvard University Press.

Langer, S.K. (1967), *Mind : An Essay on Human Feeling*, Vol. 1, Johns Hopkins University Press.

Langer, S.K. (1972), *Mind : An Essay on Human Feeling*, Vol. 2, Johns Hopkins University Press.

LATE (London Association for the Teaching of English), (1965), *Assessing Composition*, Blackie.

Loban, Walter (1963), *The Language of Elementary School Children*, National Council of Teachers of English.

Loban, Walter (1976), *Language Development: Kindergarten through Grade Twelve*, National Council of Teachers of English.

Marshall, Christopher (1978), 'Criteria Internalised by Impression Markers in Assessing the Written Composition of Eleven and Fifteen year olds'. Unpublished M.Ed. dissertation, University of Exeter.

McCarthy, D.A. (1954), 'Language Development in Children', in Carmichael, L. (ed.) *A Manual of Child Psychology*, John Wiley, N.Y. 492—630.

McIntosh, Angus, 'Patterns and Ranges' in *Language* XXVVII (1961), p. 33.

Milic, Louis T. (1969), *Stylists on Style: A Handbook with Selections for Analysis*, Chas. Scribner and Sons, N.Y.

Moffett, James (1968), *Teaching the Universe of Discourse*, Houghton, Mifflin, Co. Boston.

National Assessment of Educational Progress (1972), *Writing Objectives* for 1973–4 Assessment, NAEP, Lincoln Tower, 1869 Lincoln Street, Denver, Colorado, 80203.

NATE (1973), *Language in Context*, National Association for the Teaching of English.

Odell, L., Cooper, C.R., Courts, C. (1978), 'Discourse Theory: Implications for Research' in Cooper, C.R. and Odell, L. (eds.), 1978, (see above).

Peel, E.A. (1971), *The Nature of Adolescent Judgement*, Styles Press, London.

Peters, R.S. (1967), *The Concept of Education*, Routledge and Kegan Paul.

Peters, R.S. (1972), 'The Education of the Emotions', in Dearden, R.F., Hirst, P.H. and Peters, R.S. (1972), (see above).

Piaget, J. (1932), *The Moral Judgement of the Child*, Routledge and Kegan Paul.

Piaget, J. and Inhelder, B. (1969), *The Psychology of the Child*, translated H. Weaver, Routledge and Kegan Paul.

Piercy, Marg. (1976), *Living in the Open: Poems*, Alfred A. Knopf, N.Y.

Pringle, Kellmer M. (1974), *The Needs of Children*, Hutchinson.

Ross, M. (1978), *The Creative Arts*, Heinemann Educational Books.

Schonell, F. (1948, 4th ed.), *Backwardness in Basic Subjects*, Oliver and Boyd.

Sebeok, T.A. (ed.) (1960), *Style in Language*, Massachusetts Institute of Technology.

Shotter, J. (1974), 'The Development of Personal Powers', in Richards, M.P.M., *The Integration of a Child into a Social World*, Cambridge University Press.

Singer, R.D. and Singer, A. (1969), *Psychological Developments in Children*, W.B. Saunders Company, Philadelphia.

Stevens, Frances (1970), *English and Examinations*, Hutchinson Educational.

Stratta, L., Dixon, J., Wilkinson, A. (1973), *Patterns of Language Exploration of the Teaching of English*, Heinemann Educational Books.

Strongman, K.T. (1978, 2nd ed.), *The Psychology of Emotion*, John Wiley and Sons.

Taylor, Gordon T. (1979), 'The Development of Language, 9–15', unpublished M.Ed. dissertation, University of Exeter.

Thornton, G.H. (1901), *The Self-Educator in English Composition*, Hodder and Stoughton.

Thorndike, E.L. (1944), *Teachers' Word Book of 30,000 Words*, Bureau of Publications, Teachers' College, Columbia University, N.Y.

Torbe, M. and Protherough, R. (1976), *Classroom Encounters: Language and English Teaching*, Ward Lock.

Tough, Joan (1977), *The Development of Meaning*, Unwin.

Way, Brian (1967), *Development Through Drama*, Longman.

Wilkinson, A. (1978), 'Criteria of Language Development' in *Educational Review*, 30, No. 1, 13–33.

Wilkinson, A., Barnsley, G., Hanna, P. and Swan, M., (1979), Assessing Language Development' in *Language for Learning*, Vol. 1, No. 2, Language in Education Centre, University of Exeter.

Wilkinson, A. and Wilkinson, E. (1978), 'The Development of Language in the Middle Years', in *English in Education*, 12.1, 42–52.

Wilkinson, A. and Hanna, P. (1980), 'The Development of Style in Children's Writing', in *Educational Review*, 33, No. 1.

Witcombe, Christine M. (1979), 'Developmental Aspects of Children's Language in Junior School', unpublished M.Ed. dissertation, University of Exeter.

Wiseman, S. (1949), 'The Marking of English Composition in Grammar School Selection', *British Journal of Educational Psychology*, 19, 200–9.

Witkin, R.W. (1974), *The Intelligence of Feeling*, Heinemann Educational.

Wright, D. (1971), *The Psychology of Moral Behaviour*, Penguin.

Wright, D. and Croxen, M. (1976), *Moral Development. A Cognitive Approach*, Open University Press.

Yarlott, Geoffrey (1972), *Education and Children's Emotions*, Weidenfeld and Nicholson.

Yerrill, K.A.J. (1977), 'A Consideration of the Later Development of Children's Syntax in Speech and Writing: a study of parenthetical, appositional and related items', unpublished Ph.D. thesis, University of Newcastle.

The authors and publishers would like to thank the following for permission to reproduce extracts:

Houghton Mifflin Company, Boston for James Moffett, *Teaching the Universe of Discourse*, 1968; Macmillan Education for James Britton *et al.*, *The Development of Writing Abilities* (11-18) (Schools Council Research Studies) 1975; The Massachusetts Institute of Technology Press, Cambridge, Mass., for Roman Jakobson's diagram from Thomas Sebeok, *Style in Language*, 1960; ILEA for poems from *Hey Mister Butterfly*, 1978 (ed. Alasdair Aston).